Venture Capital and Firm Performance

This book provides an analysis of the impact on underpricing and long-term performance of venture capital in IPOs, and of the ownership characteristics of venture capital companies. It investigates the performance of IPOs in Korea during the dot-com bubble-and-bust period. The book looks at venture capital firms and their participation, their reputation, and conflicts of interests, particularly in the context of the development of a new secondary stock market in an emerging market and these factors affect the pricing and performance effects of IPO firms.

This book is a useful reference to those interested in promoting an active KOS-DAQ type of stock market, and understanding how venture capitalists and their institutional affiliation may reduce information asymmetry and add value of IPO firms.

Jaeho Lee is Associate Professor at the Department of International Business and Trade, Kyung Hee University, Seoul, Korea. He was Research Fellow for Centre for Business Research at the University of Cambridge and Birmingham Business School. He won the 2010 Best Paper Award from the Korean Association of Small Business Studies for his paper on venture capital and its impact on firm valuation.

Routledge Studies in International Business and the World Economy

For a full list of titles in this series, visit www.routledge.com/Routledge-Studies-in-International-Business-and-the-World-Economy/book-series/SE0358

Venture Capital and Firm Performance

The Korean Experience in a Global Perspective

Jaeho Lee

LONDON AND NEW YORK

First published 2018
by Routledge

2 Park Square, Milton Park, Abingdon, Oxfordshire OX14 4RN
52 Vanderbilt Avenue, New York, NY 10017

Routledge is an imprint of the Taylor & Francis Group, an informa business

First issued in paperback 2020

British Library Cataloguing-in-Publication Data
A catalogue record for this book is available from the British Library

Library of Congress Cataloging-in-Publication Data
A catalog record for this book has been requested

ISBN: 978-1-138-06195-8 (hbk)
ISBN: 978-0-367-59474-9 (pbk)

Typeset in Galliard
by Apex CoVantage, LLC

To my parents and parents-in-law who have devoted their lives to the economic development of Korea and the support of their families

Contents

Figures

Tables

Acknowledgements

First of all, my gratitude goes to Professor Alan Hughes (Judge Business School, University of Cambridge) for his invaluable academic guidance and constant encouragement. I also would like to express my thanks to Professor Douglas Cumming (Schulich School of Business, York University) and the late Professor Ajit Singh (Faculty of Economics, University of Cambridge). Professor Cumming has been very helpful with useful feedback and advices for venture capital research in many occasions since I started my academic career. It was my privilege to have an opportunity to contribute to the *Oxford Handbook of Venture Capital* (edited by Professor Cumming, Oxford University Press) as an author. The late Professor Singh was instrumental in enriching my insight on how venture capital can promote economic development in an emerging market.

Abbreviations

AIM	Alternative Investment Market
AMP	(Denmark) Autoriseret MarkedsPladsb
BHAR	Buy-And-Hold Abnormal Return
BW	Billion (Korean) Won
CAR	Cumulative Abnormal Return
CEO	Chief Executive Officer
Co.	Company
CPA	Certified Public Accountant
CTAR	Calendar Time Abnormal Return
DCF	Discounted Cash Flow
EASDAQ	European Association of Securities Dealers Automated Quotation
EED	European Enterprises Development
ERISA	Employee Retirement Income Security Act
EU	European Union
Euro.NM	Euro "New Markets"
EVCA	European Venture Capital Association
FSC	Financial Supervisory Committee
FSS	Financial Supervisory Service
GBP	Great Britain Pound
GDP	Gross Domestic Product
HML	High Minus Low
ICT	Information and Communication Technology
IPO	Initial Public Offering
IR	Initial Return
ITEQ	Irish Technology Quotation
JASDAQ	Japanese Association of Securities Dealers Automated Quotation
KDBC	Korean Development Bank Capital
KIC	Korean Industry Classification
KIS	Korea Information Service
KOSDAQ	Korean Securities Dealers Automated Quotation
KRW	Korea Won
KSDA	Korean Stock Dealers Association
KSE	Korean Stock Exchange

KTB	Korea Technology Bank
KTI	Korean Technology Investment
KVCA	Korean Venture Capital Association
LBO	Leverage Buy-Out
LPF	Limited Partnership Fund
LSE	London Stock Exchange
LTD.	Limited
M&A	Merger and Acquisition
MBI	Management Buy-in
MBO	Management Buy-Out
MW	Million (Korean) Won
NASDAQ	National Association of Securities Dealers Automated Quotation
NM	(Finland) New Market (List)
NVCA	National Venture Capital Association
OECD	Organisation for Economic Co-operation and Development
OTC	Over-The-Counter
R&D	Research and Development
RF	Risk-Free
RMRF	Return of Market (minus) Risk-Free rate
SBIC	Small Business Investment Company
SBMF	Size and Book-to-market ratio Matched Firm
SBMP	Size and Book-to-market ratio Matched Portfolio
SEO	Second Equity Offering
SIMF	Size and Industry Matched Firm
SMB	(Norway) Small and Medium Business (List)
SMBA	Small and Medium Business Administration
SME	Small and Medium Enterprise
SWX	SWiss eXchange
USD	US Dollar
VC	Venture Capital
VCC	Venture Capital Company
WR	Wealth Relative

1 Introduction

1.1 Background to the research[1]

Initial public offerings (IPOs) have attracted a great deal of attention from academic researchers and financial practitioners. In particular the IPO market around the late 1990s and early 2000s addressed a lot of interesting questions about the pricing and performance of IPO companies. In this era, small and medium-size enterprises (SMEs) based on information and communication technology realised huge gains on their stock market debut. Although numerous studies have documented this aftermarket high initial return (or interchangeable underpricing) even before this period, the degree of the initial return was unprecedentedly high during this period (Ljungqvist and Wilhelm, 2003). Many researchers have wondered why the underpricing increased and the issuers "didn't get upset about leaving money on the table in IPOs" (Loughran and Ritter, 2002). During this period the IPO market was regarded as a catalyst, attracting new issues by innovative and high-technology-oriented SMEs, which were seemingly growing without interruption with the advent of the new knowledge economy. The enormous growth of NASDAQ in the United States fostered the financing of high-tech SMEs and resulted in the establishment of similar types of stock markets in other countries. Most of these markets were born in the late 1990s, including AIM in the United Kingdom and the Euro.NM network in Europe. KOSDAQ (Korean Securities Dealers Automated Quotation), the secondary stock market in Korea, was launched in 1996 following this global trend, and it has played a substantial role in financing a number of Korean high-tech SMEs. The market capitalisation volume of KOSDAQ was one of the largest among global second-tier stock markets by the end of 1999. The growth of KOSDAQ was matched by a growth in the Korean venture capital (VC) industry; this pattern was also the case in other countries. However, with the collapse of global stock markets in the second quarter of 2000, the growth of KOSDAQ was brought to a halt, and it has not recovered its previous peak level of a decade ago.

The increasing underpricing in the short run, followed by underperformance in the long run, are general patterns that are found in the pricing and performance of IPOs around the globe (Ritter, 1991; Ritter and Welch, 2002; Loughran et al., 2003). KOSDAQ is not an exception in this respect. The pervasive nature of this underpricing and poor long-term performance around the globe has been explained in a number of ways. While most of the discussion has concentrated on the information asymmetry, agency problems, and conflicts of interest that come up between the issuing company, underwriter, and investor, it has been shown that a financial player who certifies and adds value to uncertain IPO firms can significantly ameliorate these problems, thereby leading to less underpricing and better long-run performance. A venture capital company, which features private, long-term, and risky equity finance with the aim of ultimately realising abnormal returns, has been considered an institution that can play this role for an IPO company (Wright and Robbie, 1998).

This book is an investigation of the performance of IPOs in Korea during this rapidly changing dot-com bubble-and-bust period (1999–2001), which is already about fifteen years ago but is still worth analysis in terms of venture capital participation, reputation, and conflicts of interests, particularly in the context of the development of a new secondary stock market in an emerging market. In a country such as Korea, in which firms generally relied on banks or other financial institutions, the remarkable expansion of KOSDAQ indicated that the Korean economy was experiencing a period of transition from a bank-based financial system to a newly emerging stock market-based financial system, even though the banks still played a major role in financing the national business system. The stock market-based financial system was promoted as an engine for economic growth by the Korean government following the foreign exchange crisis that occurred in 1997. However, the growth of KOSDAQ was widely criticised. Questions were raised about the pricing of IPO firms, especially their valuation relative to the fundamentals of the firms. The acute decline of KOSDAQ prices after March 2000, along with the global stock market crash, highlighted these questions. In this book, I focus on the role that reputable financial institutions such as banks may play in ameliorating the information asymmetry and agency conflicts inherent in high-tech SMEs and in adding value to them so that the companies' IPO pricing and long-term performance do not deviate much from their original valuation at IPO. These reputation and related governance issues have been a major concern of scholars of international comparative financial systems (Mayer, 2002) and of those of stock market development and economic systems (Singh, 2003). The theoretical discussion and empirical analysis highlighting the role of highly reputable VCs and financial institutions in the valuation and long-term performance of IPO companies, in particular, with the dataset in an emerging market such as Korea in the volatile dot.com bubble-and-bust period (1999–2001) should be of interest to academic researchers, financial practitioners, and policy makers dealing with emerging market issues in major markets (including US/Europe ones).

There has been much theoretical and empirical research on the relationship between IPO performance and venture-capital-backing in the US and European settings. Numerous studies document underpricing in the short run and underperformance in the long run in the pricing of IPOs of common stock in global stock markets. Most of the discussion in the underpricing literature has concentrated on the information asymmetry problem that comes up between issuer, investor and underwriter. It examines the role of a reputable financial player cer-tifying uncertain IPO firms as a way to significantly reduce the information gap. This decreases the degree of underpricing. IPO firms supported by reputable financial players would also be expected to show outperformance in the long term, because in order to maintain their reputational capital they would only bring better-quality IPO firms to the market and add further value to the firms following their due diligence before IPO.

The role of a venture capital company as a certifying agent and value-adding financial player for the IPO firms arises from several sources. Venture capital-ists can develop expertise in the financing of technology-based firms and other SMEs. Venture capitalists not only supply funding, but also can intervene in the ownership and management in order to closely monitor the firms. They hold shares in the firms and serve as members of board of directors. They also tend to specialise in particular industry sectors and provide consulting services for corpo-rate strategy to the firms. In order to minimise the agency costs and information asymmetries between themselves and the firms, venture capitalists employ various mechanisms such as staging of capital infusion, syndication of investment and use of convertible debt. Furthermore, facing reputational risk as repeated financial players who regularly raise new funds, venture capitalists are very cautious about the reputation build-up and often interact with other financial institutions and agencies such as underwriters. However, all venture capitalists are not the same: their quality is different. Some venture capitalists may be money-game players, being more interested in the short-term capital gain after IPO, rather than add-ing value through the mechanisms mentioned above. These venture capitalists incur conflicts of interest between issuing companies and investors, unlike the reputational venture capitalists.

The ownership structure of venture capitalists themselves may also affect IPO firm performances. Contrary to US and UK venture capitalists, who are mostly independents, Korean venture capitalists are generally captives of financial institu-tions or other corporate venturing companies. This feature of the Korean venture capital industry is rather closer to that of Germany and Japan. It might be expected that Korean venture capital companies will generally act as the same kind of certify-ing and value-adding financial agents. It is also likely, however, that the ownership of venture capitalists may result in different investment behaviour in relation to IPO firms, thus leading to different IPO performance. In a situation where a stock market experiences an enormous growth and the following sharp decline, as KOS-DAQ did in the very volatile stock market situation over the period 1999–2001, the potential certification or conflict of interests factors that can be caused by ven-ture capitalists' affiliation with other financial institutions is an intriguing research topic. I therefore examine the impact of the quality of venture capital companies, especially in terms of its ownership structure and reputation on IPO performance. In particular, I test the possibility of a positive impact of bank-affiliated venture capitalists such as an information advantage of banking institutions, and a negative impact of security company-affiliated venture capitalists where conflicts of interest may lead to the tendency towards overvaluation of IPO firms.

To examine these issues required a substantial programme of data collection on the short- and long-term performance of IPO firms and their ownership structures, and the ownership and reputational characteristics of the venture capitalists who invested in the firms. The dataset is one of the original contributions of this book.

Measuring short-run underpricing in the Korean economy also poses methodological problems. Stock Market regulation in Korea imposed a daily limit of stock price changes on KOSDAQ and the limit changed in the period analysed in this book. This meant that I had to create a measure which adjusts for this, and which estimates when the suppressed price changes could be identified. The finance literature related to long-term performance methodology is also not straightforward. It suggests the use of buy and hold abnormal returns (BHARs). However, there are many benchmarks used to measure BHARs. I calculated BHARs employing five benchmarks that are recommended and commonly used in recent literature. Instead of deciding on the superiority of one method over another, I compared and interpreted the variations in performance they produced and use them as test of the robustness of our results to changes in benchmarks I employ univariate parametric and non-parametric tests and multivariate regression analysis in order to test our hypotheses.

This book analyses the determinants of IPO performance in a very particular national setting, KOSDAQ, in a very particular period 1999–2001 which is divided into "hot" and "cold" stock market situations. Very few studies in the literature have analysed Korean IPOs in this period. The detailed analysis of KOSDAQ will allow for an independent set of tests of IPO underpricing and the long-term performance and update the previous results in other studies. I expect that the academic readers of this book can understand the underpricing and long-term performance pattern of KOSDAQ IPOs over the period 1999–2001 when KOSDAQ experienced a dramatic surge and the following abrupt decline and how VC-backing and other reputational and institutional effects influenced the firm performances. This research could also give investors a new insight into the Korean IPO market, especially by comparing the performance of VC-backed and non-VC-backed IPOs. The Korean financial regulatory agencies could also benefit from this research by getting insights into the differences between successful and unsuccessful IPOs and the role of venture capital participation, and the quality and ownership of venture capitalists. This could assist in the design of a financial regulation system to foster high-quality venture capitalists and to help the conventional Korean venture capitalists to review their activities so as to bring about successful IPOs. The research in this book could also provide an input into developing-country government thinking in relation to promoting an active KOSDAQ type of stock market, and how the participation of venture capitalists and their institutional affiliation with large shareholders may lead to reducing information asymmetry and add value of IPO firms. It will also demonstrate the way in which these effects may be overwhelmed by the euphoria of stock market booms.

1.2 Chapter plan

This book is organised as follows.

In Chapter 2, I provide an institutional description of the venture capital industry and the IPO market in Korean and other major countries. I introduce the institutional framework of venture capital, set out recent trends in the venture capital industry, and provide an account of the institutional framework of initial public offerings and IPO markets.

In Chapter 3, I review the literature regarding underpricing, and the long-term performance mechanisms of the certification and the value-adding role provided by venture capitalist. I derive the hypotheses for our empirical tests. I deal with how the information asymmetry between investors and issuers and the hot issue market phenomenon can affect underpricing and how the disappearance of information asymmetry and the timing of IPOs can influence long-term performance. I deal with the certification and value-adding role of venture capitalists, including internal mechanisms to minimise uncertainty, monitoring and screening functions, and external activities. I also discuss the impact of venture capitalists' institutional affiliation with banks and security companies on the performance of IPO firms. I introduce the universal banking perspective and discuss how it applies to the certification and conflict of interests that a financial institutions-affiliated VC may cause. Following the literature review, I derive twelve testable hypotheses.

In Chapter 4, I present the dataset and discuss the methodology to be used to test the hypotheses. I document the sources of data and discuss sample selection issues. I give an account of the concepts and definitions of stock market performance in terms of underpricing and long-term performance and explain various types of benchmarks that will be used in order to adjust raw long-term performance. I set out the specification of the univariate tests and the multivariate regression model I use in Chapters 5, 6, and 7. In particular, I describe the independent dummy variables and several control variables that will be used in multivariate regressions and specify the multivariate regression models that I implement in order to test our hypotheses.

In Chapter 5, I describe the main characteristics of our IPO samples by comparing VC-backed and non-VC-backed IPOs. I cover the trend in IPOs, their industry distribution, and set out IPO sample characteristics, including ownership structure, sources of funds, and financial and operating performance prior to IPO. I compare these characteristics of KOSDAQ IPO samples with that of other major countries.

In Chapter 6, I report the results of a univariate and a multivariate analysis of underpricing. I compare underpricing across different types of IPOs: VC-backed and non-VC-backed, hot and cold issue market, age (young and old), market capitalisation (small and big), and industry (high-tech and non-high-tech), respectively. This analysis across different classification of IPOs is extended by cross-classification in more detail. I also compare underpricing across IPOs grouped by the institutional type of VC-backing (bank-affiliated, security company-affiliated, other institution-affiliated and non-VC-backed). I also report the result of multiple regressions on underpricing, which were carried out for IPOs for whole sample period, IPOs in the hot market, and IPOs in the cold market, respectively.

In Chapter 7, I present the results of univariate and multivariate analysis of long-term performance. I compare the long-term performance of IPOs, grouped by venture-capital-backing (VC-backed and non-VC-backed), hot issue market (hot and cold market), age (young and old), market capitalisation (small and big), industry (high-tech and non-high-tech), and the degree of underpricing (low and high), respectively. I also extend this analysis by cross-classification in more detail. I compare the long-term performance of different types of VC affiliation: bank-affiliated, security company-affiliated, other institution-affiliated and non-VC-backed. I document the result of multiple regressions on long-term performance, which were implemented for the hot-market period and the cold-market period, respectively.

In Chapter 8, I conclude the book by summarising the previous chapters and documenting an implication of the research.

Note

1 Parts of this section appeared in Ch.26 "The Impact of Venture Capital Participation and Its Affiliation with Financial Institutions on the Long-term Performance of IPO Firm: Evidence from Korea in Hot and Cold Market Periods" by Jaeho Lee from *Oxford Handbook of Venture Capital*, edited by Cumming, Douglas (2012) and has been re-used in this chapter by permission of Oxford University Press.

2 Institutional description of the venture capital industry and the IPO market

2.1 Overview

I deal with the institutional aspects of the venture capital industry and the IPO market in this chapter. I document the basic concept and structure of the venture capital industry and the IPO market, and present the trend of venture capital investment and of the IPO market over the years in Korea and other major countries. The organisation of this chapter is as follows.

In Section 2.2, I introduce the definition and the main structure of venture capital investment and define terms that appear frequently in this chapter. I document the various stages of venture capital investing from seed investment to IPO and describe each step of venture capital investment decision-making. I then address the question how important venture capital financing is in the financing growth cycle of entrepreneurial firms that are often characterised as small and uncertain. I move on to give an account of the trend of Korean and other countries' venture capital industry. I review the Korean venture capital industry over the period 1999–2001 and present the venture capital investment data in terms of disbursements of venture capital, funding stage and size of investment, venture capital investing by industry and year, venture capital commitments, and sources of venture capital investment. The Korean data are compared with those of other major countries.

In Section 2.3, I set out the main structure of the IPO market and introduce some important terms. I explain why IPO is important for investment realisation and where IPO holds its position among various means of exit from venture capital investment. I account for the way IPO activity is related to stock market (and economic) conditions. After that, I present various statistics of KOSDAQ and other countries' IPO markets. The history of KOSDAQ is briefly reviewed and then KOSDAQ is compared with KSE (the main stock market in Korea) in terms of market capitalisation, number of listed companies, and IPO numbers of each year. I then describe the legal aspects of KOSDAQ listing requirements. These KOSDAQ data and legal aspects are compared with those of other stock markets such as NASDAQ and AIM, which were the main conduits of high-tech firms' IPOs in the USA and UK in the late 1990s and early 2000s.

2.2 The Institutional framework of venture capital

2.2.1 The definition of venture capital and its main features

Venture capital is generally defined as the investment by professional investors in entrepreneurial firms that are characterised as uncertain and suffering from information asymmetries. Venture capital is characterised as private, long-term-based, and risk-equity finance where the primary reward is an ultimate capital gain after the investee entrepreneurial firm is listed in the stock market (Wright and Robbie, 1998).[1] Venture capital investment appears as a professionally managed pool of capital that is invested in the equity-linked securities of private entrepreneurial ventures, not as a one-off investment, but as sequential investments, depending on the various growth stages in the development of entrepreneurial firms (Sahlman, 1990). In order to be actively involved in the management of the firms they fund, venture capitalists typically become members of the board of directors, retaining important economic rights in addition to their ownership rights (Sahlman, 1990).

The main form of organisation in the venture capital industry is the limited partnership (such as incorporated venture capital companies and publicly traded closed-end funds), with the venture capitalists acting as general partners and the outside investors as limited partners, even though the venture capital company is often organised as a subsidiary of financial or industrial corporations or independent small business investment companies (for example, SBICs in the USA). I focus our description of this form of organisation on limited partnerships and subsequent investment in entrepreneurial firms (portfolio companies) in this sub-section. Venture capitalists make contracts with both outside investors who supply their funds (limited partners) and entrepreneurial firms in which venture capitalists invest.[2] The legal structure of contracts between venture capitalists and limited partners generally leaves complete authority over decision-making matters to the venture capitalists. Limited partners do not choose the entrepreneurial firms that their money goes to, and they are prevented from taking a role in the management of the venture capital partnership. Given the possibility of conflicts of interests in this situation, contracts are designed with several key provisions to

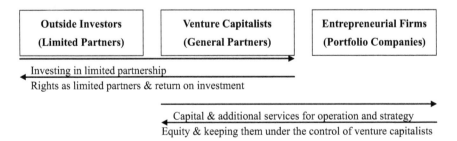

Figure 2.1 The contract flow between outside investors and venture capitalists and between venture capitalists and entrepreneurial firms

protect the limited partners from the venture capitalists' decision-making when it goes against the limited partners' interests (Sahlman, 1990).[3] Venture capitalists and entrepreneurial firms are also likely to have an information asymmetry problem. Both of them may have different perspectives about the projects they focus on, and, even with the same information, they are likely to disagree on certain issues, for example, whether they should continue or abandon the project and how they should cash in on investments (Sahlman, 1990). Contracts between them are typically designed in a way such that venture capitalists keep control of entrepreneurial firms. The most common tool for controlling entrepreneurial firms is the staging of the infusion of capital and the use of convertible preferred stock, which will be documented in detail in Chapter 3. Venture capitalists also devise a compensation scheme in which the manager of the firm receives common stock with subsequent stock options that will not pay off unless the entrepreneurial firm's project leads to eventual capital gain. However, as no contracts between them can specify every possible situation that they will face, venture capitalists typically choose to get involved in the operation of the company.[4]

2.2.2 Life Cycle of the financing of entrepreneurial firms and venture capital investing stages

Entrepreneurial firms have a tendency to get an idea for a potential project but to suffer from insufficient capital to fund it. They are generally small-medium enterprises (SMEs) that belong to high-tech industries. The great uncertainty in their investment and the information asymmetry between them and external financiers may lead to an inability to finance their projects. A bank will not provide entrepreneurial firms with debts, if they own intangible assets that are not market-tested, and thus are extremely difficult to value as collateral. Stock investors will invest in them as long as they are confident that abnormal returns will be realised by a big success on the part of the firms.

I can imagine a funding cycle that these firms rely on as they grow, depending on firm size, age, and information availability. Berger and Udell (1998) show a financial growth cycle that small business firms (including entrepreneurial firms) experience as they become older, larger and less opaque. Figure 2.2 shows this financing cycle in a stylised pattern. Smaller/younger/more opaque firms rely on their insider finance,[5] trade credit, or angel finance. As the firms grow, they gain access to intermediate finance on the equity side (such as venture capital) and on the debt side (such as bank and financial companies). Finally, if the firms keep on growing, they may gain access to public equity and debt markets. Although this growth cycle paradigm clearly shows the typically changing financing pattern of an entrepreneurial firm, it is not intended to fit all SMEs or entrepreneurial firms. Rather, it gives a general idea of which financing source they can gain access to at each growth stage.

Venture capital generally comes after the firms are financed by insider finance and angel finance (Berger and Udell, 1998; Fenn and Liang, 1995). Our data on the venture capital industry in Korea and other major countries in the following

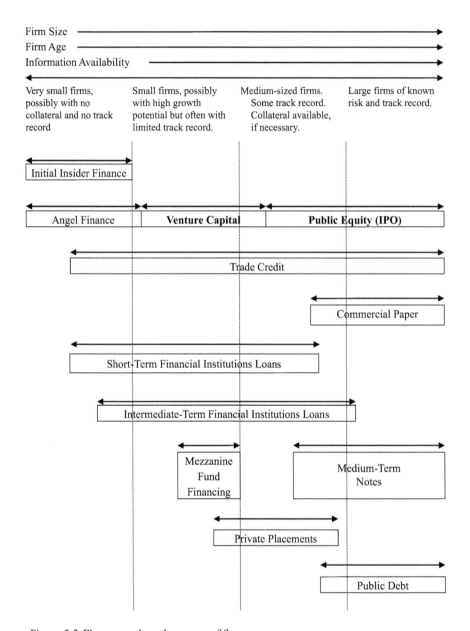

Firm Size

Firm Age

Information Availability

| Very small firms, possibly with no collateral and no track record | Small firms, possibly with high growth potential but often with limited track record. | Medium-sized firms. Some track record. Collateral available, if necessary. | Large firms of known risk and track record. |

Initial Insider Finance

Angel Finance | Venture Capital | Public Equity (IPO)

Trade Credit

Commercial Paper

Short-Term Financial Institutions Loans

Intermediate-Term Financial Institutions Loans

Mezzanine Fund Financing

Medium-Term Notes

Private Placements

Public Debt

Figure 2.2 Firm growth and sources of finance

[This figure is drawn from Berger and Udell (1998)]

sub-section 2.3 show that a high proportion of venture capital investment is concentrated in the expansion stage of the entrepreneurial firms, which are already supported financially by insider finance and angel finance for their seed and start-up financing. Venture capital would come in for the business that has been successfully test-marketed, and is in need of financing full-scale marketing, production and product development (Berger and Udell, 1998). The general pattern that venture capital comes before public debt (generally from banks) shows that the "financing pecking order"[6] can be reversed in order between external debt (from banks) and external equity (from venture capitalists). In a situation where entrepreneurial firms can be expected to cause moral hazard with debt financing, they obtain finance from venture capitalists (external equity), who are willing to accept the high-growth and high-risk entrepreneurial firms, before they obtain external public debt. Garmaise (1997) argued that the reversed pecking order between external equity and external debt could result if venture capitalists are assumed to have superior information to entrepreneurs over certain issues

Table 2.1 The stages of venture capital investing

---

1 *Seed*
   - A portfolio firm has not yet fully established commercial operations, and may also be involved in continued research and product development.
2 *Early stage*
   - A portfolio firm is implementing product development and initial marketing, manufacturing and sales activities.
3 *Start-up Stage*
   - A portfolio firm is completing development and this may include initial marketing efforts. It may be in the process of organising or it may already be in the business one year or less, but it has not yet sold its products commercially.
4 *Later stage*
   - A portfolio firm is in the stage of initial expansion of a company that is producing, shipping and increasing its sales volume.
5 *Expansion*
   - A portfolio firm is beyond the early stage of development that is focused on growing the company. The firm in the stage of expansion is normally manufacturing and shipping products. Though producing revenues, it may or may not yet be recording net income.
6 *Balanced*
   - This term is used when a venture fund investment strategy includes an investment strategy in portfolio companies at a variety of stages of development (seed, early stage, later stage, expansion, or leverage buyout) or with no particular stated investment strategy.
7 *Mezzanine financing*
   - A fund investment strategy involving subordinated debt (the level of financing senior to equity and below senior debt).
8 *Leveraged Buyout (LBO)*
   - Acquisition of a product or business, from either a public or private company, utilising a significant amount of debt and little or no equity (usually a ration of 90%debt to 10% equity).

Sources: NVCA (2001) and Plummer (1987)

which are crucial in determining the success of the projects that entrepreneurs accomplish.[7]

However, even though venture capital financing is more concentrated in the stage that has passed seed or start-up, it is known to cover almost all the different stages that the firms face. In reality, venture capitalists have their own indicated areas of specialisation of a private equity fund (NVCA, 2001). According to the jargon that is prevalent in the venture capital industry, those different stages of funding are usually expressed as *Seed, Start-up, Early, Later, Expansion, Mezzanine, Balanced, and Leveraged Buyout.*

2.2.3 The venture capital investment process

The investment activity of a venture capitalist can be seen as a systematic process involving several different steps. Researchers generally agree that there are five steps in the venture capital investment process. According to Tyebjee and Bruno (1984), this process can be analysed into five sequential steps: (1) deal origination, (2) deal screening, (3) deal evaluation, (4) deal structuring, and (5) post-investment activities.

Deal origination, the first step, is the stage at which potential opportunities for investment are recognised by venture capitalists. To find promising entrepreneurs, venture capitalists first make efforts to get to know them in various ways, such as advertising their name in industry directories and attending special conventions, trade shows and conferences for entrepreneurial firms and VC funding. However, a number of proposals come from a network of referrers, instead of starting from scratch. Fried and Hisrich (1994) showed in their analysis of 18 venture capitalists' operations that the introduction of deals was generated from a variety of sources: investment bankers, outside investors in the limited partnership, commercial banks, management of portfolio firms, and management consultants.

Deal screening, the second step, is a screening process by which venture capitalists seek to concentrate on a set of deals by selecting manageable and promising ones. Since venture capitalists typically have small staffs and must screen the relatively large number of potential deals, they tend to select the deals that they are familiar with, particularly in terms of the technology, product and market scope of the entrepreneurial firm. This leads to reducing all the proposals to a more manageable number for more in-depth evaluation. Tyebjee and Bruno (1984) documented that the screening stage is based on four criteria: (1) "the size of the investment proposal and the venture fund", either of which is the minimum and maximum limit of the investment, (2) "technology and market sector", which is expected to be a future dark horse, (3) "geographical location of the firm", which keep travel time and expense at manageable levels when the venture capitalists regularly meet entrepreneurs, (4) "stage of financing" matters. As I have seen, venture capitalists vary in the timing of their financing. Tyebjee and Bruno's (1984) study shows that venture capitalists rarely invested seed capital and their capital generally went to the firms in the stage of expanding operations.[8]

Deal evaluation phase, the third step, involves an assessment of the future return and risk of each deal with financial and accounting information and other qualitative or relevant information. While the conventional DCF (Discounted Cash Flow) is often used, the most common method is to see where the funded entrepreneurial firm meets an acceptable IRR (Internal Rate of Return)[9] (Wright and Robbie, 1996). Wright and Robbie (1996) also state that price earnings multiples based valuation methods were popular in the 1990s.

Tyebjee and Bruno (1984) found that the five evaluation criteria based on subjective assessment were normally used by venture capitalists: (1) "market attractiveness", which is determined by the size, growth and accessibility of the

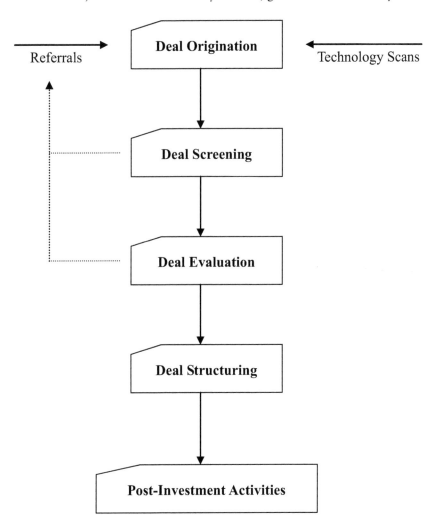

Figure 2.3 Decision process model of venture capital investment activity

This figure was drawn from Tyebjee and Bruno (1984)

market, (2) "product differentiation", which is determined by the ability of the entrepreneur to prevent competitors from a high profit margin through patents, (3) "managerial capabilities" of the CEO, which result from his/her skills in managing several business functional areas, (4) "environmental threat resistance", which represents the degree to which the firm is resistant to unmanageable difficulties from the environment; for example, outdated technology, elasticity of product sale to economic condition and barriers of entry to competitors, (5) "cash-out potential", which reflects the extent to which the venture capitalist feels that the investment can be liquidated or cashed in at the exit stage.

Deal structuring phase, the fourth step, comes if the outcome of the evaluation phase is positive. Venture capitalists begin a negotiating process with the potential entrepreneur about the amount, form, and price of the investment. The contracts also involve control rights of venture capitalists, protective covenants that limit the moral hazard of entrepreneurs, performance-related clauses that encourage entrepreneurs to achieve the agreed-upon performance goals, as explained above.

Post-investment activities, the fifth step, include a formal representation on the board of directors, consultation with the management by providing information on the market, product and suppliers through various networks. In this phase, venture capitalists finally help entrepreneurs to find the exit way such as merger/acquisitions or IPO (Initial Public Offering) which would generate a public financial market to gain abnormal returns for the investment.

2.3 Trend of the Korean and other countries' venture capital industry

2.3.1 Overview of the Korean venture capital industry

The Korean venture capital industry experienced dramatic growth over the late 1990s, after many years of negligible activities in the venture capital market. Korea ranked third in terms of venture capital investment as a share of GDP among the leading OECD countries over the period 1998–2001, following the USA and Canada, and had the largest venture capital market relative to its economy among Asian countries (OECD, 2003). The venture capital market had remained stagnant until 1997 when Korea was deeply affected by the East Asian Financial Crisis. However, it started to see a significant increase in 1998 and reached a peak of KRW 2,000 billion (0.63 per cent of GDP) in 2000, almost quadrupling from 1998. However, in 2001, Korean venture capital investment experienced a steep decline due to the worldwide economic recession, but less so than other OECD countries.

The remarkable growth of Korean venture capital investment was prompted by the government policy which was designed to amend the fundamental flaw that had made the country vulnerable to the 1997 financial crisis. The Korean government attributed one of the main causes of the Korean financial crisis to intrinsic structural problems, mainly caused by the big conglomerates (*chaebols*)-concentrated industry policy and implemented an intensifying structural reform to withdraw support toward uncompetitive groups of big conglomerates and to launch new promising technology-oriented SMEs. Moreover, this period had seen the advent of a strong economy in which high-technology firms with computer hardware and software and internet communication were regarded as the driving forces behind the significant growth of the global economy. As a result of considering these policy implications, diverse policy tools designed so as to enhance the role of technology-oriented SMEs in the Korean economy were introduced in this period (SMBA, 2001). The Small and Medium Business Administration (SMBA), the government agency which offers administrative and legal support to SMEs, introduced "Venture Business", a special legal category of firms, under the 1997 Special Measures Law for Fostering Venture Businesses, so as to ease the establishment and development of small, high-technology-based firms, and it provided the firms that are classified into this category with favourable treatment for their operation and finance. (For example, when one or more venture capitalists invest in a firm exceeding 10 per cent of its outstanding capital for over six months, the firm was designated as a Venture Business.) Furthermore, in order to boost the size of venture capital that invests in small, high-tech firms, the SMBA introduced the 1998 Special Measures Law for Facilitating Small and Medium Business Investment Venture Capital Company. The 1997 and 1998 Laws mentioned induced a significant growth in the venture capital industry, whose two main investment channels are Venture Capital Companies (VCCs) or Limited Partnership Funds (LPFs).[10]

In Figure 2.4, it is shown that, since 1998, the size and the number of VCCs and LPFs had increased dramatically. The number of VCCs more than doubled from 72 in 1998 to 145 in 2001, while that of LPFs more than quadrupled from 93 in 1998 to 395 in 2001. The total assets of VCCs more than doubled from KRW 1 trillion to KRW 2.2 trillion in 2001, while the amount of capital invested

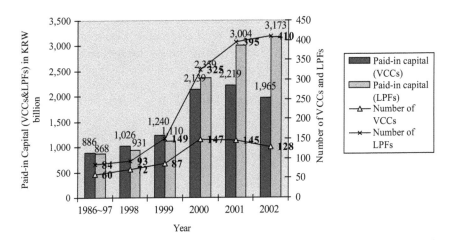

Figure 2.4 Investment by VCCs and LPFs, 1986–2002

Source: Internal data from KVCA (2003)

in LPFs more than tripled from 900 billion in 1998 to 3 trillion in 2001. Many firms funded by VCCs and LPFs went to KOSDAQ which was designed to facilitate IPOs of small and medium high-technology firms and recorded remarkable stock market returns after IPOs.

As in the cases of other major countries, the Korean venture capital industry experienced a sharp decline during 2001, after a period of huge growth in the late 1990s and 2000, accompanied by the steep drop of worldwide public equity markets. The KOSDAQ index increased by more than five times during the several years to March 2000 and then decreased considerably, coupled with the global decline in technology stocks in April 2000 (KVCA, 2001). The KOSPI (Korea Composite Stock Price Index) exceeded 1,000 points in early January 2000 but halved to around 500 one year later. Generally, the IPO firms (whether funded by venture capital companies or not) that realised the very high stock market returns had to suffer from the sharp decline of stock prices. In this situation, the optimistic times of the late 1990s with the prospect of further growth in the venture capital industry were overshadowed by the collapse of technology stock in the global equity stock market, leading to reduced investment. During 2001, fewer venture capital companies were successful in raising capital. At the same time, venture capital companies attracted very few limited partners for venture funds in comparison with the period of 1999–2000. This situation was often described as a "venture winter" in which venture capital financing activities froze and new Korean companies had difficulties in getting the venture capital they needed.

A lot of firms, in reality, had little difficulty in finding venture capital funding as long as they had a business plan under the title of technology or the internet. Their business models were not in doubt. However, the KVCA yearbook (2001) shows that venture capitalists demanded of Korean technology companies, which made up the majority of the companies that received venture capital, that they became more concerned with customer requirements and market opportunities rather than just being involved with technology alone. The slowdown in the Korean venture capital investment had been continuing since mid-2000, coupled with the lagged venture-capital-backed IPO market trend. However, it was expected that this venture capital investment in Korea would rebound in the near future and that venture capitalists would focus their screening and evaluation activities on areas with strong unique intellectual property and better prospects for investment returns (KVCA, 2001).

2.3.2 Comparison of Korean venture capital industry with those in other countries

2.3.2.1 Venture capital disbursements[11]

The Korean venture capital industry grew sharply in late 1990s to cultivate the development of high-tech SMEs. After many years of nearly negligible investments in portfolio companies markets until 1997, venture capital funds remarkably increased the amount of capital that they invested in portfolio firms. In

1998, the venture capital industry invested USD 280.9 million in 21 new firms, but invested USD 1.66 billion in 136 firms in 1999 and USD 2.83 billion in 567 firms in 2000, showing an enormous growth of investment in portfolio firms: the total value of disbursements jumped by 490.5 per cent from 1998 to 1999 and an additional 70.9 per cent from 1999 to 2000, and the number of the firms invested leapt by 547.6 per cent from 1998 to 1999 and by a further 316.9 per cent from 1999 to 2000 (See Figure 2.5). However, the Korean venture capital industry saw a sharp fall in venture capital disbursement, with venture funds disbursement dropping to USD 452.8 million in 2001, down by 84.0 per cent from the previous year. Only 24 companies were successful in gaining venture capital in 2001, down by 95.8 per cent from the preceding year. The laggard venture capital activity during 2001 brought the industry back to the levels last witnessed in 1998, in terms of the total amount invested as well as the number of companies in which they invested. This trend of decreasing investment in portfolio firms was also seen in many other countries over the year.

This extraordinary growth in the Korean venture capital industry during 1999 and 2000 is in line with the increasing trend of venture capital investment in other major countries over the same year (See Table 2.2). In general, the amount of venture capital disbursement, referred to as investments in portfolio companies, significantly increased during 2000 throughout the world. In the USA, the total amount invested in portfolio companies by the venture capital industry rose by 74.3 per cent from USD 59.3 billion in 1999 to USD 103.4 billion in 2000, showing a 74.3 per cent increase. The number of companies that venture capital funds invested in increased from 3,969 in 1999 to 5.412 in 2000, which shows a 36.4 per cent rise. In the UK, venture capital disbursements increased by 7.2 per cent from 1999 to 2000 at USD 12.4 billion, although the number of companies invested in was reduced to 1,254, down from 1,321. Other major European

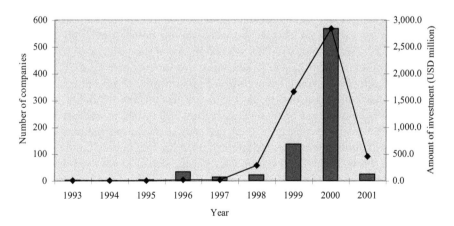

Figure 2.5 Venture capital disbursements in Korea by year

Sources: KVCA (2001)

Table 2.2 Venture capital disbursements by country

	1999		2000		Change (%) of Amount	Change (%) of Number of Firms
	USD million	Number of Firms	USD million	Number of Firms		
USA	59,371.8	(3,969)	103,493.5	(5,412)	74.3	36.4
UK	11,582.9	(1,321)	12,415.6	(1,254)	7.2	−5.1
France	2,837.1	(2,545)	4,996.4	(2,994)	76.1	17.6
Germany	3,181.5	(2,081)	4,490.5	(3,012)	41.1	44.7
Korea	**1,658.9**	**(136)**	**2,834.7**	**(567)**	**70.9**	**316.9**
Italy	1,791.7	(390)	2,796.8	(646)	56.1	65.6
Sweden	1,286.1	(819)	2,166.6	(702)	68.5	−14.3
Netherlands	1,722.2	(872)	1,804.9	(789)	4.8	−9.5
Spain	728.1	(314)	1,061.6	(389)	45.8	23.9
Switzerland	443.1	(254)	589.7	(237)	33.1	−6.7
Belgium	677.8	(504)	532.2	(483)	−21.5	−4.2
Finland	250.8	(364)	361.7	(398)	44.2	9.3
Norway	266.9	(172)	278.8	(256)	4.5	48.8
Denmark	116.8	(150)	258.1	(253)	120.9	68.7
Ireland	105.7	(173)	210.1	(205)	98.6	18.5
Poland	N/A	N/A	190.3	(102)	N/A	N/A
Greece	71.5	(45)	183.7	(78)	156.9	73.3
Portugal	119.8	(95)	172.4	(161)	43.8	69.5
Austria	89.6	(91)	153.5	(151)	71.3	65.9
Iceland	24.2	(75)	130.0	(179)	437.8	138.7
Czech Republic	N/A	N/A	114.9	(32)	N/A	N/A
Hungary	N/A	N/A	48.0	(51)	N/A	N/A
Slovakia	N/A	N/A	0.9	(9)	N/A	N/A

Sources: KVCA (2001), NVCA (2001), EVCA (2001)

countries clearly show the remarkable growth of venture capital disbursements over the same period. In France, the total amount invested in 2000 grew by 76.1 per cent, amounting to USD 5.0 billion, while the number of companies reached 2,994, up from 2,545. In Germany, investments rose by 41.1 per cent compared with 1999, going from USD 3.2 billion to USD 4.5 billion. In Italy, total disbursements increased by 56.1 per cent from USD 1.8 billion to USD 2.8 billion in amount and by 65.6 per cent from 390 to 646 in number of firms. Although Sweden experienced a 68.5 per cent rise in disbursements at USD 2.2 billion in 2000, it witnessed a decline by 14.3 per cent in the number of port-folio firms. From Table 2.2, it can be seen that the size of Korean venture capital disbursements in 2000 ranks top 5 among 23 countries whose venture capital statistics were published by major venture capital associations. Only the USA (USD 103.5 billion), the UK (USD 12.4 billion), France (USD 5.0 billion), and Germany (USD 4.5 billion) surpassed Korea (USD 2.8 billion) in 2000, which shows how dramatically the Korean venture capital industry had grown during this period.

Compared with the USA (5,412), the UK (1,980), France (2,994) and Germany (3,012), the number of firms invested in by venture capital stands at only 567 in Korea, which does not show as much significant difference from other countries as the amount invested. This indicates that the average amount invested per portfolio firm was very large.

2.3.2.2 Funding stage and size of investment

A noticeable characteristic in the Korean venture capital industry is that venture capital investment tended to be concentrated in the expansion stage (See Table 2.3). From 1993 to 2002, this stage had been the single category to gain investment capital every year. In 1999, 59.9 per cent (USD 994.8 million) of the total investment amount (USD 1.66 billion) was directed towards the expansion stage, while this proportion sharply declined in 2000 to 27.0 per cent (USD 764.6 million). However, in 2001, the proportion bounced back, with 59.3 per cent (USD 268.5 million) of the total investment amount (USD 452.8 million) going towards the expansion stage. From Table 2.3, it can be seen that very few companies could raise funds at the seed and start-up stages. In total, only 0.2 per cent (seed) and 2.5 per cent (start-up) of venture capital was invested in the companies at the initial stages, whereas a relatively greater portion of venture capital was drawn to the other early initial stage at 4.9 per cent. Moreover, it also shows that venture capital companies spent a great deal of money in acquisition activity. In total, the largest proportion of investment was directed at acquisition activity (46.4 per cent), which is close to the investment spent on fostering SMEs from the seed stage to the later stage (48.8 per cent).

The investment trend in Korea in which venture capital focuses on the expansion stage rather than on seed and start-up is also similar to those in other countries in 2000 (See Table 2.4). Among 23 countries, almost all the countries show that a larger proportion of investment went into the expansion stage, except Finland and Ireland. In the US, the investment in the expansion stage (USD 76.7 billion) more than tripled compared with that in the start-up stage (USD 23.8 billion). In the UK, the largest investments were made in the expansion stage with the amount being USD 4.2 billion, while only about one third of expansion stage investment was made in the start-up stage (USD 1.5 billion). In France, venture capital invested in the expansion stage at USD 1.8 billion, which is larger than the total of seed and start-up investment (USD 1.1 billion). In Germany, expansion stage investment represented USD 2.1 billion, while start-up and seed investment remained at USD 1.6 billion in total.

However, in Finland the investment in the start-up stage (USD 106.3 million) was slightly larger than that in the expansion stage (USD 106.0 million) and also in Ireland more investment was made in the start-up stage at USD 103.7 million than in the expansion stage at USD 94.5 million. This concentration of venture capital investment in the expansion stage indicates that venture capital financing generally occurs at the stage when investee firms have a track record, however

Table 2.3 Venture capital investing in Korea by stage by year

Year	Seed		Start-up		Other early stage		Expansion		Later stage		Public market		Acquisition		Special situations		Total	
1993					2.1	(1)	0.4	(1)									2.5	(2)
1994							0.0	(1)									0.0	(1)
1995			0.0	(1)			0.0	(1)			0.4	(1)					0.4	(3)
1996	0.0	(1)					15.8	(32)									15.8	(33)
1997					1.2	(2)	10.8	(11)									11.9	(13)
1998			0.3	(2)	0.7	(3)	90.1	(14)			157.9	(1)	32.0	(1)			280.9	(21)
1999	0.5	(1)	3.7	(7)	8.4	(23)	994.8	(98)	10.0	(3)	0.2	(2)	616.3	(2)	25.0	(1)	1,658.9	(137)
2000	10.3	(7)	131.1	(72)	229.0	(209)	764.6	(293)	2.2	(2)	0.1	(2)	1,675.5	(6)	21.9	(1)	2,834.7	(592)
2001	0.4	(1)	1.1	(3)	20.8	(5)	268.5	(13)			42.0	(1)	120.0	(1)			452.8	(24)
Total	11.2	(10)	136.1	(85)	262.1	(243)	2,145.0	(464)	12.2	(5)	200.6	(7)	2,443.8	(10)	46.9	(2)	5,258.1	(826)

Sources: KVCA (2001). The amount of venture capital investment is in USD million. The figures in parentheses are the number of firms invested in.

Table 2.4 Venture capital investment by stage in 2000 in the countries

	Seed		Start-up		Expansion		Replacement		Buyout	
USA	N/A	N/A	23,840.5	N/A	76,781.1	N/A	N/A	N/A	2,871.9	N/A
UK	60.7	(7)	1,458.0	(455)	4,226.9	(577)	102.6	(39)	6,566.9	(176)
France	66.2	(120)	1,021.6	(977)	1,774.4	(1033)	230.8	(149)	1,903.2	(335)
Germany	369.0	(285)	1,187.6	(809)	2,018.2	(1110)	124.3	(28)	790.8	(88)
Korea	**10.3**	**(7)**	**360.1**	**(281)**	**766.8**	**(295)**	**21.9**	**(1)**	**1,675.5**	**(6)**
Italy	124.1	(69)	384.2	(175)	910.2	(197)	93.4	(16)	1,284.2	(33)
Sweden	26.8	(81)	187.6	(282)	314.7	(171)	2.0	(6)	1,635.0	(28)
Netherlands	0.4	(4)	350.3	(213)	984.6	(288)	134.2	(70)	335.6	(63)
Spain	2.7	(22)	185.7	(110)	535.5	(196)	38.9	(11)	298.4	(21)
Switzerland	2.4	(10)	52.3	(57)	118.0	(70)	11.9	(7)	405.1	(33)
Belgium	75.2	(61)	174.2	(158)	245.8	(183)	5.1	(4)	31.6	(12)
Finland	21.2	(72)	106.3	(157)	106.0	(87)	3.6	(5)	124.7	(29)
Norway	4.9	(13)	93.1	(103)	176.2	(110)	0.4	(3)	4.2	(3)
Denmark	1.1	(13)	30.8	(71)	118.9	(86)	29.4	(18)	77.2	(15)
Ireland	1.3	(3)	103.7	(77)	94.5	(64)	5.1	(5)	5.6	(2)
Poland	2.6	(10)	36.5	(25)	148.6	(52)	1.8	(4)	0.0	(0)
Greece	0.0	(0)	8.6	(12)	103.9	(43)	71.0	(16)	0.0	(0)
Portugal	0.0	(0)	28.9	(46)	97.9	(70)	3.0	(2)	42.7	(11)
Austria	10.8	(37)	45.7	(25)	83.3	(53)	0.0	(0)	13.6	(3)
Iceland	0.8	(15)	33.4	(76)	64.3	(63)	0.0	(0)	31.2	(2)
Czech Republic	0.0	(0)	14.7	(8)	81.8	(19)	17.9	(5)	0.0	(0)
Hungary	0.9	(5)	0.6	(3)	27.1	(22)	0.0	(0)	19.5	(5)
Slovakia	0.0	(1)	0.0	(1)	1.3	(7)	0.0	(0)	0.0	(0)

Sources: KVCA (2001), NVCA (2001), EVCA (2001). The amount of venture capital investment is in USD million. The figures in parentheses are the number of firms invested in

limited, with growth potential, and they need more money to expand their business (Berger and Udell, 1998).

A noteworthy point from Table 2.4 is that, in several countries, venture capitalists make more investments in buyout than in the stages of fostering entrepreneurial firms: seed, start-up and expansion. In 2000, not only in Korea, but also in the UK, France, Italy, Sweden, Finland and Switzerland, buy-out financing consisted of the largest amount of venture capital investment. In the UK, buyout investment was nearly 52 per cent (USD 6.6 billion) of total investment (USD 12.4 billion). In France, buyout investment amounted to USD 1.9 billion, representing 38 per cent of total investment (USD 5.0 billion). In the other countries, buy-out financing makes up 45 per cent (Italy), 75 per cent (Sweden), 35 per cent (Finland) and 69 per cent (Switzerland). This indicates that, in many major European countries, buyout investment is regarded as the primary form of venture capital investment. While US venture capital investment tends to be directed towards the needs of entrepreneurial firms at the early and expansion stages, European venture capital considers buy-back investment as significant as other investments that aim to foster entrepreneurial firms (Black and Gilson, 1999).

2.3.2.3 *Venture capital investment by industry*

In Table 2.5, it is shown that Korean venture capital investment is concentrated in the industry sectors of high technology. The information, communication and computer-related industries are the most important sectors for Korean venture capital. In total, from 1993 to 2001, out of 800 firms that were provided with venture capital, 167 companies (20.8 per cent), 233 companies (29.1 per cent), and 110 companies (18.2 per cent) were from the communication industry, computer-related industry, and other electronic industries, respectively, totalling 510 companies (63.7 per cent). Overall, although these high technology industries generally account for a similar proportion of all investments every year, there is a slight change in the importance of each industry. Communication companies represented 23.5 per cent of total investments in 1999, 21.0 per cent in 2000, and 20.8 per cent in 2001. Computer-related companies occupied 35.3 per cent in 1999, 30.2 per cent in 2000 and 25.0 per cent in 2001. These two industries show a slight decline in venture capital investee firms through the years. However, other electronic companies show a slight increase in the proportion of total investee firms, up from 12.5 per cent in 1999 to 13.1 per cent in 2000 and 16.7 per cent in 2001. The biotechnology industry emerged as an important sector in 2000, opening new investment opportunities for venture capital. The number of biotechnology firms that received venture capital funding amounts to 42 out of 567 companies in 2000. Biotechnology firms accounted for only 2.2 per cent of total investment in 1999, but the proportion of total investment rose to 7.4 per cent in 2000 and to 4.2 per cent in 2001.

The dominance of high technology industry in venture capital investment is also confirmed in other countries (See Table 2.6). In 2000, US venture capital companies invested in 4,374 firms (80.8 per cent) that belong to the communication,

Table 2.5 Venture capital investing in Korea by industry by year

Year	Bio-technology	Communications	Computer related	Consumer related	Energy	Industrial products	Medical/ health	Other	Other Electronics	Total
1993								2		2
1994									1	1
1995			1	1				1		3
1996		5	4	5		6		9	4	33
1997		2	2			1	1	2	5	13
1998	1	4	1	2		1		7	5	21
1999	3	32	48	5	1	6	3	21	17	136
2000	42	119	171	18	2	29	15	97	74	567
2001	1	5	6	1				7	4	24
Total	47	167	233	32	3	43	19	146	110	800

Sources: KVCA (2001). Figures are number of firms.

Table 2.6 Venture capital investment by industry in countries worldwide

	Communi-cation	Computer	Other Elec.	Bio-tech	Medical	Energy	Consumer	Indus-trial	Chemi-cals	Automa-tion	Other Manuf.	Trans-port.	Finan-cial	Other serv.	Agricul-ture	Cons-truction	Other
USA	3,026	1,109	239	180	341	73	141	237	39	36	128	39	36	179	17	58	303
France	558	486	126	121	99	5	353	191	62	179	30	12	87	143	6	25	97
Germany	262	530	56	186	162	18	240	25	20	11	76	23	50	68		32	157
UK	264	270	76	27	141	14	137	81	12	8	31	14	8	52	8	6	20
Netherlands	88	157	9	32	22	8	52	49	6	6	13	4					51
Sweden	124	141	23	28	60	9	23	29			13	4	15	32			34
Korea	**119**	**171**	**74**	**42**	**15**	**2**	**18**	**29**									**97**
Italy	128	53	3	7	18	4	44	27	7	3	47	8	29	48	14	14	36
Belgium	86	92	11	32	8	1	35	23	1	5	14	4	5	43	2	8	47
Spain	72	41	7	7	13	7	52	49	21	3	9	3	7	44	6	11	8
Finland	65	77	15	31	54		20	18	9	3	21	3	4	9	2	13	5
Norway	47	41	7	5	27	10	22	7	2	5	7	5	10	17	9		19
Denmark	9	29	13	54	20		11	16	4	4	2	2	4	7			18
Switzerland	3	60	19	6	19		3	16	3	9	9		6	9			13
Iceland	29	48	2	9	13	4	4	9			2	2	15		2		15
Ireland	34	57	15	2	6	2	15	3		2	8			3	2	5	3
Portugal	17	9	2		1	4	9	15	3		26			19	1		21
Austria	26	21	3		13		10	13	1	8	10	3		3	3		5
Poland	34	14				1	2	4			6	4	7	11	3		4
Greece	11	7			6		22	2			11			4			4
Hungary	13	4			4		2	3						2	4		9
Czech Republic	13	7			2		3	3			5					2	
Slovakia							3	1			3		1			1	

Sources: KVCA (2001), NVCA (2001), EVCA (2001). Figures are number of firms.

computer-related and other electronic industries, followed by medical products (6.3 per cent) and biotechnology (3.3 per cent). In the UK, those three high-tech industries account for about 50 per cent (610 firms) out of total investee firms (1,254 firms), with the remaining investment being distributed among all industries, compared with the US case. In a lot of European countries, the concentration of venture capital in three high technologies amounts to more than 40 per cent in terms of the number of firms that received venture capital funding: France (44.8 per cent), Sweden (50.6 per cent), Switzerland (46.9 per cent), Belgium (45.3 per cent), Finland (45.0 per cent), Norway (41.1 per cent), Ireland (69.7 per cent). In Germany, although the top three high technology industries reflect 36.1 per cent (848 firms) out of the total (2,346 firms), venture capital investment is evenly distributed among all industries, compared with other countries.

In the Netherlands, industrial product industry receives fairly large investment (12.6 per cent, 81 firms), preceded by communication (13.7 per cent, 88 firms) and computer-related industry (24.5 per cent, 157 firms). In Spain, consumer-related industry stands as the second largest industrial sector (14.4 per cent, 52 firms), preceded by communication (20.0 per cent, 72 firms). In Denmark, biotechnology (26.7 per cent, 54 firms) is the largest industrial sector for venture capital investment, which is greater than the sum of the investee firms in the top three industries (25.2 per cent, 51 firms).

2.3.2.4 Sources of venture capital companies and limited partnership funds

Venture capital companies in Korea can be classified into four groups by who is the largest shareholder in them (See Figure 2.6). More than half (55 per cent) of venture capital companies were founded by corporate venturing companies. Bank-affiliated venture capital companies represent 21 per cent, securities-company-affiliated venture capital 4 per cent and private individuals 20 per cent. Figure 2.7 also shows the sources of limited partnership funds that were established for the purpose of investing in small, young and high-tech firms in Korea, in terms of capital commitment. The leading shareholders of limited partnership

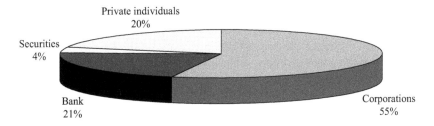

Figure 2.6 Shareholding composition of Korean venture capital companies by founder type in 2001

Source: KVCA (2001)

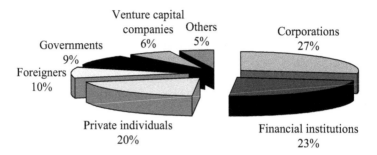

Figure 2.7 Shareholding composition of limited partnerships in Korea in 2001
Source: KVCA (2001)

funds come from corporations (27.5 per cent), followed by financial institutions including banks (23.7 per cent), private individuals (19.7 per cent), foreigners (9.5 per cent), government (8.8 per cent), venture capitalists (6.2 per cent) and other (4.6 per cent).

In other countries, there exist diverse structures of limited partnership sources (See Figure 2.8). In the USA and the UK, pension funds are the leading type of limited partnership funds in 2000. In the USA, this category committed 40.0 per cent of the capital raised by general partners (venture capitalists). The remaining sources come from banks (23.0 per cent), individuals (12.0 per cent) and corporations (4.0 per cent). In the UK, although the pension funds are the largest contributor (40.1 per cent) to the capital committed in limited partnership funds, the proportion of banks is relatively small (9.6 per cent), compared with the USA. Two more countries among 23 countries where pension funds are the largest limited partners are Sweden (35.1 per cent) and Denmark (46.5 per cent). However, in other European countries, the main source of limited partnership is banks. Banks are the largest capital contributors in limited partnership in France (38.8 per cent), Germany (29.0 per cent), Italy (42.9 per cent), Spain (42.5 per cent), Ireland (24.5 per cent), Poland (32.6 per cent), Greece (43.5 per cent), Portugal (64.8 per cent), Austria (48.0 per cent), the Czech Republic (63.2 per cent), and Hungary (93.4 per cent). In the other European countries, large financial institutions and mutual funds take a large role in investing in limited partnership. In the Netherlands, insurance companies (17.3 per cent) and the fund of funds[12] (19.3 per cent) are the major investors in limited partnership. Insurance companies are also the leading type of investor in Finland (34.6 per cent) and Norway (22.5 per cent). In a country such as Slovakia, where venture capital financing started more recently, the government made the whole venture capital commitment. In a few countries, corporate venturing companies are one of the main sources of limited partnership: France (13.0 per cent), Italy (26.4 per cent), Netherlands (18.5 per cent), Belgium (22.7 per cent), Norway (16.8 per cent), and Ireland (10.6 per cent). In Finland and Germany, governments contribute 20.1 per cent and 16.4

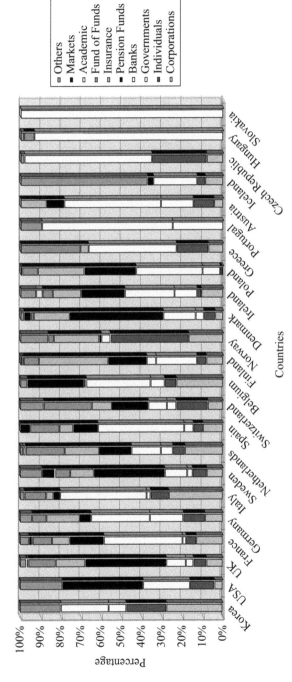

Figure 2.8 Composition of limited partnerships by partner type in 2000

Source: KVCA (2001), NVCA (2001), EVCA (2001)

per cent of capital committed, respectively. In Norway, individuals are the largest source (38.2 per cent) of limited partnership.

2.4 Institutional framework of IPO

2.4.1 IPO and its importance as investment realisation

A venture capitalist invests in an entrepreneurial firm with his own capital or in the form of a limited partnership as a general partner for a certain time. Since the venture capitalist has an expectation of obtaining a huge gain in return for his long-term investment, investment realisation and how (and when) it will be achieved is an important issue. The investment of the venture capitalist is finally realised by means of diverse investment realisation methods: IPO (Initial Public Offering), trade sale (merger and acquisition), MBO (Management Buy-Out),[13] MBI (Management Buy-In)[14] etc. There is clear evidence of the heterogeneity of the features and the timing of these various realisation methods, depending on the preference of the entrepreneurial firm and venture capitalist, corporate governance structure, stock market condition and the institutional differences of each country (Wright, Robbie et al.,1993; Wright and Robbie, 1998; Cumming and MacIntosh, 2003). However, in the context of venture capital investment, most attention has been given to investment realisation through IPO (Barry, Muscarella et al.,1990; Megginson and Weiss, 1991; Lerner, 1994; Jain and Kini, 1995; Ljungqvist, 1999; Brau, Brown et al.,2004 etc.). IPO has been believed to be one of the best ways of investment realisation because of its potential super returns (Bygrave, Hay et al.,1999).

IPO takes place when the equity is sold to the general public for the first time in the stock market. IPO indicates that a growth firm has reached a point at which it needs considerable new capital from the public market in order to implement its second-generation production technology after its seeding, start-up and development stages (Brealey and Myers, 1999). Going-public firms are no longer the firms with no track records that have attracted private capital only by displaying their high growth potential to private investors. They are medium-sized or large firms having track records and substantial assets, parts of which are available for collateral to loans (Berger and Udell, 1998). IPO provides private investors with the chances to sell their illiquid investment in a liquid public market (Ritter, 1998). Once the stock is publicly traded, this augmented liquidity permits the company to raise capital on more favourable terms from a large number of diversified investors than if it had to compensate a limited number of investors in a privately closely held firm context (Ritter, 1998).

However, along with these benefits, there are costs. An IPO firm should pay the cost of preparing a prospectus that ensures that it is qualified to go public by supplying clear evidences of its soundness in liquidity and profitability, and a promising prospect in its operation. It is required to supply the information on the firm regularly to the government regulators and public investors even after IPO. IPO firms not only pay the direct costs of legal, auditing and underwriting fees on a one-off basis, but also the indirect costs of management time and effort spent on implementing the offering in the IPO process. IPO leads to a fundamental transformation of strategy, structure, personnel, control processes and standard operating procedures. Managers of IPO issuing firms begin to undergo a completely new experience of intense scrutiny and monitoring from public capital market participants (Jain and Kini, 2000).

On the part of venture capitalists, IPO presents an opportunity to exit from their investment by selling some of the outstanding shares.[15] This IPO exit mechanism functions as a benchmark that enables outside capital providers to evaluate both the relative skill of venture capital managers and the profitability of limited partnership relative to other kinds of investment (Gompers, 1996). IPO is a turning point in the investment strategy of a venture capitalist. The venture capitalist is rewarded by abnormal returns after having taken long-term and risky investment decision and rearranges its capital and management resources to another growth entrepreneur.

2.4.2 Heterogeneity of investment realisation and IPO

In general, among those means of exit, IPO is regarded as the most desirable exit by venture capitalists. In particular, it is known that US venture capitalists normally seek to exit from investments by means of successful IPOs. According to Venture Economics (1988), IPO is the most frequently used and preferred investment realisation by venture capitalists. In its survey,[16] 35 per cent was accounted for by IPO, whereas the next most common method was acquisition by another company, which accounted for 22 per cent. Venture Capital Journal states that almost all (96 per cent) of the IPOs yielded positive returns for the venture capitalists, while only 59 per cent of the acquisitions did so.[17] Moreover, this preference for IPO over other exit methods is related to the fact that IPO means a "partly" realised investment and reserves the chances to get extra capital gain while venture capitalists retain ownership. Acquisition and trade sales, on the other hand, usually indicate a "total exit" by venture capitalists, which implies that there are no more chances for further gains (Abbott and Hay, 1995). However, despite the enthusiasm for IPO, there are clear indications that venture capitalists' approach to investment realisation is very flexible. This is the case especially for European countries. Relander, Syrjanen et al. (1994) shows that though IPO is the most preferred investment realisation route even in European countries, in practice, a trade sale to a third party is the most common form. They stated that a trade sale generally takes place "when a threshold for an IPO is not reached or because an attractive but unforeseen acquisition proposal is received".[18]

It seems that the preference for each exit route is strongly influenced by the strength of the stock market and the economic conditions. Bygrave, Fast et al. (1989) state that the significant growth of pension funds since the ERISA "prudent man" rule was eased at the end of the 1970s led to the surge of venture capital in the US and the stock market peaked in 1983 as a result. What with the abundant supply of venture capital and the great demand of the potential entrepreneurial firms that lacked sufficient funding, IPOs backed by venture capitalists hit their highest point in 1983. When the US economy recovered after a long depression during the later 1980s, venture capital annual return went up to above 20 and the annual numbers of IPOs and the average offering size renewed the previous records. Murray (1995) also gives evidence of the UK case that when the UK stock market was very strong in 1993, venture-capital-backed IPOs increased: from July 1992 to June 1993, venture-capital-backed flotation represented 48 per cent of the total of the 75 IPOs. In the late 1990s, when the IPO market had been dominated by the firms based on new technology, some of which did not show any concrete earning growth, the number of IPOs had dramatically increased over this period. However, when the US stock market showed a dramatic decline after the second quarter in 2000, it deeply affected the IPO market, resulting in the significant fall of venture-capital-backed IPOs.[19]

When the stock market situation is not favourable, M&A rises as an alternative for investment realisation instead of IPO. When the stock market is in stagnation or is extremely volatile, so that it does not guarantee record-breaking returns, venture capitalists and entrepreneurs postpone or cancel an offering and tend to consider M&A as an exit strategy (Gannon, 1998). Moriarty (1999) shows that, after the slowdown of the US IPO market in 1997, M&A activity among entrepreneurs grew. The number of M&A through the third quarter in 1998 increased to 199 in 1998, from 107 through the third quarter in 1997 and the ratio of venture-capital-backed IPOs to venture-capital-backed M&A decreased to 59.7 per cent from 95.3 per cent through the two periods. NVCA (2001) reports that the drop-off in the IPO market in 2000 for venture-backed companies allowed M&A deals to reach record levels, as 275 companies were acquired for a total amount of USD 69 billion. In the UK, there is a survey which shows that entrepreneurs consider MBO as an important exit strategy: the majority of venture capitalist respondents regarded MBO as the most important exit route when they were in this economic recession (BVCA, 1990). Respondents believed that MBO would be applied to later stage financing when it reflects the problems of recession, rescue-type, refinancing deals. They thought that MBO provides entrepreneurs with the ability to supply capital when the firms remain basically sound, but are financially constrained as the finance sources such as borrowing and new equity become less readily available during a recession period. It can be said, despite the fact that IPO is considered as the most preferred form of exit, that if the stock market is in a downturn, or does not develop well enough to allow buyers and sellers of issues to benefit from sustainable capital gains and abundant liquidity, it may not be selected as an exit option.[20]

2.4.3 The IPO process and valuing IPOs

Even though the global stock markets have considerable variety in the process of IPO, they share many key characteristics. As is shown in Figure 2.9, after the company takes the decision to go public, it interviews potential financial advisors, such as investment bankers and lawyers, who will support the whole IPO process. With the help of the existing auditors, the company prepares quarterly and

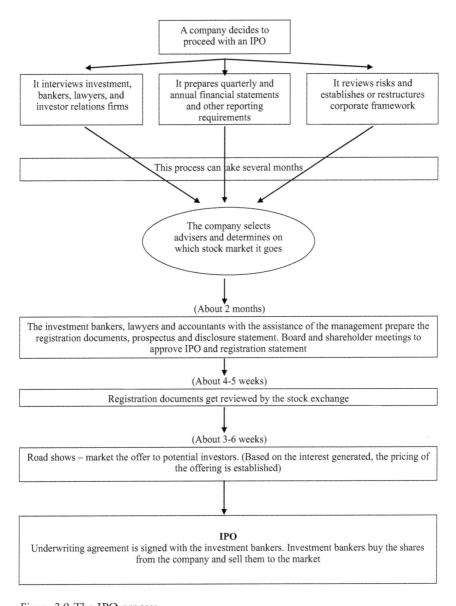

Figure 2.9 The IPO process

This figure was originally drawn from Rutschmann (1999) and Piccino and Kierski (1999) and was revised to reflect the Korean context.

annual financial statements and other reports which are required to be included in the registration documents and prospectus. The company often restructures its organisation by reviewing potential risks in the business, and assesses potential litigation and tax liability (Piccino and Kierski, 1999). After that, the company selects one or more investment banks and lawyers and decides on which stock market it will be floated. Lawyers provide legal services such as drafting and reviewing the prospectus, providing advice on shareholder structure, IPO litigation risk and disclosure requirements. The investment bank has a legal responsibility to conduct "due diligence" through the all the stages of preparing IPO. Due diligence requires itself with a detailed investigation into the authenticity of information provided by the going-public company (Roll, 1996). The investment bank evaluates the performance of the company, provides a high degree of advice on the long-term strategy and daily operation of the company and positions the company in the market in order to obtain comparable valuation on the issue.

One of the important things that the going-public company and investment banker have to do is to value (price) the offering. As a rule, valuing IPO is no different from valuing other stocks. The traditional financial techniques such as discounted cash flow (DCF) method and firm comparison analysis are used. However, in practice, since many IPOs are of young growth firms in high technology industries, historical accounting information has only limited value in predicting future profits and cash flows (Ritter, 1998). Accordingly, an initial valuing depends greatly on how the market is valuing other comparable companies and how intense the demand in the companies is (Piccino and Kierski, 1999).[21]

Analysts in the investment bank produce a periodic report that explains the history and business of the company to assist investors in understanding the position of the company. When the application for the registration successfully passes regulatory inspection, the company has got a preliminary prospectus and implements a marketing campaign for the offering. The company and the investment bankers hold a "road show" in major cities, where they make presentations in front of prospective investors. Through this event, the investment bank stimulates interest in the issue, attracting large institutional investors and small personal investors so that shares may be sold to them.

Based on the demand on the issue ascertained at the road shows, the company and the investment bank determine the offer price and the size of the offering.[22] Except for the shares allotted to small personal investors, shares in the offering are usually allotted to large institutional investors and underwriter syndicates. Bygrave, Hay et al. (1994) state that, in general, one third is allocated to a so-called "institutional pot", which is a group of large institutional investors who are active enough in the IPO market for their trading behaviour to be easily predicted. The remaining shares are placed among underwriter syndicate members who undertake to buy the shares and sell them to investors when the trading of shares begins in the market. Investment bankers typically act as market makers, in other words, they participate vigorously in the trading of the company's stock and thus provide liquidity.

On the part of venture capitalists, an opportunity to sell part of their existing shareholding and to sell the remaining part at a follow-on secondary offering if the company performs up to their expectations is given. However, venture capitalists are typically under the regulation of a lock-up period during which shares cannot be sold, thus they should wait until the lock-up period expires to liquidate their shareholding.[23]

2.5 Trend of Korean and other countries' IPO markets

2.5.1 Overview of KOSDAQ

Behind the considerable growth of the venture capital industry in Korea since the late 1990s was the existence of a well-functioning IPO market. The KOSDAQ (Korean Securities Dealers Automated Quotation) stock market, the over-the-counter stock market in Korea, took a lead in all the IPO listings over this period. KOSDAQ was established in July 1996 to promote the advancement of high-technology firms and SMEs (Small and Medium Enterprises) into the public stock market. The Korean government, after the 1980s, realised that the *chaebol* (big conglomerates)-dominated and volume-oriented export economy policy would reach its limit, so it recognised the necessity to transform the Korean economic structure in a way such that more SMEs, especially high technology-oriented companies, would contribute to the further growth of the Korean economy. To do this, the Korean government introduced a lot of industrial policies that stimulate the economic activities of SMEs, such as extending tax favours and financial support in order to foster their growth. However, the local stock market, KSE (Korean Stock Exchange)'s listing requirements were too rigorous for SMEs to go public, which made it all the harder for rapidly growing SMEs and entrepreneurs to raise enough funds through the channel of the public equity market. The Korean government took the decision to pave an alternative route that enables SMEs and entrepreneurs to obtain direct financing from the stock market and announced in 1987 the "Market Organisation Plan for Vitalising the Stock Trading of SMEs". As a result of this plan, the KSDA (Korean Securities Dealers Association), arranged an OTC (over-the-counter) market in April 1987, and, as the number of traded companies increased, the government authorised the KSDA to organise the KOSDAQ, which is the Korean version of NASDAQ, the secondary stock market in the USA.[24]

KOSDAQ had been going through its fledgling stage before 1997, when the Asian Financial Crisis clouded the Korean economy. However, the financial crisis was, in a sense, a disguised blessing to SMEs financing and the development of KOSDAQ. In a situation where the high-debentured and uncompetitive chaebols collapsed, the government used this opportunity to reform the Korean economy by lifting up the SMEs' position in the Korean economy. As was mentioned in the above overview of the Korean venture capital industry (section 2.3.1), the governments enforced the measures to expand the role of high technology-oriented SMEs in 1998, especially by enhancing their financing. In 1999, a new administrative measure designed to promote IPOs in KOSDAQ was implemented: for example, some listing requirements were eased and tax incentives were given to the KOSDAQ-listed companies. What with the government efforts to stimulate the direct financing of SMEs through KOSDAQ and the unprecedented expansion of IT investment in computer hardware/software and online internet businesses, KOSDAQ experienced dramatic growth from mid-1999. As shown in Table 2.7, The KOSDAQ index more than tripled from 75.18 points at the end of 1998 to 256.14 points by the end of 1999. Market capitalisation volume increased astoundingly from KRW 7.89 trillion in 1998 to KRW 98.7 trillion in 1999. Total trading volume in 1999 was KRW 8.75 trillion, representing an increase of more than 40 times relative to that in 1998. However, following the decline of the global stock market and the downfall of the IT boom in 2000, KOSDAQ suffered a dramatic drop from the previous year in terms of market index and market capitalisation volume.

The KOSDAQ market index plummeted about 80 per cent from 256.14 points at the end of 1999 to 52.58 points at the end of 2000. The total market capitalisation volume shrank to about one third from KRW 98.7 trillion to KRW 29 trillion in twelve months. The KOSDAQ index made a rally in 2001 (72.21 points at the year-end) but fell to the lowest level since 1997 (44.36 points at the year-end) in 2002. However, during the period 1999–2001, venture-capital-backed IPOs account for more than 40 per cent of all the IPOs each year. As is shown in the part on the basic characteristics of our 372 IPO samples in Chapter 5, venture-capital-backed IPOs represented 50 per cent of all the IPOs in 1999, 44 per cent in 2000 and 42 per cent in 2001.

Table 2.8 shows that KOSDAQ had been fast-growing relative to KSE. The number of listed firms in KOSDAQ increased significantly from 453 at the end of 1999 to 721 at the end of 2001 and surpassed the number of KSE-listed firms at the end of 2002 by 843 to 683. Over this period, most of the going-public companies selected KOSDAQ rather than KSE to list their shares. This occurred because the Korean government allowed KSDA to apply more relaxed standards for listing requirements to going-public high-tech SMEs, providing them with easier access to the stock market. By the end of 2000, KOSDAQ had 608 companies with the market capitalisation amounting to KRW 29 trillion, about 15.4 per cent (KRW 188 trillion) of KSE.

Table 2.7 Major yearly statistics of KOSDAQ

	1997	1998	1999	2000	2001	2002
KOSDAQ index	97.25	75.18	256.14	52.58	72.21	44.36
Total Capital Stock Value	3,495	5,408	13,061	15,128	14,735	14,616
Total Outstanding Stocks	719,475	1,167,115	4,089,875	7,076,907	8,414,065	10,517,566
Market Capitalisation	7,069	7,892	98,704	29,016	51,818	37,403
Trading Volume	47	206	8,754	51,050	94,393	78,182
Trading Value	1,166	1,607	106,808	578,490	425,180	294,091

Sources: KSDA (2003), Unit of statistics is KRW billion won or thousand shares

Table 2.8 Comparison of major yearly statistics between KOSDAQ and KSE

	1998		1999		2000		2001		2002	
	KOSDAQ	KSE	KOSDAQ	KSE	KOSDAQ	KSE	KOSDAQ	KSE	KOSDAQ	KSE
Market Index	75.18	562.46	256.14	1028.07	52.58	504.62	72.21	693.7	44.36	627.55
Trading Volume	56	5,494	2,525	6,003	4,826	5,199	6,967	11,599	7,175	15,689
Trading Value	293	43,696	42,676	91,294	19,366	27,396	29,058	60,083	19,033	40,591
Market Cap	7,892	137,798	98,704	349,504	29,016	188,041	51,818	255,850	37,403	258,681
Daily Avg. Trading Volume	3	275	126	300	284	306	367	610	378	826
Daily Avg. Trading Value	15	2,185	2,134	4,565	1,139	1,612	1,529	3,162	1,002	2,136
No. of Listed Companies	331	748	453	725	604	704	721	689	843	683
Listed No. of Shares	1,167	11,444	4,090	17,326	7,049	19,639	8,414	19,578	10,518	26,463
Weighted Avg. Stock Price (KRW)	6,762	12,041	29,300	20,418	4,129	9,622	6,154	12,609	3,546	9,811

Sources: KOSDAQ (2003) Units are KRW Billion and Million Shares. Trading Volume and Trading Value are the sum of each day in December.

However, the market capitalisation volume and trading volume of KOSDAQ are smaller and more volatile than those of KSE. The market capitalisation volume in KOSDAQ rose to KRW 51.8 trillion at the end of 2001, but dropped to KRW 37.4 trillion billion at the end of 2002, while that in KSE increased to KRW 255.8 trillion billion at the end of 2001 and maintained the same level (KRW 258.6 trillion) at the end of 2002. Trading volumes totaled KRW 4.8 trillion during December 2000, reaching 90 per cent of trading volumes (KRW5.2 trillion) of KSE in the same month. However, in later years, the gap in trading volumes in the same month between the two stock markets has not been narrowed.

2.5.2 Comparison of KOSDAQ with other IPO markets

2.5.2.1 Market profile

In Table 2.9, it is shown that KOSDAQ is one of the most successful second-tier stock markets in the OECD countries. The number of IPO companies rose from 453 in 1999 to 843 in 2002, showing about a 90 per cent increase.

In terms of the listed companies, KOSDAQ is bigger than any other stock market, except for the NASDAQ (3,725 companies in 2002) and Canadian Venture Exchange (2,504 companies in 2002), being followed by AIM (Alternative Investment Market) in the UK (704 companies) and Neuer Markt in Germany (240 companies), the Swedish O-List market (235 companies), and the French Nouveau Marche (154 companies). From the point of view of market capitalisation shown as the percentage of GDP, KOSDAQ is also ahead of most other countries with 22.0 per cent in 1999, following NASDAQ (56.5 per cent) and the Swedish O-List market (28.3 per cent). Only these three countries show a two-digit percentage. The success of KOSDAQ indicates that the government's attempt to nurture the IPO market for high-tech SMEs has taken effect, at least, from a quantitative point of view.

However, it can be seen that the global economic slowdown and the sluggish performances of technology-based stocks led KOSDAQ to decline significantly from its peak. The percentage of market capitalisation vis-à-vis GDP dropped considerably from 22.0 per cent in 1999 to 5.0 per cent in 2002, though KOSDAQ still ranks fourth in these statistics among OECD countries. I can see that, since mid-2000, the global second-tier stock markets had suffered from a serious drop in market value. NASDAQ, which had surpassed all the other stock markets since its establishment in 1971, witnessed a substantial downfall in its market value, with its market capitalisation percentage out of GDP continuing to decline from 56.5 per cent in 1999 to 16.5 per cent in 2002. The other stock markets were no exception to this rule, being deeply affected by the decreasing market value of the companies.

Table 2.10 shows that the KOSDAQ market index trend was in line with other major second-tier stock markets. The dramatic rise in 1999 and the fall since 2000 in KOSDAQ was also experienced in NASDAQ, where the stock market index increased 85.6 per cent during 2000 but fell – 39.3 per cent in 2000. AIM

Table 2.9 Second-tier stock markets in OECD countries

Country (stock market)	Year of creation	Number of initial public offers (IPOs)				Number of quoted companies				Market capitalisation (per cent GDP)			
		1999	2000	2001	2002	1999	2000	2001	2002	1999	2000	2001	2002
United States (NASDAQ)	1971	485	397	63	40	4,829	4,734	4,109	3,725	56.5	36.9	28.9	16.5
Canada (Canadian Venture Exchange)	1999	2,425	403	330	122	2,358	2,598	2,688	2,504	1.7	10.2	12.7	9.7
Korea (KOSDAQ)	1996	160	250	181	176	453	604	721	843	22.0	5.6	9.5	5.0
United Kingdom (AIM)	1995	67	203	109	78	347	524	629	704	1.5	1.6	1.2	1.0
Germany (Neuer Markt)	1997	132	132	11	1	201	338	326	240	5.7	6.0	2.4	0.5
Sweden (O-List)	1988	N/A	N/A	24	9	150	228	240	235	28.3	24.0	23.3	18.5
France (Nouveau marché)	1996	32	52	9	2	111	158	164	154	1.1	1.7	1.0	0.5
Norway (SMB List)	1992	3	7	7	3	78	77	79	79	4.2	1.8	1.5	1.2
Italy (Nuovo Mercato)	1999	6	32	5	0	6	40	45	45	0.6	2.2	1.2	0.6
NASDAQ Europe	2001	—	—	N/A	N/A	—	—	49	43	—	—	—	0.2
Finland (NM List)	1999	N/A	N/A	N/A	N/A	N/A	17	16	15	N/A	0.7	0.3	0.2
Spain (Nuevo Mercado)	2000	—	N/A	N/A	N/A	N/A	12	N/A	14	—	3.4	N/A	N/A
Switzerland (SWX New Market)	1999	6	11	1	0	6	17	15	9	N/A	3.0	0.9	0.2
Ireland (ITEQ)	2000	—	N/A	N/A	N/A	—	7	8	8	—	3.6	1.7	0.7
Denmark (Dansk AMP)	2000	3	0	1	3	3	3	4	7	0.1	0.1	0.1	0.1
Japan (Mothers in Tokyo)	1999	2	27	7	8	2	29	32	N/A	0.2	0.1	0.1	0.1
Japan (Hercules in Osaka)	2000	—	N/A	43	N/A	—	N/A	N/A	N/A	N/A	N/A	0.3	N/A
Netherlands (EURO.NM Amsterdam)	1997	1	2	—	—	13	15	—	—	0.3	0.2	—	—
Belgium (EURO.NM Belgium)	1997	6	3	—	—	13	16	—	—	0.2	0.2	—	—
Europe (EASDAQ)	1996	N/A	N/A	—	—	56	62	—	—	—	—	—	—
Austria (Austrian Growth Market)	1999	N/A	N/A	—	—	2	2	—	—	0.01	0.01	—	—

Sources: OECD (2003) (Compiled by OECD Secretariat from national sources) In 2001, EURO.NM (EURO.NM Belgium and EURO.NM Netherlands) and EASDAQ merged and became NASDAQ Europe. Japan Hercules in Osaka stock market was previously NASDAQ Japan.

Table 2.10 Comparison of major yearly statistics among KOSDAQ, NASDAQ and AIM

	KOSDAQ	NASDAQ	AIM
Market Index			
1998	75.18 –	2,192.7 –	801.6 –
1999	256.14 (240.7)	4,069.3 (85.6)	1,932.7 (141.1)
2000	52.58 (−79.5)	2,470.5 (−39.3)	1,437.8 (−25.6)
2001	72.21 (37.3)	1,950.4 (−21.1)	897.8 (−37.6)
2002	44.36 (−38.6)	1,335.5 (−31.5)	602.9 (−32.8)
Market Capitalisation			
1998	6.6	2,588.8	7.4
1999	87.2	5,204.6	21.7
2000	22.9	3,597.1	22.3
2001	39.2	2,899.9	16.9
2002	31.5	1,997.6	16.5
Trading Volume			
1998	205,654	202,040,229	6,921,384
1999	8,674,393	270,108,214	21,258,520
2000	51,050,314	442,752,966	39,510,300
2001	94,393,120	471,216,589	28,166,600
2002	78,181,894	441,665,958	24,791,760
Trading Value			
1998	1.4	5,758.6	3.2
1999	94.3	11,013.2	8.7
2000	457.3	20,395.3	20.3
2001	321.4	10,934.6	7.1
2002	248.0	7,254.3	5.7

Sources: KOSDAQ (2003), NASDAQ Newsroom (2003), LSE (2003). Parentheses in the market index are the rate of change compared to the last year-end's market index. Market capitalisation and trading value of each year in KOSDAQ and AIM were converted to USD based on the exchange rate at each year-end. Units are billions dollars and thousand shares.

also went through the same pattern of rise and fall in the same period with 141.1 per cent increase in 1999 and – 25.6 per cent decrease in 2000. The market capitalisation volumes of KOSDAQ have remained very tiny, relative to those of NASDAQ over the years; they surpassed AIM in 1999, with KRW 87.2 billion in 1999, about four time as large as the market capitalisation volume of AIM (USD 21.7 billion). The trading value, the sum of all the equity turnovers across the year, also shows that KOSDAQ overtook AIM in 1999. The trading value in KOSDAQ in 2000 was USD 457.3 billion, while the trading value in AIM in the same year remained USD 20.3 billion.

2.5.2.2 Listing requirements

Before a company goes public in KOSDAQ, it must satisfy the prerequisites for listing on KOSDAQ. A security company acting as the underwriter for the

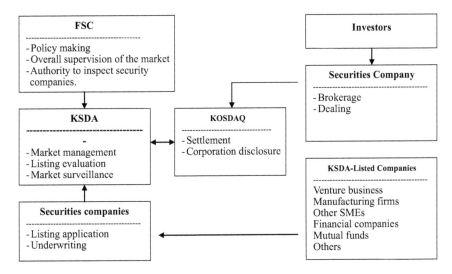

Figure 2.10 KOSDAQ Stock market flowchart

This chart is drawn from KSDA (2001).

firm appraises the issuer's capability to comply with the listing requirements and then files a preliminary application form with KSDA (Korean Securities Dealers Association). Along with this, the going-public firm is required to register itself with FSC (Financial Supervisory Committee). If the issuers' stocks are judged by KSDA and FSC to be eligible for listing, by meeting the listing requirements, KSDA permits the listing.

All the issuing companies must satisfy the share distribution requirement. In principle, all the issuing companies should have a minimum of 500 minority shareholders who own more than 30 per cent of shares altogether. In this case, they can put up 10 per cent or more of the total outstanding shares at the IPO. However, if the minor shareholders (a minimum of 500) have less than 30 per cent of shares, the issuing companies put up 20 per cent or more of the total outstanding shares at the IPO. Listing requirements apply differently to "Venture Businesses" and "Ordinary Businesses".

The Venture Business that is designated as such by SMBA, as explained in Section 2.3.1, has no obligation to meet the listing requirements for the minimum years of establishment, size of capital, debt-to-equity ratio and profitability. However, the Ordinary Business should satisfy the following minimum requirements: three years or more of incorporation history; KRW 500 million or more of paid-in-capital; 100 per cent or less than 100 per cent of debt-to-equity ratio, or less than 1.5 times the average debt ratio of the same industry sector; positive ordinary income during the most recent fiscal year. Other than these requirements, the same listing requirements apply to the Venture Business and the Ordinary Business. The listing requirements for the KOSDAQ IPO firms are summarised in Table 2.11.

Table 2.11 Listing requirements in KOSDAQ

Categories	Ordinary Business	Venture Business
Quantitative and Legal Requirements		
Years of incorporation	3 years or more	-
Paid-in capital	KRW 500 million won or more	-
Debt-to-equity ratio	100 per cent or less than 100 per cent, or less than 1.5 times the average debt ratio of the same industry sector	-
Profitability	Positive ordinary income during the most recent fiscal year	-
Share distribution	The number of minimum small shareholders is 500. If they have 30 per cent or more than 30 per cent of outstanding shares, 10 per cent is the minimum requirement the company should put up at IPO. However, if they have less than 30 per cent of outstanding shares, the minimum to be put at IPO is 20 per cent. (Foreign firms: 300,000 shares or more to more than 100 minority shareholders)	
Auditor's opinion	Either "qualified" or "qualified with reservation"	
Transfer of shares	No limitations on transferring shares in the corporation's constitution	
Face value of the share	KRW 100, 200, 300, 1000, 2500, 5000	
Lawsuits	No lawsuits that will affect the business significantly. If the company goes bankrupt, the reasons must be resolved within 6 months of the listing application date	
Standing auditor	Companies with total assets of more than KRW 100 billion in the most recent fiscal year should employ a Standing auditor.	
Independent director	Companies with total assets of more than KRW 100 billion in the most recent fiscal year should employ an Independent director.	
Qualitative Requirements		
Truth of application statements	No false description or expression in the contents of the preliminary application and the documents attached thereto. Such a company should not fail to describe or express material information therein.	
Financial stability	For an enterprise whose current ratio, quick ratio, loan dependency ratio or financing cost ratio, etc. are inferior to the average ratios of the industry to which it belongs, then the financial stability of such an enterprise is significantly low considering its loan composition ratio, fund management plan, etc.	
Ownership of the venture capitals and listing agent	No record of any officer or employee of a venture capital company investing in shares of stock, etc. of the concerned venture business to be listed for his own account, regardless of the titles thereof; and no record of any officer or employee in charge of listing affairs of a listing agent investing in shares of stock, etc. of a company to be listed for his own account, regardless of the titles thereof, except succession and testamentary gift, etc.	

Categories	Ordinary Business	Venture Business
Qualitative Requirements		
Establishment of the proper disclosure organisation	Material data related to the management of the company, such as a CPA audit report, etc. must be disclosed in a legal manner and the company must maintain a management system to disclose financial status, business performance and so on in a timely manner.	
Compliance related to laws and regulations	No difficulties in ordinary business activities under the sanctions related to violations of statutes. No significant danger in the company's financial status due to the bankruptcy of affiliate companies or the possibility thereof. No significantly inappropriate reason for a company to list with KOSDAQ for investor protection considering the nature of the business.	

Source: KSDA (2003)

Table 2.12 Financial listing requirements in NASDAQ

Categories	Standard 1 Marketplace Rule 4420(a)	Standard 2 Marketplace Rule 4420(a)	Standard 3 Marketplace Rule 4420(a)
Stockholder's equity	USD15 million	USD 30 million	–
Market value of listed securities	–	–	USD 75 million
Total assets	–	–	USD 75 million
Total revenue	–	–	USD 75 million
Income from continuing operations before income taxes (in latest fiscal year or 2 of last 3 fiscal years)	USD 1 million	–	–
Publicly held shares	1.1 million	1.1 million	1.1 million
Market value of publicly held shares	USD 8 million	USD 18 million	USD 20 million
Minimum bid price	USD 5	USD 5	USD 5
Shareholders (round lot holders)	400	400	400
Market makers	3	3	4
Operating history	–	2 years	–
Corporate governance	Marketplace Rules 4350 and 4351	Marketplace Rules 4350 and 4351	Marketplace Rules 4350 and 4351

Source: NASDAQ (2003). For Standard 3, a company must satisfy one of the following: the market value of listed companies or the total assets and the total revenue requirement. Publicly held shares are defined as total shares outstanding less any shares held by officers, directors, or beneficial owners of 10 per cent or more. Round lot holders are shareholders of 100 shares or more.

There is considerable diversity in listing requirements among global stock markets, so it is very difficult to compare the listing requirements on KOS-DAQ with those on other stock markets directly. In the case of AIM, the listing requirements are not very stringent. Companies do not need to have reached a certain size or have any particular years of establishment. Moreover, they are not required to distribute shares to minor shareholders, unlike KOSDAQ. In NAS-DAQ, there are several quantitative listing requirements for different categories of standards, requiring the minimum size of equity, total assets, profitability, etc. A company must meet all of the requirements under at least one of three listing standards.

Stockholders' equity is required to be USD 15 million or more (Standard 1) and USD 30 million (Standard 2). In Standard 3, a company must meet one of the following requirements: USD 75 million or more of market value of listed securities or USD 75 million or more of total assets and USD 75 million or more of total revenue. A company must distribute at least 1.1 million shares to the public in all three schemes. However, the requirement on the market value of publicly held shares is more stringent in Standard 3 (a minimum of USD 20 million). While KOSDAQ has a particular requirement on minority shareholders, NASDAQ has a "round lot holders" requirement: shareholders who own 100 shares or more must be at least 400 or more. A company needs to have a business history of at least two years under Standard 2, but other standards have no requirements concerning the operating history. Companies listed on NASDAQ are required to maintain a high degree of corporate governance, outlined in the NASDAQ Marketplace Rules.[25]

2.6 Implication of the chapter

In this chapter, I have reviewed the institutional aspects of the venture capital industry and the IPO market and described the recent trend of the Korean and other countries' venture capital industry and IPO market. It was shown that the Korean venture capital industry and IPO market had experienced dramatic remarkable growth since the late 1990s, which highlighted the private and public financing of high-tech oriented SMEs. Korea ranked the third in terms of venture capital investment as a share of GDP and the number of second-tier stock market-listed firms among the leading OECD countries. The venture capitalist investment was shown to be concentrated in the expansion stage and high-technology sector, which is similar to other countries. The growth of KOSDAQ is in line with that of other global second-tier stock markets that was followed by the ICT stock boom in the late 1990s. This sharp growth of Korean venture capital industry and the IPO market provides us with a peculiar setting for empirical study, especially in comparison with that of other countries. In the following chapter, I review the literature in terms of the relationship between the venture capital investment and the performance of the firms that the venture capital companies back, and derive several testable hypotheses for our empirical analysis.

Notes

1 The definition of venture capital is different across countries. The above definition is prevalent in the US context in terms of the relationship between the venture capital investment and initial public offering. However, the definition of venture capital in the European context includes a broader scope of venture capital investment, which is inclusive of seed, early, expansion, mezzanine (late), turnaround and buyout transactions (Cumming, 2002)

2 According to a seminal paper by Sahlman (1990), the contracts have certain similar characteristics, particularly: (1) staging the commitment of capital and preserving the option to abandon; (2) using compensation systems that are directly linked to value creation; (3) preserving ways to force management to distribute investment proceeds. These elements of the contracts present three fundamental problems: (1) the sorting problem – how to select the best venture capital organisations and the best entrepreneurial firms; (2) the agency problems – how to minimise the present value of agency costs; (3) the operating-cost problem – how to minimise the present value of operating costs, including taxes.

3 Sahlman (1990) sums up the key provisions: (1) the limited life of the venture capital fund; (2) limited partners' right to withdraw from funding the partnership by reneging on their commitments to invest beyond the initial capital infusion; (3) a compensation system structured so as to give the venture capitalists the appropriate incentives, so that venture capitalists are typically entitled to receive 20 per cent of the profits generated by the fund; (4) prohibition provisions to prevent venture capitalists from serving their own interests; for example, venture capitalists' self-dealing (being more able to buy stock in the portfolio on preferential terms or receiving distributions different from those given to the limited partner); (5) venture capitalists are required to commit a certain per centage of their effort to the activities of the fund.

4 Venture capitalists sit on the board of directors, help recruit and compensate key individuals, work with suppliers and customers, help establish tactics and strategy, play a major role in raising capital, and help structure transactions such as mergers and acquisitions (Sahlman, 1990).

5 Insider finance can be defined as funds offered by the start-up team and CEO, their families and friends before and at the time of business inception.

6 Pecking order theory states that the information asymmetry problem between investor and investee affects the choice between internal and external financing and between new issues of debt and equity securities. This results in a pecking order of financing choices, in which the investment is financed first with internal funds, reinvested earnings primarily; then by new issues of debt; and finally with new issues of equity (Myers and Majluf 1984). This pecking order theory reflects the preference of financing on the part of investee firms. If they have internal funds sufficient for their investment, they do not need to rely on external finance. If they issues debt or equity over internal funds, despite the fact that they have enough cash flow to cover the potential projects, it may give outside investors a wrong impression that the their financial structure will deteriorate. Moreover, an optimistic firm that predicts that its profit will increase in the future does not issue equity at present because it thinks that it can sell the more expensive equity later on. Rather, it issues debt now, thus lowering the financial cost. Furthermore, a firm whose profit is expected to be not very good may try to issue the stock at present because they will not be able to draw the equivalent money in the future. But, its attempts to issue equity would force the stock price down and get rid of any advantage in the future. To avoid this, the firm does not issue equity, but ends up issuing debt.

7 Garmaise (1997) argued that while it seems reasonable to argue that entrepreneurs have a superior informational advantage over certain aspects of their project, such as the feasibility of their project's technology, it may be plausible to assume that venture capitalists have superior information over a project's marketability and its operational implementation.

8 Other researchers show that different criteria are used for the screening phase. MacMillan, Zemann et al. (1987) show that venture capitalists think highly of "entrepreneurial personality" and "experience", with less emphasis on market, product and strategy. Muzyka, Birley et al. (1995) emphasise "good management team" and "reasonable financial and product market" characteristics.

9 Average annual yield of an investment, where the interest earned over a period of time is the same as the original cost of the investment.

10 Venture capital in Korea is invested in two ways established by the 1986 SME Establishment Assistance Law: Venture Capital Companies (VCCs) or Limited Partnership Funds (LPFs). The VCCs must be registered with the SMBA as a corporation that provides capital mainly to start-ups. It is entitled to receive government assistance in the form of low-interest loans, equity funding and tax benefits, but must invest a certain share of its portfolio in small firms less than seven years old. The LPFs, which are pooled funds where each investor receives profit in proportion to the amount invested, are generally launched and managed by VCCs. Legally, all LPFs must receive a certain share of financing from VCCs (SMBA, 2001).

11 Disbursement means an investment by a venture capital company into a portfolio company.

12 A mutual fund which invests in other mutual funds.

13 MBO (Management Buy-Out) is defined as management's purchase of all outstanding shares from venture capitalists.

14 MBI (Management Buy-In) is defined as the purchase of company shares owned by venture capitalists by an outside investor who leaves the management unchanged.

15 IPO company is set up partly to sell new shares (which is called the *primary* offering) to raise additional cash for the company. It is also set up partly to sell the existing shares (which is called the *secondary* offering) owned by the venture capitalists and its founders.

16 It included 544 venture capital investments made between 1970 and 1982.

17 Also, according to *Venture Capital Journal*, average gain of IPO was more than 150 per cent, but that of other major exit ways such as acquisitions, buy-backs and secondary sales was less than 50 per cent.

18 Petty, Bygrave et al. (1994) argue that trade sales provide more immediate full liquidity of an investment than is possible in an IPO, while it deprives the entrepreneur of the management and control over the firm. Wright et al. (1993) surveys the investment realisation preferences of venture capitalists in four European countries and documents that trade sale is the favourite exit form in UK, France, and Holland. They argue that trade sale is attractive because of the ability to achieve actual realisation of cash.

19 *Business Week* (May 7, 2001) reports the contrasting beginning of two IPO years in the US: "The first quarter (of 2001) was the worst for IPOs since the end of 1990, with just 24 deals offered. Compare that with 121 in the opening quarter of 2000". Total IPO in NASDAQ decreased from 397 in 2000 to only 63 in 2001.

20 Wright and Thompson et al. (1994) state that the preferred form of investment realisation will vary between countries and also in the same country over time, depending on the state of development of buy-out, stock and corporate asset markets, and economic conditions that affect the feasibility of investment realisation types and their timing.

21 Piccino and Kierski (1999) document the factors to be considered when valuing IPO firms. The IPO firm should be positioned in the market to obtain comparable company valuations. Comparable companies in the same industry sector will be used as benchmarks, which are, for example, based on price-earning ratios, sales multiples, and long-term EPS growth estimates. A qualitative analysis of the company's growth prospects is also important. Market opportunity, the company's leadership position in the market and the industry, its technology, time to market advantage as well as particular features should be critical. Moreover, the IPO valuation has to take the long-term growth prospects into account. IPO has to be priced reasonably in line with the EPS growth prospects. In addition, the merger market value as well as the public market value should be taken into account. The merger market value reflects the control aspect, which, in most cases, commands high premiums due to potential takeover bids. The control premium value should be treated as a potential upside.

22 The revision of offer price after finding out the market demand is called "book-building" During the marketing campaign ("road show") period, the underwriter investigates potential buyers, their willingness to purchase the IPO stocks and the price which they think is reasonable. Through this process, a demand curve of the quantity and price of the stocks to be sold is constructed and the offering price is then based on this information (Ritter, 1998).

23 In US, there was a 180-day lock-up period. In Korea, the lock-up period was 6 months, if a venture capitalist had had shareholding for less than 6 months, and 3 months if it had had it for more than 6 months.

24 The introduction of KOSDAQ needed the amendments in the Securities and Exchange Act (Article 172) in 1996. KOSDAQ mediated the trading of KSDA-listed stocks and OTC bonds through a central processing agent, matching all buy and sell orders received from securities companies. KSDA organised the KOS-DAQ Committee to prop up the market's efficiency and integrity in 1998 (KSDA, 2001).

25 NASDAQ corporate governance requirements include the following sub-section: distribution of annual and interim reports, solicitation of proxies, independent directors, conflicts of interest, audit committees, shareholder approval, shareholder meeting, stockholder voting rights, quorum, auditor peer review (NAS-DAQ, 2003).

3 Literature review and formulation of hypotheses[1]

3.1 Overview

Numerous studies have documented the fact that aftermarket underpricing in the short run and underperformance in the long run are observed in the pricing of Initial Public Offerings (IPOs) of common stock, and they have attempted to understand the meaning of these phenomena. While most of the discussion has concentrated on the information asymmetry problem that comes up between issuer, underwriter and investor, it has been shown that a financial player who certifies uncertain IPO firms can significantly reduce the information gap, thus decreasing the degree of underpricing, and, furthermore, can contribute to the development of business operations and management in the long term. If they lack this kind of certification and value-adding services, IPO firms can face serious conflicts of interest between themselves and investors, thus being required to underprice their shares and later experiencing worse stock price performance. In much of the literature, a venture capital company has been considered as an institution that alleviates the information asymmetry that is inherent between issuing firm and investor and enhances the value of the firm through its ownership and management.

In this chapter, I review the literature regarding underpricing and the long-term performance of IPO firms and the certification and value-adding role of venture capitalists. Moreover, given the setting of the empirical study in KOSDAQ, which has experienced a dramatic growth since 1999, I proceed to take our discussion a step further by considering how different organisations of venture capital companies can affect the performance of IPO firms. I assume that not only the presence of venture capitalists,[2] but also the ownership structure of venture capitalist companies has a significant meaning for the performance of IPO firms. Following our literature review and discussion, I derive twelve testable hypotheses that can be examined by using IPO data for the KOSDAQ market during the period 1999–2001.

The remainder of this chapter is organised as follows. In Sections 3.2 and 3.3, I look at the pattern of underpricing and long-run underperformance of IPO stocks in the worldwide stock markets in order to see how these two anomalies in the pricing of IPOs are prevalent. Sections 3.4 and 3.5 deal with how the information asymmetry between investors and issuers affects underpricing and long-term performance. I also consider how these relationships may be affected by the state of the stock market, in particular, the impact of 'hot' or speculative market booms. In Section 3.6, I cover the certification and value-adding role of venture capitalists, which are explained in detail in relation to internal mechanisms designed to minimise uncertainty in entrepreneurial firms; monitoring and screening functions through participation in the ownership and management of the entrepreneurial firms; and external activities, such as forming a close relationship with other financial players. Section 3.7 discusses the impact of different organisation forms of venture capitalists on the performance of IPO firms. Our research focuses on how banking organisations can effectively certify IPO firms and add value for them through a venture capital subsidiary by using the "information advantage" that they acquire through close monitoring of the firms with which banks have an on-going lending relationship. In Section 3.8, following the discussion of the certification and value-adding role of venture capitalists, twelve hypotheses are derived.

3.2 The immediate aftermarket underpricing[3] phenomenon

It is well known that stocks going public are frequently associated with large initial returns (the price change measured from the offering price to the market price on the first trading day). A number of researchers have reported that IPO stocks exhibit such underpricing. Ritter (1991) states that IPOs of common stocks show a pattern of abnormally large returns on their first trading day in the US. In his article, the average underpricing and hence initial return from the sample was estimated at 16.4 per cent. Furthermore, as reported in Loughran, Ritter et al. (1994, 2003), this phenomenon of underpricing was experienced in every country with a stock market. Table 3.1 shows a summary of the average initial

Table 3.1 Average initial returns of IPO firms in worldwide stock markets

Country	Authors	Sample Size	Time period	Average IR
Australia		381	1976–1995	12.1
Austria		83	1984–2002	6.3
Belgium		86	1984–1999	14.6
Brazil		62	1979–1990	78.5
Canada		500	1971–1999	6.3
Chile		55	1982–1997	8.8
China		432	1990–2000	256.9
Denmark		117	1984–1998	5.4
Finland		99	1984–1997	10.1
France		571	1983–2000	11.6
Germany		407	1978–1999	27.7

(*Continued*)

Table 3.1 (Continued)

Country	Authors	Sample Size	Time period	Average IR
Germany*	Franzke (2003)	300	1997–2002	49.8
Greece		338	1987–2002	49.0
Hong Kong		857	1980–2001	17.3
India		98	1992–1993	35.3
Israel		285	1990–1994	12.1
Italy		181	1985–2001	21.7
Japan		1,689	1970–2001	28.4
Japan *	Kirkulak. (2002)	456	1997–2001	35.9
Korea		477	1980–1996	74.3
Korea *	Kim and Park (2002)	347	1999–2001	143.8
Malaysia		401	1980–1998	104.1
Mexico		37	1987–1990	33.0
Netherlands		143	1982–1999	10.2
New Zealand		201	1979–1999	23.0
Norway		68	1984–1996	12.5
Portugal		21	1992–1998	10.6
Singapore		441	1973–2001	29.6
South Africa		118	1980–1991	32.7
Spain		99	1986–1998	10.7
Sweden		332	1980–1998	30.5
Switzerland		120	1983–2000	34.9
Taiwan		293	1986–1998	31.1
Thailand		292	1987–1997	46.7
Turkey		163	1990–1996	13.1
United Kingdom		3,122	1959–2001	17.4
United Kingdom*	Levis (2001)	240	2000	60.1
United States		14,840	1960–2001	18.4
United States*	Ljungqvist and Wilhelm (2003)	2,178	1996–2000	35.7

Note: This table is an updated version of Loughran, Ritter et al. (1994) and Loughran, Ritter et al. (2003). Full references to the articles cited in these articles can be found in Loughran, Ritter et al. (2003). New articles added by this author are marked with a * and full reference is added. Initial returns are mainly the difference between the offer price and the first-day closing price, but in some cases they are the difference between the offer price and the closing price of some days or some weeks after the trading began, reflecting price increases that did not fully realise at the first day (Loughran, Ritter, et al.,1994).

returns on IPOs in a number of countries around the globe. Among 34 nations surveyed in Loughran, Ritter et al. (2003), no stock markets realised less than 0 per cent on average on the initial returns of going public firms across the years, which indicates that offer prices of IPO stocks on average were underpriced. Only four countries (Austria, Canada, Chile, and Denmark) show less-than –10 per cent initial returns on average over the period surveyed in the literature.

Many of the initial returns are concentrated in the range from 10 per cent to 30 per cent (in countries such as Australia, Belgium, Finland, France, Germany, Hong Kong, Israel, Italy, Japan, the Netherlands, New Zealand, Norway, Portugal, Singapore, Spain, Turkey, the United Kingdom and the United States). However, 12 countries out of 33 exhibit considerably higher initial returns, which are over 30 per cent. These countries include Brazil (78.5 per cent), China (256.9 per cent), Greece (49.0 per cent), India (35.3 per cent), Korea (74.3 per cent), Malaysia (104.1 per cent), Mexico (33.0 per cent), South Africa (32.7 per cent), Sweden (30.5 per cent), Switzerland (34.9 per cent), Taiwan (31.1 per cent), and Thailand (46.7 per cent). Though not contained in Loughran, Ritter et al. (1994), more recent empirical studies on IPO underpricing which cover a shorter period, in particular for the samples of late 1990s and early 2000, also demonstrate higher returns: US (35.9 per cent) in Ljungqvist and Wilhelm (2003), UK (60.1 per cent) in Levis (2001), Germany (49.8 per cent) in Franzke (2003), Japan (35.9 per cent) in Kirkulak (2002) and Korea (143.8 per cent) in Kim and Park (2002). Underpricing in Korea appears to be very high, compared with that of all other countries, except China and Malaysia.

Ritter and Welch (2002) have documented the fact that underpricing phenomenon was especially remarkable in the late 1990s, in which the "new economy" paradigm and "technology and internet stock boom" prevailed over the global economy. If I take the example of the US, this phenomenon seems very evident. The average initial return of IPO stocks was 18.4 per cent over the period 1960–2001. But, if I separate this return into different periods, the underpricing was 14.5 per cent in 1980 and reached 65.0 per cent in 1999 and 2000, but fell back to 14.0 per cent in 2001 in the US (Ritter and Welch, 2002).

It seems that large initial returns (underpricing) that are realised on the first or early days of trading are a universal phenomena that are observed in the global stock markets. Although underpricing became considerably larger in the years 1999 and 2000, it was consistently found in the previous years, too.

3.3 Poor long-term performance phenomenon

It was also reported that IPO stocks showed, on average, a poor longer-term performance, relative to a variety of benchmarks (Ritter, 1991; Loughran, Ritter et al.,1994; Loughran and Ritter, 1995; Ritter and Welch, 2002). Loughran and Ritter (1995) report that the underperformance of IPO firms reached 20.0 per cent over the period 1970–1990. According to Ritter and Welch (2002), the average benchmark-adjusted three-year buy-and-hold return of IPO stocks in the US was – 23.4 per cent during the period 1980–2001.

This long-run returns contrast sharply with the high initial returns (18.4 per cent) that US IPO firms recorded during 1960–2001. This deteriorating long-term performance of IPO stocks is not limited to the US. Table 3.2 displays the long-term performances of IPOs in other stock markets. Among 12 countries (excluding the US) surveyed by Ritter (1998), only two countries recorded positive three-year IPO returns (Korea: +2.0 per cent, Sweden: +1.2 per cent).

Table 3.2 Long-term performances in worldwide stock markets

Country	Authors	Sample size	Time period	Average long-term
Australia		266	1976–1989	–46.5
Austria		57	1965–1993	–27.3
Brazil		62	1980–1990	–47.0
Canada		216	1972–1993	–17.9
Chile		28	1982–1990	–23.7
Finland		79	1984–1989	–21.1
Germany		145	1970–1990	–12.1
Japan		172	1971–1990	–27.0
Japan *	Hamao, Pecker et al. (2000)	355	1989–1994	–10.7
Korea		99	1985–1988	2.0
Singapore		45	1976–1984	–9.2
Sweden		162	1980–1990	1.2
United Kingdom		712	1980–1988	–8.1
United Kingdom *	Espenlaub, Garrett et al. (1999)	249	1986–1991	–8.0
United States		4,753	1970–1990	–20.0
United States *	Ritter and Welch (2002)	6,249	1980–2001	–23.4

Note: This table is based on the collection of empirical results of long-term abnormal returns around the globe in Ritter (1998). Full references to the articles cited in this review can be found in Ritter (1998). New articles added by this author are marked with a * and full reference is added. The long-term returns are typically measured as 3 years buy-and-hold returns, which are defined as $100 * [1+ R_{ipo,T}]/(1 + R_{m,T})] - 100$, where $R_{ipo,T}$ is the average total return on the IPOs from the market price of the first trading day until three years; $R_{m,T}$ is the average of benchmark returns, which is either a market return or a matching-firm return over the same interval.

Almost all of the stock markets surveyed in this table exhibit negative three-year IPO returns. While the UK (–8.1 per cent) and Singapore (–9.2 per cent) showed higher-than-minus 10.0 per cent three-year IPO returns, other countries recorded significantly worse three-year performances: Australia (–46.5 per cent), Austria (–27.3 per cent), Brazil (–47.0 per cent), Canada (–17.9 per cent), Chile (–23.7 per cent), Finland (–21.1 per cent), Germany (–12.1 per cent), and Japan (–27.0 per cent). More recent studies that are not contained in Ritter (1998) also show the negative long-term performance: Japan (–10.7 per cent) in Hamao, Packer et al. (2000), and the UK (–8.0 per cent) in Espenlaub and Garrett et al. (et al. (1999). The Korean case surveyed in Ritter (1998) shows that Korean stock market outperformed other stock markets in the long run. This Korean long-term performance is based on Kim, Krinsky et al. (et al. (1995). These authors argue that the existing theories on the long-term performance (Miller, 1977; Shiller, 1990) do not apply to the case of Korean IPOs, but it is more likely that this outperformance was caused by the Korean stock market boom that continued from the late 1980s until the early 1990s. Their study excludes the late years associated with the dob.com bubble and subsequent corrections.

Considering the fact that all these countries recorded very high initial returns at the initial stage of trading in the stock markets, these poor long-term performances seem to be another anomaly in the pricing of IPO common stocks. From an investor's viewpoint, the price pattern of large underpricing and poor long-term performances may present opportunities for active trading strategies to produce superior returns (Ritter, 1991). The underpricing and long-term performance effects have led to a major debate on the reasons for their existence and the pattern of returns across different types of IPOs.

3.4 Rationales for underpricing

3.4.1 Information asymmetry between issuer and investor

A lot of theoretical and empirical research has been undertaken in order to grasp the meaning of the underpricing. Mainly, the discussion has been concentrated on the information asymmetry problem that may exist between issuer and investor. In the literature that explains underpricing in terms of the information asymmetry that is inherent between IPO issuer and investor, underpricing is the intended result of the issuer attempting to attract investors to buy IPO shares.

3.4.1.1 The lemons problem, signalling and underpricing

When issuers face the "lemons problem",[4] they need to separate themselves from the lower-quality issuers by pricing the IPO below its true value, which lower quality issuers find it hard to imitate. Issuers are able to get back the costs of IPO underpricing by selling the shares they retained at a higher price after IPO than they would have without signalling. Their signal is reinforced by the announcement of high dividends (earnings) after IPO (Allen and Faulhaber, 1989), future issuing activities by selling additional shares on more favourable conditions (Welch, 1989), retained ownership (Grinblatt and Hwang, 1989), or analyst coverage (Chemmanur and Fulghieri, 1998).[5]

The two rationales, according to this hypothesis, are the following ones. One is that capable issuers have an ability to underprice their stocks, "leaving good money on the table". They expect that they will sell their seasoned issues at a higher price. The other, which is contrary to the former, is that issuers can sell the IPO stocks to investors at a higher price than would otherwise be the case by sending a kind of positive signal to the market. Investors will perceive the issuers as less risky and more promising and will be willing to pay a higher price to buy the stock. This is basically an argument about "reputation" and has been documented in numerous signalling models, which will be reviewed later in this chapter and will be adapted for the empirical analysis to a Korean empirical setting.

Signalling theories of IPO underpricing focus on the ability of informed issuers to convey favourable/unfavourable private information to less-informed investors by selling the IPO issues at a discount. Allen and Faulhaber (1989) document a signalling equilibrium model that "initial owners of high-quality firms separate themselves from their lower-quality counterparts by retaining more shares and pricing the IPO below its true value, which can be inferred by uninformed investors from the IPO signal". As the signal contains the high quality of the firm, so the after-market share price rises reflecting the signal. Issuers are able to get back the costs of IPO underpricing by selling the shares they retained at the IPO at a higher price than they would have sold them without signalling. It can be said that, in their model, the underpricing phenomenon is an ability to underprice the issue by communicating the firm's favourable private information to the issuing firms retaining shares in the firm. Firms are ready to distinguish themselves as good firms from bad firms by incurring a cost that the less successful firms cannot profitably sustain. In this model, investors update their prior beliefs about the value of the firm by its earnings or dividend policy. High dividends (earnings) after the IPO will be more effective in revising the market's beliefs about firms that underprice more. The model implies that the better firms will underprice more, will have higher earnings, will initiate dividends earlier, will have a higher payout ratio, and will experience a more favourable reaction to the dividend announcement.

Welch (1989) formalise the notion that good firms underprice in order to "leave a good taste in investors' mouths". His hypothesis is that the owner's incentive to underprice is stimulated by their intention to sell additional securities on more favourable conditions. Though the entrepreneur of a high quality firm will underprice, he will be compensated at the time of the seasoned issue by a higher price for the shares. The underpricing is a believable signal if the imitation costs for the low quality firm are high enough. The implication of the author's model is that firms who underprice more see a less unfavourable response at the time of the second stock issue.

Grinblatt and Hwang (1989) have developed a theoretical model of IPO valuation and bivariate signalling mechanisms that hold that entrepreneurs' retained ownership is positively linked to the use of underpricing. In their model, the mean and the variance of the company's cash flows are unknown to investors; however, retained ownership and the offer price are used as signals of the unknown parameters. They claim that these three implications are unique to their model: 1) Given the variance of the firm's cash flows, the degree of underpricing is positively related to the entrepreneurs' fractional holdings; 2) Given the entrepreneurs' fractional holdings, firm value is positively related to the degree of underpricing; 3) Given the variance of the firm's cash flows, firm value and the degree of underpricing are positively related.

3.4.1.2 *"Winner's curse" and underpricing*

Another rationale for the underpricing is the "winner's curse" explanation. (Rock, 1986). Rock's model focuses on the information asymmetry model based on the observation that investors can be divided into two categories: well-informed investors vs less-informed investors. He relates underpricing to the "winner's curse" faced by less-informed investors. Since shares are usually sold at a fixed price, rationing of shares will take place if the issue is oversubscribed owing to a strong demand on them. Issuing firms are assumed to have less information than potential investors. They cannot forecast the market price accurately. However, they can form an anticipation of the value of their shares. Informed investors who know the true market value will only subscribe to issues that are priced below their true value. In contrast, uninformed investors are assumed to subscribe to all issues equally. Well-informed investors will subscribe to underpriced issues in order to earn an abnormal return. However, less-informed investors will be allocated all of the undesirable overpriced issues avoided by well-informed investors. Consequently, less-informed investors face the "winner's curse" and will not purchase the IPO stocks unless they are given an underpricing incentive.

3.4.2 *Information asymmetry between issuer, investor and underwriter*

3.4.2.1 *Market feedback and adjustment of the offer price*

Where the bookbuilding method[6] is used for the setting of the offer price, investment bankers may underprice IPOs in order to induce regular investors to reveal their information about their truthful valuations of the firm. To encourage their honesty, the underwriters compensate investors by means of underpricing. Furthermore, in order to induce truthful revelation for a given IPO, the investment banker must underprice issues for which favourable information is revealed by more than those for which unfavourable information is revealed (Ritter, 1998). This leads to a prediction that there will only be partial adjustment of the offer price from that contained in the preliminary prospectus to that contained in the final prospectus. In other words, the IPOs for which the offer price is revised upwards will be more underpriced than those for which the offer price is revised downwards (Barry, Gilson et al.,1998; Loughran and Ritter, 2002). Barry, Gilson et al. (et al. (1998) present this pattern from their empirical data. According to them, IPOs where offer prices relative to the file price range were higher realise an average initial return of 30.22 per cent, whereas IPOs where offer prices were lower realise 3.54 per cent.[7]

3.4.2.2 *Underwriters' superior knowledge in market conditions*

Another explanation for the underpricing of new issues comes from the observation that underwriters take advantage of their superior knowledge of market conditions to underprice offerings. Baron (1982) and Baron and Holmstrom (1980) suggest that underpricing arises due to the information asymmetry and conflicts of interest between underwriters and issuing firms. The authors assume that investment bankers acting as agents on behalf of issuing firms are on the side of buying clients. Investment bankers as underwriters find it easy to sell off the common stocks that they are in charge of when they take side with buy-side clients. In this pre-IPO process, underwriters use their superior knowledge of market conditions to underprice offerings. When investment bankers find it hard to sell the issuers' shares, they underprice them in order to facilitate the offering process. Ritter (1998) documents the fact that when less sophisticated issuers, especially investment banking firms, go public, they underprice themselves by as much as other IPOs of a similar size. He observed that investment bankers have been successful at convincing clients and regulatory agencies that underpricing is normal for IPOs.[8]

3.4.2.3 *Reputable underwriter (and auditor) and alleviation of underpricing*

Because these information asymmetry hypotheses assume that issuers and under-writers should underprice their shares to attract investors, if information asym-metry problems disappear, there should, in theory, be no underpricing. Some of the literature related to "reputation" states that issuers can alleviate the degree of information asymmetry by employing highly prestigious underwriters, auditors or financial advisors in the process of IPO.

Service differentiation in the market for underwriting can be explained within the asymmetric information and agency costs perspectives. Within the agency framework, to be serviced by a high quality underwriter will lessen the expected high agency costs experienced by IPO firms (Jelic, Saadouni et al.,2001). Fur-thermore, the choice of a high quality underwriter could be viewed as a signal-ling device where only firms with more favourable information can choose high quality underwriters (Titman and Trueman, 1986). The researchers who argue for the role of reputable financial players in the process of IPO argue that issuing firms are able to avoid underpricing when they send information about the IPO firms to the market. This indicates that, even though they have room to under-price, they do not have to do it just in order to attract investors.

Numerous studies of IPOs investigate the relationship between underwriter prestige and initial returns (Logue, 1973; Beatty and Ritter, 1986; Titman and Trueman, 1986; Johnson and Miller, 1988; Carter and Manaster, 1990; Meg-ginson and Weiss, 1991; Carter, Dark et al.,1998; Paudyal, Saadouni et al.,1998; Chen and Mohan, 2002; Logue, Rogalski et al.,2002). Higher-quality under-writers are more likely to adjust offer prices upwards during the IPO process. IPO firms are willing to pay for these reputable services, because their reputation allows the underwriters to be effective in pre-market activities which are inclusive of marketing, pricing and distribution of IPO shares (Logue, Rogalski et al.,2002). Researchers generally find that the more prestigious underwriters' involvement in the IPO has the impact of lessening the underpricing of IPO firms. Logue (1973) and Beatty and Ritter (1986) were among the first to develop a measure of underwriter reputation. Using Rock's (1986) framework, Carter and Manaster (1990) modelled the role of the investment banker's reputation and showed that more prestigious investment bankers are linked to less risky IPOs. Carter, Dark et al. (et al. (1998) conducted an empirical analysis of the relationships of ini-tial returns and three-year performance of IPOs and found that IPOs managed by more reputable underwriters are associated with less short-run underpricing. Highly prestigious underwriters were expected to reduce the information asymmetry by means of their high quality due diligence services in the process of IPO.

Holland and Horton (1993) examined the relation between the reputation of the professional advisors involved in IPO (specifically, the sponsor, the accountant and the auditor) and short-term performance. They found that more reputable auditors are linked to lower initial returns, which can thus be interpreted as lower underpricing. In this case, firms issuing with renowned institutions do not have to underprice the issues. Instead, they have the power to pull up the issue price, which reflects the true value of the firm, or to overprice the issue. This indicates that a positive signal of the firm can raise the bidding price, so leading to less severe underpricing. The involvement of reputable agencies that seem to act to raise the value of the firms will be acknowledged by the market. Moreover, the empirical results supporting the association of reputable financial players in the process of IPO with underpricing are found elsewhere in literature, too. When a privately-held firm goes public, market investors have less publicly available data than from publicly-traded firms, because privately-held firms are less required to disclose information about the firm. This difference in regulatory environment offers a good setting for analysis of the role of the auditor in signalling information about the firm to the investors (Beatty, 1989). A widely held view suggests that the employment of a nationally famous audit firm will increase the offer price (reduce the initial return) received by the IPO firms. This is why IPO firms consider switching auditor prior to listing (Beatty, 1989).

As I have discussed previously, the firm's established owners have an incentive to minimise underpricing because it transfers wealth from themselves to the new investors. However, when the public investors have a doubt that the entrepreneurs have an incentive to hide their private information, causing the typical "lemon" problem discussed above, the entrepreneurial firms need to hire an agent who can credibly attest the quality of the firms. Reputable underwriters, as I discussed above, are among those that the going-public firms want to associate themselves with. And, furthermore, reputable auditors are among those who can certify the uncertain entrepreneurial firms. The rationale behind this is particularly important, because (1) auditors deal with the financial statements that contain the most crucial information about the firms (Kinney, 1986) (2) auditors have an incentive to audit the firms in accordance with accounting principle since their reputation capital may be reduced by *ex post* revelations of errors or misstatements (Palmrose, 1988). Kinney (1986) suggests that different audit firms provide auditing services of different quality and that auditing firms may not be homogeneous. "Since the nature and extent of agency costs and information asymmetries vary across the firms that attempt to minimise these related costs, the auditing services demanded will be heterogeneous". This heterogeneity may lead CPA firms to differentiate themselves on the basis of investment in reputable capital in order to facilitate the attestation function (Kinney, 1986). Palmrose (1988) has documented the fact that since auditing firms, having invested more in reputable capital, have greater incentives to reduce application errors, the information disclosed in the accounting reports audited by these firms will be more precise, other things being equal. Uninformed investors will be allowed to estimate more precisely the firm value when highly reputable auditors attest an accounting report, thus reducing the uninformed investors' *ex ante* uncertainty. This advantage generated by the use of reputable auditors will be reflected in the pricing of IPO firms in the market. "Value-maximising owners of IPO firms will choose the auditing firm with reputation capital that equates the marginal benefit of less underpricing with the marginal cost of a higher quality audit" (Beatty, 1989).

Beatty (1989) shows that the auditor compensation premium is significantly larger for the *ad hoc* "middle six (sized auditing firms) than for smallest-nine audit firms" in the US, indicating that the privately-held going-public firms should pay the price needed to induce a reputable auditor to investigate their financial statements. Simunic and Stein (1987) suggest that auditor product differentiation in the dimensions of control, credibility and product line motivates the management's auditor choice in the IPO market. They conclude that the form of the underwriter agreement, the proportion of common stocks held by outsiders after the IPO, and a measure of uncertainty are related to the choice of the auditing firm. Beatty (1989) has provided evidence that larger and less risky IPO firms tend to hire "Big Eight" audit firms in the US. To prove the relationship of underpricing with auditor reputation, two proxies (auditor size and compensation to auditors) for auditor reputation are used in their hypotheses and the results of both tests provide support for the inverse relations between auditor reputation and IPO initial return.

Titman and Trueman (1986) have presented a signalling model that shows which auditor quality provides useful information to investors in assessing the value of the IPO firm. Two features of their model lead to a signalling of the IPO firm's value. First, high quality auditors are those individuals with a comparative advantage in making a report on the firm's information. Second, the firm is needed to pay a price premium for this higher quality audit. "These two expected costs of hiring the high quality auditor exceed the expected benefits of misclassification for the low firm value IPOs". As Beatty (1989) has argued, this cost-benefit analysis leads the entrepreneur to choose an appropriate audit firm that is able to signal the value of the firm to the market. Signalling models assume that the firms sending costly signals to the market cannot be duplicated easily by the firms who do not possess the signalled characteristic. In the IPO markets, by employing nationally famous auditing firms, firms appear to signal their credibility to the market.

3.4.3 Hot issue markets[9] and the high-technology stocks boom in 1999–2000

Information asymmetry theories assume that there tends to be a problem of the placement of shares among investors, because the supply of shares is supposed to exceed the demand on them in their model. However, these theories may have some difficulties in explaining the severe underpricing of IPOs during the late 1990s, in which it was impossible to leave shares unsold because of the strong interest on the part of a lot of investors. In this case, underpricing may be interpreted as the outcome of irrational behaviour by investors in "hot" markets, not because of the information asymmetry between issuer, underwriter and investor. In addition, a body of literature has emerged focusing on the firm characteristics of the IPO stocks in 1999–2000 which highlights the role of high-technology IPO stocks in the increasing pattern of underpricing during that period.

High initial returns have a tendency to be followed by a rising IPO volume and vice versa (Ibbotson, Sindelar et al.,1994; Lowry and Schwert, 2002; Lowry, 2003). It may be natural that, when IPO volumes are rising, initial returns will be lowered because the increased transaction supply volume in the stock markets is expected to have the effect of watering down the market, leading to a reduction in the return on the stock investment. But for the considerable time period during which the stock market is "hot", the initial returns went up. Aggarwal and Rivol (1990) have argued that a huge amount of underpricing was caused by "market fads" which can be defined as temporary overvaluation of the IPO firms by investors in the early IPO stage. Higher levels of noise trading are likely to happen not in accordance with rational expectations of the firms' value, but in accordance with irrational over-optimism.

The increased underpricing phenomenon in the late 1990s and early 2000 has also been linked to investor over-optimism in high-technology stocks. The core argument is that high-technology firms were valued on the basis of their growth potential and factors other than the historical information and accounting data, despite their insufficient tangible assets and uncertain future profitability. Amir and Lev (1996) point out that a new and more adequate method of evaluating internet stocks by non-financial measures began to arise, since the internet industry was evolving at such a rapid speed that the quantitative data might not be useful for pricing these firms. Following this argument, Rajan and Servaes (1997) attribute underpricing to over-optimism about the earning potentials and long-term growth prospects of going-public firms. Diverse unconventional measures are shown to be related to a positive first-day stock market return: "web traffic" which is supposed to create future growth potential through network effects and customer relationships (Rajgopal et al.,2000); frequency of visits to the website and the pages viewed per visitor (Trueman, Wong et al.,2000); the spin-off of a high-technology firm from a parenting company (Schill and Zhou, 1999); and the announcement of company name change to internet related. com names (Cooper, Dimitrov et al.,2000).

Hand (2000) states that selling and marketing administration expenses are positively related to the high initial returns rather than to revenues. He also states that it can be argued that larger losses and expenses generate higher market values because investors consider these expenses as reflecting investments in intangible assets which can lead to a high revenue in the future. In this case, high forecasted earnings for one year and in the long run in the IPO prospectus are very important in pricing IPO stocks.[10] Demers and Lev (2000) also find that internet companies' expenditures on knowledge, customer acquisitions and technology are considered as the capitalisation of assets by investors. Perotti and Rossetto (2000) offer a model to appraise internet firms' investments as "platform investments", i.e. an innovative distribution and production infrastructure which increases access to customers, producing a set of entry strategic options in an uncertain market which will be exercised once demand ensures profitability. The authors claim that a company establishing an industry standard, which would control the market by means of the investment, would benefit from its advantageous position to develop applications that could adjust to consumer demand.

On the other hand, some authors argue that too much reliance was placed on the growth prospects of the firms, so that a realistic analysis of their future profitability was neglected, which was reflected in the dramatic downfall of the high technology stocks boom after mid-2000. Schultz and Zaman (2001) argue that the market was irrationally overpricing internet stocks, and managers were in a rush to make their companies public so as to seize the market share and first-mover advantages. However, in an industry in which economies of scale allow only a few firms to survive, a lot of firms could not ensure that the high stock market returns of the initial IPO stages would continue.

3.5 Rationales for poor long-term performance

Theoretical models that explain the phenomenon of long-term underperformance of IPO stocks are not as well developed as the case of short-term underpricing. Many factors can affect the long-run performance, so it is quite difficult to figure out the association of the stock market performance after three or five years with IPO characteristics. I outline three theories of the long-term underperformance and discuss how the reputation of financial agents such as underwriters can alleviate poor long-term performance.

3.5.1 Disappearance of the information asymmetry

This hypothesis argues that the stock market contains two kinds of investors: optimistic and pessimistic. When a great deal of uncertainty about the value of the IPO exists, the valuations will be much higher in the case of optimistic investors than in the case of pessimistic investors. When the trading has commenced, the IPO stocks price will depend on the investment behaviour of optimistic investors who have a great interest in the firms. However, as time goes on and more information becomes known to the market, the divergence of opinion between optimistic and pessimistic investors will narrow and the market price will drop (Miller, 1977 and 2000).

Miller (1977), for example, documents the fact that the prices of new issues are not set by the evaluation of the typical investor, but by the small minority who think highly enough of the investment merits of the new issue to include it in their portfolio. The divergences of opinion about a new issue are greatest at the moment when the stock is issued. "It is the frequent case that, at the time of IPO, the company has not started operations, or there is uncertainty about the success of new products or the profitability of a major business expansion. Over time this uncertainty is reduced as the company acquires a history of earnings or lack of them, and the market indicates how it will value these earnings. With the passage of time and the reduction in uncertainty, the appraisal of the top x per cent of the investors is likely to decline even if the average assessment is not changed. This would explain the poor performance of a group of new issues when compared to a group of stocks about which the uncertainty does not decrease over time".

3.5.2 Underwriters acting like impresarios

The "impresario" hypothesis argues that investment bankers act like the impresarios who manage musicians and entertainers. Just as impresarios reduce the ticket price to create an excess demand for the concert tickets and avoid empty seats, underwriters underprice IPO stocks to generate excess demand for the purchase of stocks. This hypothesis implies that the companies with the highest initial returns should have the lowest following returns, because the offer price was not based on the firms' fundamental values, but on the underwriters' deliberate intention to induce excess demand (Shiller, 1990), According to this hypothesis, a hot market appears when underwriters discover that the public investors are ripe for the fad for IPOs and they let high initial returns run for a while to create publicity and good will for the IPOs (Shiller, 1990). It is natural that the stocks listed during the period of the artificially created hot market turn out to show lower subsequent returns. Shiller found that only 26 per cent of the underwriter respondents did any analysis of the appropriate offer price based upon the firm's underlying value.

3.5.3 Timing of IPOs using windows of opportunity

When there is an abundance of optimistic investors who think highly of the growth potential of companies that are going public, the large cycles in volume of IPOs may reflect an attempt to "time" IPOs by firms so as to jump on the bandwagon of hot investor sentiment (Schultz, 2003). It is plausible that although the firms come to IPO more frequently, taking advantage of normal business cycle activity, the large swings in volume of IPO, as shown by Ibbotson, Sindelar et al. (et al. (1994),[11] seems to be difficult to explain merely by normal business cycle activity.

Aggarwal and Rivoli (1990) argue that IPO markets are easily subject to 'fads' which can be argued "to be a temporary overvaluation caused by over-optimism on the part of investors". When the fads appear in the IPO market, high initial returns are the result of a temporary overvaluation by investors in early trading. In this case, the aftermarket is not seen as efficient, so that high initial returns are not the result of underpricing by underwriters, but are caused by inefficient stock markets that are moving up due to temporary investor sentiment towards over-optimism. The authors argue that, although it is not possible to prove the presence of fads in stock markets, it is possible that price movement patterns are consistent with the fads explanation. They document the existence of poor long-run performance as plausible evidence of the fads phenomenon that can be observed in early trading. Roughly speaking, if the long-run price drops below the offer price at the IPO, the IPO stock may have been overpriced instead of being underpriced.

If investors avail themselves of the over-optimism that is prevalent in the IPO market and rush into it, firms that are going public in high-volume periods are more likely to be overvalued than other IPOs. This argument has the testable implication that the high-volume periods should be related to the lowest long-run returns. This pattern indeed exists in numerous studies [Ritter (1991), Ibbotson, Sindelar et al. (1994), Loughran, Ritter et al. (1994), Loughran and Ritter (1995), Brav and Gompers (1997) and Schultz (2003)]

3.5.4 Reputable underwriters and the alleviation of poor long-term performance

I have seen above that an IPO firms' offer price could be overpriced when the firm decides to go public, taking advantage of "market fads" or "windows of opportunity" and consequently the firm's long-run stock price has a tendency to decline as the true value comes to be revealed in the market. In particular, when an underwriter acts like an "impresario" as is argued by Shiller (1990), and sets an offer price not on the basis of the firm's true value, but with the purpose of creating market demand, then the firm's stock price will fall after IPO. However, if the underwriters are financial players that frequently turn up in the IPO market, and their reputation and future operations are closely linked to the performance of the IPO firms that they bring to the IPO market, it is more likely that they are keen on bringing the good-quality firms to the IPO market and reducing the information gap between issuer and investor. If they don't do this, their reputable capital will be forfeited due to false overpricing.

Booth and Smith (1986) show that when asymmetric information prevails, the investment bank (underwriter) must also invest in its own reputable capital. In any case, the investment bank must put its reputation on the line with each new offering, or its opinion concerning firm-specific information may be useless to the investors. Carow (1999) indicates that more prestigious underwriters monitor firm managers closely when deciding new securities' issue prices. For an investment to perform these tasks, it must acquire clear and accurate information about business operations, growth prospects, and managerial strengths and weaknesses of the issuer. When a firm that was closely monitored by a more reputable underwriter goes public, it is more likely that the firm's long-term performance will not deteriorate as seriously as the one that was monitored by a less reputable underwriter. This reflects the better quality of an IPO firm that is underwritten by more reputable underwriter.

It is most likely that a more reputable underwriter will select good-quality firms so as not to lose the reputational capital that it has accumulated through time.

Chemmanur and Fulghieri (1994) propose that investors assess underwriters' reputations by measuring the quality of the firms advised by investment banks. The authors argue that investors use the investment banks' past performance, as measured by the quality of the firms in which they have previously sold equity, to assess their credibility. By marketing IPOs that have a relatively better past performance, investment banks protect and build up their reputation. Michaely and Shaw (1994) state that, in order to preserve its reputation, the prestigious underwriter screens the firms that go public and selects the less risky ones, using information that is unavailable to the public. This, in turn, reduces the uncertainty and information asymmetry between informed and uninformed investors, resulting in less heterogeneity in the amounts of information that investors have. Investors know that by subscribing to issues underwritten by reputable investment bankers they face less risk. They use the underwriter's capital as a proxy for its prestige and find that IPOs that are managed by high prestige underwriters tend to have smaller initial returns and less negative long-run returns than do IPOs that are handled by lower reputation underwriters. As a result of this discussion, I can say that more reputable investment banks want to underwrite firms that have more prospects and less risk.

While there have been many cases where underwriter reputation is associated with less underpricing, which demonstrates the role of certifying IPO firms, there has been only a small amount of research that connects underwriters' reputation and the long-term performance of IPO firms. As has been explained, this scarcity of research comes about because long-term performance reflects firms' true value and the stock market condition apart from being affected by an underwriter who acts as a financial player only at IPO time. Carter, Dark et al. (1998) examine the relationship of long-term performances and underwriter reputation and find not only that IPOs that are managed by more reputable underwriters are associated with less short-run underpricing, but also that the underperformance of IPO stocks (represented as three-year returns of IPO) observed by Ritter (1991) and Loughran and Ritter (1995) is less severe for IPOs that are handled by more prestigious underwriters. However, Doukas and Gonene (2003) find that the reputation of investment bankers that is based on the long-term performance of IPO firms is negligible.

3.6 The Certification and value-adding role of venture capitalists

I reviewed the theories on the IPO underpricing and poor long-term performance in the previous sections. The main points of the discussion were: underpricing arises as a result of information asymmetry between the issuing firm and investors, and an involvement of a reputable financial agent in the process of IPO can lessen the degree of underpricing; the poor long-term performance results from the disappearance of the information asymmetry or the overpricing of the IPO stocks at initial stage of IPO, and the participation of a reputable financial in the process of IPO can alleviate the degree of the poor long-term performance.

Our research is centred on the question whether the existence of venture capitalists in the ownership and management of IPO firms causes similar effects that a reputable financial agent can bring to the pricing and performance of IPO firms. Much of the literature in finance has regarded venture capitalists as implementing similar functions to reputable underwriters or auditors for going public firms, that is, by lessening the information asymmetry between investors and issuers, thus resulting in the reduced underpricing of IPO firms (Barry, Muscarella et al.1990; Megginson and Weiss, 1991) and better long-term performance (Brav and Gompers, 1997) by improving the firm-quality. Venture capitalists, it is argued, have their own specific tools to reduce agency costs that are intrinsic to financing uncertain entrepreneurial firms, and that play a role in raising a firm from the early development stage through the expansion and production stage to the stage of IPO or other exit routes. Our main research questions are twofold. One is: does the presence of venture capitalists in the operations of venture firms *certify the value of those firms*, leading to *less underpricing by thus reducing the information asymmetry*, as in the case of other financial players such as the underwriter and the auditor? The other is: do venture capitalists lead to *better long-term performances of IPO firms* as a result of *value-added to the firms?* So first I will review the general reasons for explaining the mechanisms by which venture capitalists play a role in relation to the underpricing and the long-term performance. Then I move on, in the next section, to the ownership structure of venture capitalists to see how this may affect underpricing and long-term performance.

3.6.1 *Mechanisms to minimise the uncertainty of entrepreneurial firms*

A high-technology boom emerged during the 1990s and a number of new entrepreneurial firms[12] operating in high-technology focused industries were formed over this period in many developing countries as well as in the advanced industrial countries. These new small high-tech industrial firms found it difficult to get finance from conventional financial institutions, let alone public investors in capital markets. This is because small high technology firms are viewed as presenting greater default risks than other traditional small firms though they are perceived as having more growth potential.

Westhead and Storey (1997) have identified four reasons for this higher risk: (1) scientists are normally the founders of high-technology firms and they often tend to lack managerial and entrepreneurial skills, (2) because the product or service is novel, it is especially difficult to assess its true value, (3) in the high technology area, products or services tend to have a shorter life cycle than in the more conventional sectors, (4) financing is often required in order to conduct research and development at the before-product/service stage. Here there is not only the uncertainty of the market itself, coming at a later stage, but also whether the research will ever lead to a product or service at all. When they do not have any profits as a result of selling products/services in the market nor do they have any tangible assets to be put up as collateral for lending, it is extremely difficult to receive financing from financial institutions.

However, venture capitalists do invest in these kind of uncertain and risky entrepreneurial firms. It can be said that venture capitalists invest in them for three reasons: (1) venture capitalists think more highly of the future prospects of the firms that are expected to bear great success, looking forward to abnormal returns in the future in return for their risky equity investment (2) venture capitalists have the know-how, skills and various networks needed to guide and help entrepreneurial firms from the early development stage through the expansion and production stage to IPO or other exit stages.

3.6.1.1 *Agency costs and information asymmetries inherent in the financing of entrepreneurial firms*

Sahlman's (1990) seminal work on venture capital financing states that the agency problem between venture capitalists and entrepreneurial firms is centred on the issue of the venture capital financing contract. The relationship between the entrepreneur and the venture capitalist can be said to be an applied version of the principal-agent relationship (Jensen and Meckling, 1976).

Conflicts may arise in such situations between the venture capitalist as principal and the entrepreneur as agent because the entrepreneur may have information that is unknown to the venture capitalist and may choose to shirk or to over-invest, creating agency costs.[13] If the entrepreneur possesses private information about the firm and chooses to continue investing in a negative NPV project using the money from the venture capitalist, the entrepreneur is undertaking inefficient continuation. As a principal, the venture capitalist finds it difficult to identify and assess correctly the outcomes or results of operations that the entrepreneurs have achieved. Another type of agency cost results from the entrepreneurs' being motivated to consume perquisites, in a way that entrepreneurs might invest in projects that have high personal returns but low expected monetary payoffs to shareholders. For example, an entrepreneur may select to invest in a certain type of project that may help build up his reputation in the high-tech industry, but will provide low expected returns to the shareholders, i.e. the venture capitalists. This agency problem shed lights on factors affecting the duration and size of venture capital investment. Venture capitalists assess potential agency and monitoring costs when they invest in venture firms. Venture capitalists are interested in how to alleviate the risks arising from entrepreneurs' private benefit-seeking behaviour, by carrying out continuous monitoring and check-ups. The amount of the monitoring costs should be negatively correlated to the expected agency costs.

Chan, Siegel et al. (1987) have developed a model in which venture capitalists improve allocational efficiency by overcoming asymmetric information. Their model illustrates the contribution of the venture capitalist as an informed intermediary who solves agency problem in a market with imperfect information. Chan begins with a world where entrepreneurs can assess the qualities of projects and their perquisite consumption, but investors are imperfectly informed about them. In a situation in which there are the investors with positive search costs and the entrepreneurs that are induced to offer unacceptable inferior projects, the "lemon" problem noted by Akerlof (1970) occurs. Only low-quality projects are offered to the investors, and they accordingly pay a price that reflects this low quality. Chan introduces the venture capitalist as an informed intermediary who plays a role between uninformed investors and entrepreneurs, reducing information asymmetry. In their model, venture capitalists induce a *Pareto-preferred* allocation, leading the investors to a higher welfare state. The venture capitalist solves the adverse selection problem and good projects can be accepted by venture capitalists.

Admati and Pfleiderer (1994) show how conflicts of interest and informational asymmetry can be effectively solved by a leading venture capitalist in the syndication of venture capital financing. They focus on the agency problem that lies in investment and continuation decisions when capital is offered in stages. They identify the over-investment problem, that is, the problem that an entrepreneur who is motivated to attract outside funds may keep on investing in a project that seems to be no longer worthy of investment. Their point is that the venture capitalist may suffer the same problem as the entrepreneur after they have become insiders by having ownership in the company. Even when the venture capitalist has learned that a project is no longer favourable, but has a possibility of success, the venture capitalist may have an incentive to attract new outside funds from other venture capitalists. The authors argue that this situation can be resolved by means of "robust" contracts in which the lead venture capitalist maintains a constant fraction of the firm's equity. This solution neutralises the venture capitalist's incentive to mislead. They show that this contract is robust in the sense that the contract is not made invalid by small changes in possible contingent outcomes.

3.6.1.2 *Instruments to minimise agency costs and information asymmetries*

Venture capitalists utilise various control mechanisms and resource allocation in venture capital investments. This indicates that the agency costs and the asymmetric information problem linked to entrepreneurial firms makes project governance enormously important. As Sahlman (1990) and Gompers (1995) have documented, three control mechanisms have significance for a venture capital financing contract. These are: (a) staging of capital infusion; (b) syndication of investment; and (c) use of convertible bonds.

3.6.1.2(a) *Staging of capital infusions*

Staged capital infusions are one of the most effective control mechanisms that venture capitalists can make use of. When prospects for venture firms are uncertain, venture capitalists can periodically evaluate the venture firms' status and can decide whether they will continue the next round of financing. The shorter the duration of each round of financing, the more frequently can the venture capitalist monitor the entrepreneur's progress.[14] Sahlman (1990) stresses the monitoring role of staged capital commitments. He noted that the venture capitalist commits only a fraction of the capital needed for the whole project of a venture firm, because the venture capitalist thinks that subsequent financing should be tied to the successful completion of intermediate objectives. Gompers (1995) examines the role that staged capital infusions take in controlling potential agency costs in young entrepreneurial firms. His evidence indicates that the staging of finance permits venture capitalists to gather information and monitor the progress of firms, maintaining the option to abandon projects periodically.

3.6.1.2(b) *Syndication of investment*

Syndication of venture financing is a mechanism through which venture capitalists resolve informational uncertainties about potential investments. One venture capital firm will originate the deal with an entrepreneurial firm and look to bring in other venture capital companies. The logic of syndication of venture financing can be quite simple. A decision-making process offered by hierarchical organisations, in which investments are made only if several independent observers agree, may be superior to one in which projects are funded after only one arbitrary decision (Sah and Stiglitz, 1986). Syndication of financing gives venture capitalists a chance to check out their own thinking against other knowledgeable sources and brings together more expertise and support. If the lead venture capitalist is very reliable source of information, others are willing to invest in the firm. Moreover, venture capital syndicating allows the venture capital firm to diversify into more investments. Another benefit of syndicating financing is that bringing in other venture capitalists to provide their own due diligence acts as a second opinion on the investment opportunities (Gompers, 1999).

3.6.1.3(c) *Use of convertible debt*

It is possible that the entrepreneurial firm pursue short-term success rather than ultimate long-term success to get more funding at each capital infusion stage. Convertible bonds can attenuate the incentives of adverse selection on the part of entrepreneurs (Gompers, 1999). By shifting resources to improving short-term goals the entrepreneur reduces the possibility of liquidation but, at the same time, increases the probability that, when refinancing, the venture capitalist will decide to exercise the debt conversion option, becoming the owner of a substantial fraction of the venture. If the terms of conversion are decided beforehand to be sufficiently favourable to the debt holder (the venture capitalist), the entrepreneur faces a situation in which good news about the prospects of the project leads to a reduction in his profit because of debt conversion by the venture capitalist. As a result, he will not engage in as much short-termistic manipulative behaviour as he would in a situation where only straight debt-equity financing is used.

3.6.2 *The value-adding role of venture capitalists*

Does venture capitalists' involvement with the operations of venture firms enhance the value of those firms? Whereas the earlier review has laid emphasis on the internal certifying role of venture capital backing through the reduction of information asymmetries, this part highlights the way that venture capitalists' internal monitoring and screening of the firms (before IPO) and external market demand creating activities contribute to the increase of the value of IPO firms.

3.6.2.1 *Ownership retention and managerial intervention*

It has long been known that high ownership concentration can increase the value of public firms (Smith, 1986; Wruck, 1989). Venture capitalists are active investors who hold considerable stakes in the venture firms that they sponsor and dispatch the executives to sit on the board of directors in the firms (Hellmann and Puri, 2002).[15]

In the US study, Barry, Muscarella et al. (1990) find that typically there are at least three venture capitalists involved in a venture firm and they hold more than a third of the total equity stake before IPO. Just after the IPO, the average venture capital stake drops to about a quarter, but, even one year after, venture capitalists still hold 18 per cent of the equity stake. In more than half of the cases, venture capitalists sell no shares.[16] Furthermore, venture capitalists hold 33.4 per cent of issuing firms' board seats before IPO and this figure does not change very much one year after the offering. Therefore, they are in a position to deeply influence the management of the firms. Barry, Muscarella et al. (1990) emphasise the importance of the holding of ownership positions by venture capitalists. They note that a venture capitalist's expertise and experience in monitoring investments can send important signals to investors at the time of IPO.

Consistent with Sahlman's (1990) view of the nature of venture capitalists' contracts with their investors and with entrepreneurs, I find that venture capitalists are willing to bind themselves to the value of a new issue by maintaining their equity positions beyond the IPO.

3.6.2.2 *Incubating firms through market specialisation and innovation promotion*

Venture capitalists' certifying and value-adding roles for entrepreneurial firms are perceived from their managerial and business assistance in incubating and bringing up the entrepreneurial firms from the early stage to IPO. A venture capitalist often specialises in a specific industry. Entrepreneurs, who are often narrow technical specialists with limited managerial and business skills, can benefit from the strategic guidance provided by venture capitalists who are often specialists in a particular industry, technology, or stage of development (Rock, 1987).

Some venture capitalists employ consulting staffs that join actively the management of portfolio companies (Gladstone, 1989). For example, venture capitalists focus on "innovation" as the source of competitive advantage and require a strong emphasis on resource allocations to R&D. VCs are considered as agents to guide entrepreneurial firms to make resource allocations that are best fitted for the industry and the market conditions pertinent to the specific IPO firm (Hellmann and Puri, 2000; Hellmann and Puri, 2002). Hellmann and Puri (2000) find that venture firms pursuing a strategy focused on innovation are attracted to the value added benefits of VC involvement and, as a result, they are more likely to seek and obtain venture capital. He also finds that the presence of VCs significantly reduces the time to market for firms pursuing innovation.

Kortum and Lerner (1998) have shown that the high-tech industry in the U.S owes its success to the vitality of the venture capital industry of the nation. They throw out a question as to whether venture capital really contributes to innovation in the high-tech industry and examine the relationship of patenting (a proxy for innovation) with venture capital-backed firms and venture capital financing. They find that venture capital expenditures are significantly associated with the increase in patenting, showing that a doubling in venture-capital-backed companies is linked with an increase of between 5 per cent and 17 per cent in successful patent applications.[17]

Venture capitalists can add values for uncertain entrepreneurial firms by providing them with business, managerial and technological skills and guidance through its own experts, or consultants, or diverse practitioners in their networks (Stuart, Hoang et al., 1999). This mechanism to lessen the agency costs in the relationship with entrepreneurs can carry positive signals in public markets.

3.6.2.3 *Building-up of reputation as repeated players*

Venture capitalists attest the quality of the information disclosed by the company at IPO. This holds that reputable venture capitalists play a similar role to underwriters and auditors in overcoming information asymmetries between well-informed insiders and less-informed outside investors (Booth and Smith, 1986; Megginson and Weiss, 1991). Investors are aware that venture capitalists have the motivation to bring firms to the IPO market at high values and "are willing to pay more for companies brought to market by venture capitalists who are better able to oversee and guide new enterprises" (Barry, Muscarella et al.,1990). Venture capitalists are very cautious in screening, selecting and monitoring portfolio firms, because they may lose their reputation by taking poorly qualified firms to the IPO market. They are not one-off, but repeated players in the IPO market.

As Espenlaub, Garrett et al. (1999) have discussed, venture capitalists are able to credibly commit themselves to the accuracy and completeness of disclosed information since false certification would lead to the loss of any valuable reputation that has been built up over time. The incentive towards truthful certification thus relies on the potential losses from cheating outweighing the gains from cheating. Venture capitalists are also able to screen potential portfolio companies by offering them contracts that only companies of a given quality will accept.

3.6.2.4 *Interaction with other financial institutions and agencies*

Venture capitalists' reputable capital is enhanced by "repeated interaction and interlocking arrangements with the market intermediaries" (Jain and Kini, 2000). Venture-capital-backed issuers are able to exert influence on institutional investors, prestigious investment bankers and analysts to support them to a great degree. Not only venture capitalists, but also investment bankers acting as agents of underwriting take part in such activities as due diligence, valuation, preparation of the prospectus, planning and implementation of the road show, generating demand, pricing, distribution and allocation of securities in the pre-IPO period. In the post-IPO period, they add value to venture firms via activities such as stabilisation, market making and research coverage by their analysts (Barber, Lehavy et al.,1998; Aggarwal, 2000; Ellis, Michaely et al.,2000). The prestige of investment banks and analysts takes reputable effect. As venture capitalists select highly renowned investment bankers in expectation of better services, their reputable activities are recognised in the market, so are associated with superior outcomes (Carter and Manaster, 1990; Carter, Dark et al.,1998; Jain and Kini, 1999). Further, as long-term players in the IPO market, venture capitalists can shape an ongoing relationship with specific investment bankers. As well-informed players, venture capitalists are able to provide those institutions with accurate and timely information about the firm. Because venture capitalists repeatedly make firms public, if they are recognised as being connected with failures in the market, they may damage their reputation and ability to bring firms public (Gompers, 1996; Brav and Gompers, 1997). By not giving false information to hype up or overprice the issuing firm's value, venture capitalists demonstrate their ability to bring an appropriate firm to the prestigious investment bankers. A reputation for competence and honesty will allow venture capitalists to establish enduring relationships with pension fund managers and other institutional investors who are vitally important as investors in venture capital funds and as purchasers of shares in IPOs (Megginson and Weiss, 1991).

3.6.2.5 *Reputation of the venture capitalist: certifying agent or money game player?*

While I have already documented the certifying and value-adding role of venture capitalists, I must point out the possibility of less-reputable venture capitalists' affecting the performances of IPO firms in a negative way (Amit, Glosten et al.,1990). That is, whereas it has been generally recognised that a venture capitalist as a financial player can reduce the concern about information asymmetry and enhance the value of firms through his expert monitoring, it has been also observed that all venture capitalists are not the same.

As seen above, Amit, Glosten et al. (1990) have questioned the value of venture capital. They assume that entrepreneurs are well aware of their technology and business, but venture capitalists cannot evaluate precisely the skill level of the entrepreneurs. Because the authors assume that entrepreneurs can finance themselves or seek other financing and that venture capital contracts are purely equity causing higher costs, high-ability entrepreneurs choose to opt out of the venture capital market. The venture capital market in their model breaks down. They argue that the lower investment returns of the 1980s in the US are attributable to the breakdown of the market in the manner that their model describes. Admati and Pfleiderer (1994) point out an agency problem that venture capitalists can bring in the same way that entrepreneurs do. Even when a venture capitalist has learned that a project is not favourable any longer, he may have an incentive to attract new outside funds from other venture capitalists. The authors argue that this situation cannot be resolved without a "robust contract" in which the lead venture capitalist maintains a constant fraction of the firm's equity.

Moreover, it is known that venture capital investment and the decision of going public move closely in line with the stock market trend. Venture capitalists tend to increase their investment when the stock market is hot and looks favourable. Venture Economics (2002) reports that US venture capital investment has increased about six times from 1996 to 2000. In 2000, USD 105 billion was raised for venture capital investment. New venture capital investment raising reached its the highest peak in the f quarter in 2000 when NASDAQ was at its peak, and began dramatically to decrease after that in line with the decline of NASDAQ index. Venture capital investment in 2002 is only just as large as the level of in 1998. This indicates that venture capitalists may be more interested in mature entrepreneurial firms that are on the threshold of IPOs, rather than in trying to incubate the firms in early stages that have a business idea, but are lacking in seed money. NVCA (2002) in the US states that venture capital-backed IPOs increased by 75 in 1999 to 233 before falling slightly to 226 in 2000 and recorded only 35 in 2001 and 22 in 2002. These statistics show that venture capitalists are passionate IPO players when the stock market is in the boom period, but that they hesitate towards IPOs when the market is not favourable.

Furthermore, it has been pointed out that the selling of IPO shares by venture capitalists is consistent with the decline in shares prices. Field and Hanka (2000), Bradley, Jordan et al. (2001) and Espenlaub, Goergen et al. (2003) have found that, around the shares unlocking day, the returns of IPO firms that were backed by venture capitalists were more aggravated compared with IPO firms that were not backed by venture capitalists. This indicates that venture capitalists sell shares more aggressively than executives, families and other shareholders. The negative effect, that is, deteriorating share prices, is much more pronounced in the case of venture capital backed IPOs. Gompers and Lerner (1998) have also found that they distribute shares to limited partners who sell the shares quickly. When distribution of shares took place, shares prices apparently continued to drop in the months after the distribution. They suggest that venture capitalists may use insider information when distributing shares, which results in more negative reactions in the stock market.

Especially, the history and experiences of venture capitalists can affect their performances. Gompers (1996) focuses on the conflicts of interest between venture capitalists and the issuing firms that they back. He provides evidence that young venture capital companies "grandstand",[18] i.e., they bring companies to the public market earlier than more established firms in order to raise their profile in the market. He also finds that this is costly both to the young venture capitalists and to other issuing firms' shareholders because the greater uncertainty and information asymmetries with younger firms indicate that IPOs sponsored by inexperienced and younger firms are more underpriced. Their long-term performance was not better, either.[19]

3.7 Institutional differences in venture capitalists' ownership and their influence on IPO performances

In addition to the influence of venture capitalists on IPO performances by means of their certification through diverse mechanisms in order to lessen information asymmetry and increase the value of the firms, I now turn to another aspect of the research agenda: the impact of different kinds of organisation of venture capitalists on the performances of IPO firms. The interest in how the ownership of venture capitalists can have an effect on the performances of venture capitalists' investee firms comes from the fact that venture capitalists' investment behaviour cannot avoid the influence of their parenting investors. In this sub-section, I discuss the relationship between venture capital and the financial system and examine how venture capitalists affiliated with large institutions, particularly banking organisations, can differently affect the performances of going public firms before/after IPO.

3.7.1 Venture capital and the stock market

Comparing capital markets in countries with stock market-based systems (USA and UK) with those in countries with bank-based systems (Germany and Japan) has gained popularity in corporate governance studies. The USA has a well-developed stock market that provides a tool for corporate control such as take-over, but a large number of comparatively small banks that keep an "arm's length" relationship with the corporations, thus play a limited role in the corporate governance. By contrast, Japanese main banks and German universal banks are few in number, but larger in size, relative to Japanese and German firms, and are said to take a primary role in corporate governance (Black and Gilson, 1998; Aoki, 1994; Roe, 1994). Each financial structure is said to have strengths and weaknesses in providing funding to companies and in improving corporate governance, respectively. Especially, a lot of discussion has taken place as to which system is favourable for technology development (Milhaupt, 1997; Black and Gilson, 1998; Black and Gilson, 1999). Since venture capitalists are primary sources for providing funds to entrepreneurial firms that have their own specific technology and good prospects for future operation, but experience a lack of funding due to their uncertain status, the discussion was narrowed down to which financial system is more advantageous to the operations of venture capital companies. How do these two different sets of legal rules and institutional settings influence entrepreneurship, innovation and the venture capital market?

From the perspective of the venture capital market, in general, the stock market-based system has been argued to be a more efficient and convenient system that enables venture firms to gain easier access to funding sources than bank-based system. The development of IT and biotechnology companies and the accompanying venture capital funding of them have been linked, and the argument has been made that they play a major role in inducing the prosperity of US economy. Advocates of an active stock market claim that the adaptability of the stock market system for corporate control enabled high-tech firms to alter their ownership structure through IPO in a very convenient way (Milhaupt, 1997; Mayer, 2002). However, advocates of a bank-based financial system claim that a stock market-based system promotes short-term investment behaviour, making long-term planning by managers difficult or impossible (Edwards and Fischer, 1994; Porter, 1992). Singh, Singh et al. (2000) argues that a stock-market-based financial system tends to overestimate the value of a firm, as is shown in the dot. com bubble in the late 1990s, and suffers from price volatility. This may have important implications for the analysis of IPO and VC performance in "hot stock market" periods.

Gilson (1996), Milhaupt (1997) and Black and Gilson (1998) claim that the viability of the venture capital industry and its potential for growth is dependent on a strong IPO market. Success in making their portfolio companies public increases the reputable capital of venture capitalists and is crucial for attracting additional capital to venture capital funds. This is obvious from empirical evidence indicating a noteworthy correlation between the number of venture-capital-backed IPO firms and subsequent new capital to venture capital funds (Black and Gilson, 1998).[20]

Their argument is based on the premise that the existence of an active stock market motivates venture capitalists and entrepreneurs to have expectations of generating huge profits from going-public firms (Gompers and Lerner, 1997). However, more basically, the advocates argue that strong IPO exit provides a more efficient mechanism that allows the parties involved to realign their assets and to rearrange control rights over the firms (Jain and Kini, 2000). They argue that this kind of mechanism cannot be copied in the bank-based system, in which the IPO market is not very viable. When IPO cannot be selected (though it may be considered to be ideal) in the bank-based system, trade sale or buy-back is regarded as a more realistic way of exit.

Black and Gilson (1998) argue that IPO is very important in the context of the relationship between the venture capitalist and the investors in the limited partnership and the relationship between the venture capitalist and the portfolio company. They argue that the aspect of "implicit contract over future control of the portfolio company in a manner that is not readily duplicable in a bank-centred system" is vital for the successful venture capital industry. As venture capital providers, who are not expert in assessing the portfolio companies, investors in the limited partnership commit their money to venture capitalists. After they have invested, they need to confirm a benchmark of the skills of venture capital managers and the profitability of venture capital funds. If the investment returns turn out be acceptable, investors will be willing to invest in future partnerships organised by the same venture capitalists. But this kind of reinvesting is not written into the first contract, so it remains "implicit" between venture capitalists and capital providers. IPO provides a good benchmark that means that capital providers can evaluate the performances of venture capitalists. Also, on the part of the relationship between venture capitalists and portfolio companies, IPO "implicitly" provides the portfolio companies with an opportunity to "call on control rights exercised by using as exit strategy". By IPO, venture capitalists generally sell their shares after some time has passed, and entrepreneurs regain their control rights over the firm.[21] Through IPO, entrepreneurs get back the call option rights that will be based on the firm's fundamentals and the market situation. Only IPO, rather than other means of exit, enables the venture capital provider and entrepreneur to exercise this kind of "implicit control rights" that cannot be written into the contract documents. IPO provides a good mechanism to fulfil their expectation of having implicit control rights in the future. Black and Gilson (1998) argue that this kind of contracts design cannot be easily duplicated in the banking-based system and that a vibrant IPO market makes this system of contracts feasible.

3.7.2 *Venture capital and the universal banking perspective: conflicts of interest*

IPOs backed by venture capital that is affiliated with investment banks provide a good testing ground for universal banking (Gompers and Lerner, 1999).[22] Some researchers began to take notice of the possibility that the institutional difference in relation to venture capital could affect the financial performance of IPO firms, because the market may treat each IPO backed by venture capitalists differently according to the ownership of the venture capital companies. The investors in the stock market may notice the possibility that investment banks or commercial banks, which have ownership in entrepreneurial firms through venture capital subsidiaries, can act as certifying or value-adding financial agents or incur conflict of interests between issuing firms and investors. There have been empirical studies that dealt with this issue: Gompers and Lerner (1999) and Li and Masulis (2003) for the US and Espenlaub, Garrett et al. (1999) for the UK (which are characterised as stock market-based system); Bessler and Kurth (2003) for Germany and Hamao, Packer et al. (2000) for Japan (which are featured as bank-based system)

While the earlier US studies approached the issue of venture-capital-backed IPOs in terms of venture capital companies' own certifying capability (Barry, Muscarella et al.,1990; Megginson and Weiss, 1991) or the influence of underwriters, auditors or other financial advisors in short-run and long-run stock market performance (Carter and Manaster, 1990), this research highlights the aspect of certification and conflict of interest when financial institutions are major shareholders of venture capital companies.

Gompers and Lerner (1999) seminally introduced the universal banking perspective in their venture-capital-backed IPO research by focusing on the conflicts of interest that can occur between underwriters who hold an equity stake in IPO firms through venture capital subsidiaries and investors. They note the possibility that, when investment banks underwrite firms in which they have shares through a venture capital subsidiary, they may incur conflicts of interest between investors and themselves. They document the fact that an investment bank has an incentive to set a high price for IPO shares as an agent and this incentive is strengthened when it has an ownership in the IPO companies as a result of more aggressive marketing. However, the investment bank is also worried about losing its reputation by pricing the firms too high. The investment banks should also consider the institutional investors, their long-term clients on the demand-side. The IPO price will be determined in equilibrium by considering all these concerns. Both how the investment banks set the offering price in the end and how the stock market reacts to their decisions depend on the a priori perceptions of investors. When investors do not take notice of these conflicts of interests (the "naïve investors" hypotheses[23]), investment banks are more likely to deliver a high price when they hold an equity stake in the firms through a venture capital subsidiary. And the issues perform significantly worse in the long run than those of other firms in which underwriters did not invest and show no differences in underpricing. On the other hand, when investors accurately anticipate these conflicts of interest (the "rational discounting" hypotheses), investment bankers only bring the "least informationally sensitive" firms which minimise the information asymmetry concern, so there should be no difference in long-term performances between IPOs underwritten by investment banks which have shareholdings in the firms through venture capital and by independent underwriters. In this case, investors require more underpricing in anticipation of the potential adverse selection problem, as discussed above (Rock, 1986).

The benefits and costs of universal banks[24] have been debated, in particular since the early 1990s, in line with the intensified discussion of financial institutions' role in the economic development of a country and the recent trend of mergers in the financial sector (Saunders and Walter, 1996; Canals, 1997). The reason why the debate on universal banking has significance for venture capital research is that venture capital companies affiliated with other financial institutions are parallel to the subsidiaries of universal banks, so the debate can be directly applied to the issue of how different organisations of venture capital companies can influence the performance of the firms that the venture capital companies back. As was suggested by Gompers and Lerner (1999), it has been pointed out that universal banks could incur some costs to investors by causing a conflict of interests between investors and themselves. Kroszner and Rajan (1994) and Puri (1994) have suggested the possibility that investment banks in a universal banking group may induce public investors to invest in the companies that turn out to be of low quality. Roe (1994) documents the public sentiment around the time of the stock market crash of 1929 in the US, which believed that banks had an incentive to take advantage of investors by issuing securities of a company with an outstanding loan when the firm's future prospects were not very promising.[25] Banks forced the issuers to pay back the loan owed to the banks.

However, Kroszner and Rajan (1997) and Puri (1996) have presented evidence that universal banks have some advantages that can act as a positive signal in the market. Kroszner and Rajan (1997) found evidence that, before 1929 in the US, banks could positively affect the market's perception of the underwriting by separating the internal securities department within the bank into a newly incorporated affiliate. Puri (1996) argues that, due to the universal banks' greater ability to access information, universal banks before 1929 in the US could induce the investors to pay a premium for issues underwritten by universal banks. Fields and Fraser (2004) find that there are no significant differences in the pricing and the performance of IPO firms that are underwritten by investment banks and those that are underwritten by commercial banks (through their subsidiaries) in the US.[26]

3.7.3 Venture capital and the universal banking perspective: information advantage

Despite the plausible conflicts of interests that universal banks can incur, they can lead to great certification roles for the issuance of the firms. This is because, as "banks", they have a great "information advantage" over other financial institutions acquired through the on-going lending relationship with a company. In this sense, when a "commercial bank" in a universal banking group (without acting as an underwriter as an "investment bank" in a universal banking group does) participates in the ownership of venture capital, this can convey a greater positive signal certifying the entrepreneurial firms.

Banking institutions can obtain a lot of information about the firms by appointing a specialist to transmit funds, screening the loan applicants, monitoring the firms' managerial performances and profits and enforcing specific contracts that discipline managers (Calomiris and Ramirez, 1996). Holding shares in a firm is considered as a mechanism of certification by means of which banks can reduce the agency costs associated with debt (Prowse, 1990; Aoki, 1994). Banking institutions are more willing to provide funding for long-term investment (Edwards and Fischer, 1994).

Aoki (2000) has documented the concept of relational financing[27] in the world of competition and has said that banks' role in gathering information by making transactions with diverse firms, thus creating "informational rents", is still very significant in funding firms. These information rents allow banks to create a reputation mechanism. In their model, banks do not just exit from the firm after IPO. Banks or their subsidiaries not only can underwrite securities, but also keep providing loans and even maintain a rescue commitment to the firms up to their maturity, that is, throughout their life cycle. As they have an information advantage, they can sustain relational financing with the firms, whether these are small, medium-sized high-tech firms, or large-sized non-high-tech firms. A bank as a relational financier whose subsidiary is a venture capital company may decrease its monitoring role from the hands-on intervention in the firms' operations before IPO to a hands-off "arm's length" type of financing after IPO, because they know the firms and their people very well already and permit the firms to have more discretion in their management. Hellmann, Lindsey et al. (2003) propose the possibility that banking organisations may invest in the venture capital industry through their subsidiaries in order to develop client relationships between themselves and their client companies for their core lending activities. Rajan (1992) analyses the trade-off between a bank-like lender who has the ability to monitor the borrower's on-going performance and public investors who cannot monitor. As the borrower's quality improves, the returns from monitoring decrease, and the most efficient capital provider shifts from the role of a monitoring bank-like lender to that of a non-monitoring investor. Diamond (1991) discusses a similar theoretical model and suggests that the optimal type of monitoring by investors depends on the firm's stage in its life cycle. When banks have lending relationships with venture firms, they may shift from close monitoring to loose monitoring even after their subsidiary sell their shares in the venture firms. They only intervene in the crises of the firms if they need to take part in rescue financing or just to put them in the merger market.

If all these certifying and value-adding functions of banks are recognised in the market, IPO firms backed by banks-affiliated venture capital companies are expected to experience less underpricing. In the US, there is some evidence of less underpricing when the firm has bank loans outstanding (James and Wier, 1990). Corporate bond issues in the US that are underwritten by Section 20 subsidiaries of commercial banks have tended to have lower yield spreads at issue for risky firms when the related bank has a loan outstanding in the firm (Gande, Puri et al.,1997). For long-term performances, there should be no abnormal returns for bank-affiliated venture-capital-backed IPOs in equilibrium when investors anticipated the certification at IPO time, as in the case of an anticipation of a conflict of interest (Gompers and Lerner, 1999). However, if bank-affiliated venture capital is still appreciated as having more credibility for the mechanism of certification than is provided by other types of venture capitalists then, after a certain amount of time has passed, and if the IPO firms reflect the value generated by this mechanism, this certification will lead to higher returns in the long run.

3.8 Major empirical evidence on venture capital-backing and IPO performances

3.8.1 Involvement of venture capitalists, underpricing and long-term performance

Many researchers have endeavoured to find any significant statistical correlations between the involvement of venture capitalists and underpricing/long-term performance. However, the results are somewhat mixed, depending on the countries, sample period and methodologies. I report the empirical evidence of underpricing and long-term performance by the order of stock market-based system countries and bank-based system countries.

Using a sample of US IPOs over the period 1978–1987, Barry, Muscarella et al. (1990) first made attempts to establish the significance of the underpricing phenomenon. They did not find any statistically significant difference in initial returns between 433 venture capital-backed firms and 1,123 non-venture capital-backed firms.[28] However, they found that the initial returns were negatively associated with the number of venture capitalists involved in the issuing company, the lead venture capitalist's age, the size of the venture capitalists' equity stakes in the issuing companies, the length of the venture capitalists' occupancy on the company boards and the number of prior IPOs in which the lead venture capitalist participated.[29] This indicates that underpricing is related to the proxy variables for the venture capitalists' management skills. It can be said that the quality of monitoring and guidance skills of venture capitalists certifies the quality of the issuing firm. However, Megginson and Weiss (1991) found that, using a sample of 320 venture capital-backed companies and 320 other non-venture capital-backed companies matched by offer size and by industry during 1983–1987, venture capital-backed IPOs reduced initial returns, that is to say, they showed less serious underpricing.[30] Moreover, they also confirmed that venture capitalists certify the venture firms with uncertainty, by showing that underpricing is significantly related to the underwriter compensation, underwriter quality (market shares of underwriters), and the age of the issuing firm. They argue that venture capitalists facilitate the IPOs of younger firms by reducing the information asymmetries that are especially associated with those firms. On the other hand, Francis and Hasan (2001), who also analyse US data for the sample period 1990–1993, found that the initial returns of VC-backed IPOs on average to be significantly higher than those of non-VC-backed IPOs.[31] Brav and Gompers (1997) find that, using the US data venture capital-backing IPOs outperform other IPOs in the long run.[32] They argue that, unlike individual investors who are susceptible to market fads, institutions such as venture capitalists act according to their valuation of the firms. They maintain their ownerships of the firms. Because institutional investors are the main sources for the purchasing of venture funds, they may be more willing to hold equity in firms that have been brought by venture capitalists with whom they have invested. The greater availability of information by venture capitalists and the large shareholdings by venture capitalists and institutional investors may make venture-capital-companies' share price less prone to investor sentiment. Especially in the case of small firms, venture capitalists' involvements make a difference. For the small firms in which individual investors, not venture capitalists (or large institutional investors) invest, underperformance is severe because there is less information availability and because of the scarcity of the certification role. Furthermore, Brau, Brown et al. (2004) examine if the presence of VC-backing results in significant differences in the underpricing and the long-term performance of US manufacturing firm in the sample period 1990–1996, and find that there are no significant differences in firm performance between both groups.[33]

Espenlaub, Garrett et al. (1999) compare the initial returns and long-term performance of 135 VC-backed IPOs and 114 non-VC-backed IPOs by using UK IPO data between 1992 and 1995. They find that there is no significant difference of initial returns between VC-backed and non-VC-backed IPOs.[34] They also contrast the market index-adjusted twenty-four and thirty-six month cumulative average abnormal returns (CAARs) between VC-backed and non-VC-backed IPOs and find that the differences in the long term between both subsamples are not significantly different.[35] They add that, however, there is no evidence of significant long-term underperformance in either of the two samples, unlike the US underperformance which was found in Ritter (1991).

Franzke (2003) analyses the underpricing of Germany IPO firms (79 VC-backed vs 160 non-VC-backed) in the period 1997–2002 and finds that the VC-backed firms do not seem to be less underpriced, thus not supporting the hypothesis of the certification of venture capitalists.[36] However, he also finds that the involvement of a prestigious venture capitalist leads to higher underpricing, thus rejecting the hypothesis that the impact of the venture capitalist reputation will be to lower underpricing. Bessler and Kurth (2003) examine the long-term performance of Germany IPO firms by using the data of 75 VC-backed and 232 non-VC-backed IPOs during the period 1998–2001 and find that the eighteen-month buy-and-hold-returns do not yield any significant difference between VC-backed and non-VC-backed IPOs, thus suggesting no apparent positive impact of venture capital financing on the performance of IPOs.[37]

Using a dataset of Japanese IPOs over the period 1989–1995, Hamao, Packer et al. (2000) find that venture capital-backing is linked to higher underpricing.[38] They also find that the long-term performance of Japanese venture capital-backing offerings is no better than that of other IPOs.[39] This implies that, in the Japanese case, the presence of conflicts of interest is reflected in the short-term and long-term stock price. They conclude that venture capital does not seem to alleviate informational problems by certifying the quality of the IPO firm in Japan. Kutsuna, Cowling et al. (2000) analyse Japanese IPOs in 1996 distinguished between VC-backed firms (59 firms) and non-VC-backed firms (50 firms) and find no specific difference of initial return and the short-term performance (after one, three and six month) between the two groups.[40] But in the empirical analysis of the relationship between the stock price growth rates and the types of venture capital investment, a high proportion of venture capital investment was associated with a more conspicuous deterioration in share price movements during the aftermarket period. However, it was also shown that the retention of shares by venture capitalists was positively associated with the aftermarket return. When the venture capitalists sold a high portion of shares, it led to the decline of the aftermarket return. The worsening aftermarket return reflects a conflict of interest between venture capitalists and outside investors.

In comparison to empirical results of the US and UK (stock market-based system countries) and Germany and Japan (bank-based system countries), there have been very few studies of Korea.[41] Kim and Park (2002), however, examine the initial return of the 347 IPOs in KOSDAQ stock market over the period from

1999 to 2001 and find that the excess initial return[42] of " Venture Business"[43] is significantly higher than non-venture business (" General Business").

3.8.2 Institutional affiliation of venture capitalists, underpricing and long-term performances

The empirical results on the association between venture capitalists' affiliation with investment banks and underpricing and long-term performance are also mixed. I also report the empirical evidence of underpricing and long-term performance by the order of stock market-based system countries and bank-based system countries.

Gompers and Lerner (1999) examine the effects of the conflict of interest between underwriters and outside investors in IPOs where the venture capital firm backing the offering is a captive subsidiary of (or affiliated with) the underwriting investment bank, by using the 885 US IPOs between 1972 and 1992. In such cases, the investment bank may have an incentive to set the offering prices too high and time offerings when the firms' value meets with the overvaluation by the market. Their study investigates whether the existence of conflicts of interest is reflected in the differences in the short- and long-term performance between offerings with underwriters affiliated with venture capitalists and other IPOs. In terms of short-term performance, Gompers and Lerner argue that if investors are expecting the adverse effects of the conflict of interest, such as the underwriter's incentive to overprice, then investors will rationally demand a "lemons discount" to compensate them, because it is likely that greater information asymmetry between the underwriter and themselves, and accordingly adverse selection from underwriters, will take place. Given this prediction, IPOs will be more underpriced; that is, the offer price will be lower (relative to fundamentals) than it would be without the conflicts of interest. They find no evidence of differences in worse long-term performance or higher initial returns between IPOs backed by underwriters-affiliated venture capitalists and those backed by the others.[44] Li and Masulis (2003) examine the impact of the affiliation of venture capitalist with underwriters on the IPO underpricing by focusing the 1996–2000 period in the US, and find that venture capital investments by lead underwriters significantly decreased IPO underpricing, whereas venture capital investments by other syndicate underwriters had no effect.[45] They argue that the certification effect of the lead underwriter is reinforced when investors have greater uncertainty about IPO valuation.

Espenlaub, Garrett et al. (1999) examine the effect of the affiliation of venture capitalists with investment banks using the UK data during the period from 1992 to 1995. They found that the cases of affiliation of venture capitalists with investment banks showed less underpricing than those of independent venture capitalists.[46] This is also consistent with the view that venture capitalists with reputable financial institutions provide more effective screening and monitoring, thus leading to the certifying of issue quality. However, when the investment bank affiliate acted as the underwriter, initial returns were somewhat higher than offerings backed by affiliated venture capitalists but where the affiliated investment bank did not sponsor the IPO.[47] They confirmed the role of reputable venture capitalists with links to reputable underwriters, but also showed the possibility that a conflict of interest may arise due to the presence of the affiliated investment bankers as underwriters. They also found that long-term stock prices with backing by underwriters-affiliated venture capitalists exhibited substantially better performances than those backed by venture capital companies that were independent of underwriters.[48] At the same time, the long-term performance of UK IPOs is positively related to the reputation of the underwriters. This implies that a conflict of interest between the affiliated underwriter and outside investors does not appear in the UK case.

By using the data of Germany IPOs over the period 1998–2001, Bessler and Kurth (2003) investigate the long-term performance of bank-affiliated VC-backed IPOs, compared with that of other VC-backed IPOs. They find that the initial return of bank-affiliated VC-backed IPOs was quite substantial, compared to that of other VC-backed IPOs. The difference of these two initial returns is significant. However, a comparison of the eighteen-month abnormal BAHRs between bank-affiliated VC-backed IPOs and other VC-backed IPOs did not reveal any significant difference.[49]

Hamao, Packer et al. (2000) report significantly worse long-term performances for venture capital-backed IPOs where the lead venture capitalist was affiliated with a security company, using a sample of IPOs issued on the Japanese IPOs between 1989 and 1995. They also found that higher average initial returns were associated with backing by venture capitalists whose parent is the lead underwriter, while all other forms of venture capital show smaller initial returns.[50] When venture capital holdings were broken down by the venture capitalists' affiliation with other institutions, the IPO firms which security companies or banking institutions had invested in the venture capital companies do not seem to outperform or underperform other IPOs.

In addition to empirical results of the US and UK (stock market-based system countries) and Germany and Japan (bank-based system countries), there is empirical evidence of the underpricing/long-term performance of Singaporean IPOs in relation to VC's institutional affiliation.[51] By using the Singaporean IPO data for 64 firms from 1987 to 1999, Wang, Wang et al. (2002) compare the underpricing and long-term performance between the IPOs backed by financial-institutions-affiliated VCs, regardless of the VCs' affiliation with underwriters, and those backed by independent VCs. They find that financial-institutions-affiliated VCs are associated with significantly higher underpricing and worse long-term performances than independent VCs.[52] They attribute this result to the better quality of the independent VCs that have more experiences of investments in high-technology firms than financial-institutions-affiliated VCs do in Singaporean context. I did not find any long-term performance studies in the period 1990–2000 for Korea.

3.9 Hypothesis formulation

The discussion that I have had so far leads us to consider twelve hypotheses that will be subjected to empirical analysis.

3.9.1 Certification and value-adding by venture capitalists and their impact on underpricing and long-term performance

As I discussed above, much of the literature regards venture capitalists as implementing similar functions to those of reputable underwriters or auditors for going public firms, that is, as lessening the information asymmetry between investors and issuers, thus resulting in a reduction of the underpricing of IPO firms (Barry, Muscarella et al.,1990; Megginson and Weiss, 1991) and in a better long-term performance (Brav and Gompers, 1997). Venture capitalists have been known to provide funding to entrepreneurial firms which suffer from a difficulty in getting finance from conventional institutions such as banks etc. due to their greater default risks (Westhead and Storey, 1997). Venture capitalists play a role in raising a firm from the early development stage through the expansion and production stage to the stage of IPO or other exit routes. When entrepreneurial firms invoke agency problems and information asymmetry, which are inherent in their uncertain operation, between investors and themselves, venture capitalists can alleviate the concerns by acting as an informed financial intermediary (Chan, Siegel et al.,1987; Hellmann and Puri, 2000). To do this, venture capitalists utilise various control mechanisms and resource allocations for venture capital investment. Venture capitalists often invest through syndicates in which one or more venture capitalists play the leading role (Admati and Pfleiderer, 1994; Gompers, 1999). Venture capitalists generally provide financing in the form of staged financing which is matched with the development in the life cycle of the entrepreneurial firms (Sahlman, 1990; Gompers, 1995). Venture capitalists may employ convertible debts in order to avoid the entrepreneurs' short-termistic behaviour which is aimed at receiving the funding at each financing round (Gompers, 1999). Entrepreneurs can benefit from the strategic guidance provided by venture capitalists who are often specialists in a particular industry or technology (Hellmann and Puri, 2000; Kortum and Lerner, 1998). Venture capitalists provide entrepreneurs with business, managerial and technological skills and guidance through their own experts, or consultants, or diverse practitioners in their networks (Stuart, Hoang et al.,1999). All the investment behaviour, funding mechanism, and strategic guidance of venture capitalists can be recognised as alleviating the information asymmetry that exists between public investors and issuing firms, thus certifying those firms to outside investors when the firms go public. Furthermore, venture capitalists are "repeated players" in the IPO market. Megginson and Weiss (1991) have documented the fact that venture capitalists certify the venture firms in the sense that they attest the quality of the information disclosed by the company at IPO. Espenlaub, Garrett et al. (1999) has stated that venture capitalists are very cautious in screening, selecting and monitoring investee firms, because they may lose their reputation by taking poorly qualified firms to the IPO market. They are not one-off but repeated players in the IPO market. Jain and Kini (2000) have argued that venture capitalists' reputable capital is enhanced by repeated interaction and interlocking arrangements with the market intermediaries. Venture-capital-backed issuers are able to exert an influence on institutional investors, prestigious investment bankers and analysts to support them to a great degree in the pre-IPO and post-IPO period. If venture capitalists want to act as long-term players in the IPO market, they had better shape an ongoing relationship with specific underwriters. Venture capitalists' certification role, which comes from their monitoring and continuing relationship, is enhanced by the choice of a prestigious underwriter (Carter and Manaster, 1990; Carter, Dark et al.,1998; Jain and Kini, 1999).

Accordingly, following this literature review, venture capital-backed IPOs in KOSDAQ will be expected to be less underpriced immediately after IPO and to show better long-term performances than IPOs that are not backed by venture capital. I expect that in the Korean stock market, venture capitalists' involvement in ownership of the entrepreneurial firms sends a positive signal to the capital markets. In a stock market such as KOSDAQ, which has a shorter track record, with only five years' stock listings and dealings, public investors will be assumed to have less accumulated information about IPOs, especially about the high-technology focused firms that prevailed during the period of our research. This indicates that public investors may suffer from the unavailability of information on the value of the firms and they are most likely to resort to the ownership side of the firms: those who are backing the firms. Korean venture capitalists are expected to have the same kind of ability to back up the entrepreneurial firms not only by means of financial support but also by means of managerial and business assistance in the US or the UK, thus to screen appropriate firms and bring the firms from a relatively early stage to successful IPOs.

> *H1a: Venture capital-backed IPOs will prove to be less underpriced, compared with other IPOs which are not backed by venture capital.*
>
> *H1b: Venture capital-backed IPOs will prove to show a better performance in the long term, compared with other IPOs which are not backed by venture capital.*

3.9.2 The reputation of venture capitalists and its impact on underpricing and long-term performance

Whereas I agree with the role of certification and adding-value of venture capitalists by means of diverse mechanisms, I also recognise that venture capitalists are not all the same. Investors differentiate their quality, capability and skills from one another. It was implied that some venture capitalists are less aware of entrepreneurs' technology and business, not to mention that they cannot appraise accurately their status as entrepreneurs (Amit, Glosten et al.,1990). More capable venture capitalists tend to concentrate on a narrow set of industries, thus showing a clear preference for certain industries They tend to concentrate their efforts in monitoring and screening firms on specific industries that are selected strategically (Barry, Muscarella et al.,1990). When multiple venture capitalists turn up in the ownership of an IPO firm, the quality of lead venture capitalist can be critical to the evaluation of the firm among the investors. Syndication of financing is recognised as a mechanism which indicates that a lead venture capitalist has persuaded other venture capitalists to participate in the financing, with the lead venture capitalist increasing incentives to monitor carefully because it has increased the risk to its own reputation by soliciting the participation of other venture capitalists (Gompers, 1999). The reputation of lead venture capitalists in the syndication of financing is greatly reflected in the expectation of investors concerning the prospects of IPO firms (Admati and Pfleiderer, 1994). When venture capitalists can invoke an agency problem in such a way that they have an incentive to draw on new funds from other venture capitalists for the firms whose prospects are not very favourable, the reputable venture capitalists who maintain a constant fraction of the firm's shares can resolve this situation (Admati and Pfleiderer, 1994).

Moreover, it has been observed that venture capitalists have a tendency to put their investment and IPO decisions in line with the stock market situation (Venture Economics, 2002). Only more capable and reputable venture capitalists can attract funding from investors for early stage financing for the firms. Less capable and reputable venture capitalists tend to focus on the mature entrepreneurial firms that are on the threshold of IPOs. It has been noticed that young and less experienced venture capitalists show a willingness to bring entrepreneurial firms to the public market earlier than what would be a more appropriate time, even when the entrepreneurs are in less-mature situation for IPOs, that is, "grandstanding" (Gompers, 1996). It was seen that young venture capital companies take IPO firms to the public market earlier than more established firms in order to raise their profile in the market. This is costly both to the young venture capitalists and to the issuing firms' other shareholders, because greater uncertainty and information asymmetries are ascertained, thus requiring more underpricing. The long-term performance of the IPO firms will not be so good, either (Gompers, 1996).

It is likely that more experienced and older venture capitalists will be more cautious in screening and selecting IPO firms and bringing them to the stock market in order to avoid the risk of losing their reputation as a result of IPOs of bad quality firms, while less experienced and younger venture capitalists are interested in promoting their reputation. Korea's venture capitalists have a relatively short history and the majority of them were established after the regulatory change in 1998, which aimed to encourage the foundation of more venture capital companies in order to promote technology financing. Therefore, not all of the Korean venture capital companies have any experience of investing in firms in the early stage and guiding them to the IPO stage. Furthermore, among about 120 venture capital companies, only about 20 of them appear in the ownership section of the IPO prospectus of IPO firms. Therefore, I expect that, in this situation, the investors in the KOSDAQ will differentiate between the qualities of the venture capital companies backing IPO firms. So I can anticipate, in our empirical analysis, that IPOs backed by venture capitalists with more reputation will be seen as reducing information asymmetry at IPO and will operate in a better way in the long run.

Accordingly, I hypothesise that:

> *H2a: IPOs backed by more reputable venture capitalists will show less underpricing, compared with IPOs backed by less reputable venture capitalists.*
>
> *H2b: IPOs backed by more reputable venture capitalists will show outperformance in the long term, compared with IPOs backed by less reputable venture capitalists.*

3.9.3 Institutional differences in venture capitalists' ownership and their impact on underpricing and long-term performance

Since the early 1990s, the role of the financial system in economic development has been one of the important issues in finance research. Especially, the comparison between the stock market-based financial system (USA and UK) and the bank-based financial system (Germany and Japan) has attracted academic attention. In general, the stock market-based capital market has been regarded as a more efficient and convenient financial system than the bank-based capital market for venture capital financing, due to its adaptability for corporate control and its easy access to exit through IPO (Gilson, 1996; Milhaupt, 1997; Black and Gilson, 1998; Mayer, 2002). However, it has also been suggested that the short-term perspective shown by investors in the stock market-based financial market could sometimes make impossible the investment that needs to be done in a long-term perspective (Porter, 1992; Edwards and Fischer, 1994; Singh, Singh et al.,2000).

IPO firms that are brought to the stock market by venture capital that is affiliated with investment banks or commercial banks provide a good empirical testing ground for universal banking (Gompers and Lerner, 1999), which was legally prohibited in the US in 1929 after the stock market crash, but which appears as the general form of banking institution in Germany. The reason why the debate on universal banking is significant for venture capital research is that venture capital companies affiliated with investment banks or commercial banks are analogous to the subsidiaries of universal banks, so that the debate can be directly applied to the issue of how different organisations of venture capital companies can influence the performance of the firms that the venture capital companies back. This issues is also important in KOSDAQ, in which a lot of IPO firms were backed by venture capital companies whose parent institutions are security companies (equivalent to investment banks in the Korean context) or commercial banks, thus raising the possibility of a conflict of interest or certification according to which kind of financial institution owns the venture capital company.

It was documented above that when a venture capital company that has a shareholding in an IPO firm is affiliated with an investment bank, in particular, if the investment bank acts as an underwriter for the IPO firm, this situation may cause a conflict of interest between the investors and the underwriter. The investment bank as an underwriter may have an incentive to set a higher offer price for IPO shares (Kroszner and Rajan, 1994). It may have an incentive to take advantage of investors by issuing shares of a company with an outstanding loan when the firm's future prospects are not very promising (Roe, 1994). Consequently, in the context of KOSDAQ, securities companies-affiliated venture capitalists may invoke the same kind of conflict of interests.

However, it was also discussed above that commercial banks-affiliated venture capital does not present the same conflict of interest that securities companies-affiliated venture capital does, because commercial banks do not (are not legally permitted to) act as underwriters directly. Banking institutions can acquire a lot of information about the firms with which they have a lending relationship through the appointing of a specialist to transmit funds, and screening and monitoring the business and the operations of the firm (Calomiris and Ramirez, 1996). It was suggested that the holding of shares in a firm by a bank is considered as a certifying and value-adding mechanism by means of which banks can decrease the agency costs associated with debt (Prowse, 1990; Aoki, 1994). Banking institutions are willing to provide funding for long-term investment (Edwards and Fischer, 1994). The banks that gain the "information rents" by means of venture capital investment and debt can have a "relational financing" relationship with the IPO firms and can take control of the extent of their intervention in the firms (Aoki, 2000). Accordingly, these kinds of certifying and value-adding functions of commercial banks-affiliated venture capital-backed IPOs can also be reflected in the investment behaviour of KOSDAQ.

Following this logic, I get a third hypothesis:

> *H3a: IPOs backed by venture capitalists in whose ownership commercial banks have participated as major shareholders will show less underpricing.*
> *H3b: IPOs backed by venture capitalists in whose ownership commercial banks have participated as major shareholders will show better long-term performance.*
> *H4a: IPOs backed by venture capitalists in whose ownership securities companies have participated as major shareholders will show more underpricing.*
> *H4b: IPOs backed by venture capitalists in whose ownership securities companies have participated as major shareholders will show worse long-term performance.*

3.9.4 *The reputation of the underwriter and the auditor, and its impact on underpricing and long-term performance*

Because the certifying agent of the venture capitalist for an IPO firm suffering from asymmetric information between the issuer and the investor originally owes its concept to other financial players, such as the underwriter and the auditor in the process of IPO, I summarise the discussion of how underwriters alleviate underpricing and contribute to the better long-term performance of the IPO firm and derive another hypothesis.

Concerning the underpricing, the discussion was concentrated on the information asymmetry problem that could exist between the issuer and the investor. When issuers face the "lemons problem", they need to separate themselves from the lower-quality issuers by pricing the IPO below its true value, which lower-quality issuers find it hard to imitate. Issuers are able to get back the costs of IPO underpricing by selling the shares they retained at a higher price after IPO than they would have been sold without signalling. Their signal is reinforced by the announcement of high dividends (earnings) after IPO (Allen and Faulhaber, 1989), future issuing activities by selling additional shares on more favourable conditions (Welch, 1989), retained ownership (Grinblatt and Hwang, 1989), or analyst coverage (Chemmanur and Fulghieri, 1998). Moreover, when investors have different information about the issuer, IPO stocks may be underpriced because too high priced stocks may lead investors and issuers to fear a "winner's curse" (Rock, 1986). Furthermore, where the bookbuilding method is used for the setting of the offer price, investment banks may underprice IPOs so as to induce regular investors to reveal their information about their truthful valuations of the firms. Through the process of "bookbuilding" and "road show", underwriters acquire information about the market demand on the shares to sell. When market demand is higher, the offer price will be set higher than the original price. When potential investors come to realise that their willingness to pay a high price will lead to a higher offer price, underwriters should offer something in return for the investors' revealing the information about the demand for the shares: underpricing and more allocation (Ritter, 1998).

Because these information asymmetry hypotheses assume that issuers should underprice their shares in order to attract investors, if information asymmetry problems disappear, there should be no underpricing. Some of the literature relating to "reputation" states that issuers could alleviate the degree of information asymmetry by employing highly prestigious underwriters, auditors or financial advisors in the process of IPO. There is a lot of empirical evidence that more reputable financial advisors are linked to lower initial returns, which can thus be interpreted as lower underpricing. The employment of a prestigious underwriter, auditor or other financial advisors to the issuing company may be interpreted by investors as a positive signal of issue value, leading to less underpricing (Titan and Truman, 1986; Holland and Horton, 1993; Carter and Manaster, 1990; Logue, Rogalski et al.,2002 etc.) Where there exists a large degree of information asymmetry, the involvement of highly prestigious financial institutions in the IPO process will reduce the extent of information asymmetry and help the issuers to set their offer price in accordance with the firms' true value.

In the long-term performance discussion, I have seen that it is more likely that underwriters will be keen to bring the good-quality firms to the IPO market, so that their reputable capital will not be forfeited by false over-pricing. Booth and

Smith (1986) show that the underwriter must also invest in its own reputable capital, putting its reputation on the line with each new offering. Carow (1999) indicates that more prestigious underwriters monitor firm managers closely when deciding new securities' issue prices. A firm that was closely monitored by a more reputable underwriter is more likely to present less severe long-term performances than one that was underwritten by a less reputable underwriter. There is empirical evidence that more reputable underwriters are associated not only with less short-run underpricing but also better long-term performance of the IPO firms (Carter, Dark et al.,1998). It has not been clearly shown by empirical tests that IPO firms audited by more reputable auditors show better long-term performances, but I can expect that firms which are better qualified for IPO and have greater prospects in the future will employ a more reputable auditor in spite of the higher costs of auditing.

From this discussion, a fourth hypothesis is derived:

> *H5a: Underwriter reputation is associated with less underpricing.*
> *H5b: Underwriter reputation is associated with better long-term performance.*
> *H6a: Auditor reputation is associated with less underpricing.*
> *H6b: Auditor reputation is associated with better long-term performance*

Notes

1 Parts of this chapter appeared in shorter and revised forms in Ch.26 'The Impact of Venture Capital Participation and Its Affiliation with Financial Institutions on the Long-term Performance of IPO Firm: Evidence from Korea in Hot and Cold Market Periods" by Jaeho Lee from *Oxford Handbook of Venture Capital*, edited by Cumming, Douglas (2012) and "The Hot and Cold Market Impacts on Underpricing of Certification, Reputation and Conflicts of Interest in Venture Capital Backed Korean IPO" by Jaeho Lee from *Korean Venture Management Review*, 12(4) (2009). Original parts have been used in this chapter with permission of Oxford University Press and The Korean Association of Small Business Studies, respectively.

2 A venture capitalist is a professional working for a venture capital company, but this is interpreted widely in the literature as an organisation that manages venture capital funds. So, in this book, the term venture capitalist is frequently used as a synonym for a venture capital company.

3 Underpricing translates directly into the initial return, defined as the return earned by an investor buying at the offering price and selling at the first-day closing price. The terms underpricing and initial return will be used interchangeably in the remainder of this book.

4 In Akerlof's (1970) model, second-hand cars, so called "lemons" are traded at a significant discount in a market characterised by asymmetric information, where not buyers, but sellers can differentiate good quality from bad quality

5 The evidence of empirical results about the signalling hypothesis is mixed. Even though there is evidence of extensive post issuing activities by IPO firms (Welch, 1989), price appreciation may be an important reason for entrepreneurs to return to the market for more funding (Jegadeesh, Weinstein et al.,1993). Michaely and Shaw (1994) found that firms with more underpricing have a weaker future earnings performance, fewer dividend payouts, smaller dividend amounts and less frequent returning to the market for secondary equity and debt issues.

6 In the "bookbuilding" process, the offer price is revised after finding out the market demand. During the marketing campaign period, the underwriter investigates potential buyers, their indication of purchasing the IPO stocks and the price which they think is reasonable. Through this process, a demand curve of the quantity and price of the stocks to be sold is constructed and the offering price is then based on this information (Ritter, 1998).

7 An interesting implication of the market feedback hypothesis is that a positively-sloped demand curve may be incurred (Ritter, 1998). Under this hypothesis, the offering price is adjusted upwards if regular investors indicate positive information. Other investors, knowing that this will only be a partial adjustment, correctly infer that these offerings will be underpriced and consequently they will want to purchase additional shares, leading to a positively sloped demand curve.

8 There rose a kind of financial theory that explains the existence of underpricing as the result of IPO allocation of the underwriter. Loughran and Ritter (2002) argue that, if underwriters are given discretion in IPO share allocation, the discretion will not automatically be used in the best interests of the issuing firm. It is plausible that underwriters may intentionally allow underpricing to take place in order to favour buy-side clients who are eager to receive IPO allocations. They argue that, when market valuation of the IPO firms is increasing, as in the late 1990s, the issuing firms can be complacent about the excessive underpricing once they learn about the aftermarket valuation that is higher than they expected. In this case, it is more likely that the underpricing is positively related to the more prestigious underwriter, because the reputation of the underwriter must be related to the ability to attract demand from investors. The identity of IPO share buyers (especially, institutional investors), their demand quantity of the shares at the road show, the offer price and offering volume adjustment after the road show can be important information to test this hypothesis. This information was not available for KOSDAQ IPO firms when I started our research. It is an interesting research agenda to investigate how venture capitalists as shareholders of the IPO firm behave in the face of a conflict of interests between issuing firm and underwriter.

9 The term 'hot' market is generally used to indicate that the impact of investors sentiment is particularly acute in periods characterised by excessive optimism or speculative bubbles often based upon particular types of IPO stocks (Aggarwal and Rivoli, 1990; Ljungqvist, Nanda et al.,2001).

10 It was reported that IPO shares whose earning per share was negative realised much higher initial returns (72.0 per cent) than those whose earning per shares was positive (43.5 per cent) during the period 1999–2000 in the US (Ritter and Welch, 2002).

11 Ibbotson, Sindelar et al. (1994) show a tendency for a strong relationship to exist between the number of offerings and the average initial returns. For example, while the average initial returns of the period 1980–89 was 15.3 per cent with offerings of 5,155, that of the period 1970–79 was just 9.0 per cent with 1,658 offerings.

12 "Entrepreneur", "Entrepreneurial firm", "high-technology firm" and "venture firm" are used interchangeably, depending on the context.

13 Williamson (1988) implies that the problem of shirking or over-investment arises when an agent has an asset which is very specific to him, and so is appropriated only by him.

14 Sahlman (1990) notes that the role of stage capital infusion is similar to that of debt in highly leveraged transactions, keeping the owner/manager on a "tight leash" and reducing potential losses from bad decisions.

15 Hellmann and Puri (2002) state that venture capitalists can have a considerable impact on the development of new firms. They find that venture capital is associated with a variety of professionalisation, such as human resource policies, the

adoption of stock option plans, and the replacement of the founder with an outside CEO.

16 This evidence in Barry, Muscarella et al. (et al. (1990) is also found in Field and Hanka (2000), who found that average ownership of the US venture capitalists immediately after the IPO was 23 per cent and this ratio dropped to 17 per cent one year after the IPO. However, they find that venture capitalists tend to sell off considerable number of shares that they have held on the day of expiration of their share lock-up. On the contrary, Hamao, Packer et al. (et al. (2000) find that, in Japan, the average shares that lead venture capitalists hold are 5.92 per cent, less than a half of the stake documented in similar studies of the US. Also, they found in Japan the post-issue IPO equity share held by the lead venture capitalist declines by around 40 per cent of the pre-IPO share. This implies that venture capitalists cash out either during the offering or its aftermath.

17 The authors raise a concern that there may be an endogenous variable, that is, "the arrival of entrepreneurial opportunities" that are correlated with venture capital investment and patenting. To avoid this problem, they exploit the major discontinuity point in the history of venture capital industry. The 1979 clarification of the "prudent rule" of ERISA (Employee Retirement Income Security Act), a policy shift that freed pension investors to invest in venture capital was considered in their analysis. Actually, this policy shift leads to a dramatic increase in the funds committed to the venture capital. They assume that this type of exogenous change should identify the role of venture capital, because it is unlikely to be related to the entrepreneurial opportunities. Even after presenting this causality problem, the result still shows that venture capital funding has a strong positive influence on innovation.

18 He names the phenomenon as "grandstanding" in the sense that venture capitalists want them to be seen in the best position, that is, in the "grandstand" where a block of seats commands the best view for racehorses.

19 Barnes and Mccarthy (2002) find that, by using the UK data, the companies backed by young venture capital companies are indeed younger at IPO than those backed by older venture capital companies. However, there is little evidence to suggest greater underpricing for young VC-backed companies.

20 Black and Gilson (1998) provide some evidence regarding the relationship between the number of venture capital-backed firms and the amount of new venture capital commitments in each year. They find that, with a one-year lag, the change in the number of IPOs and the resulting change in the amount of new venture capital that was committed were positively correlated.

21 It can be argued that entrepreneurs regain their control rights if they buy-back the share from the venture capitalists. However, provided that venture capitalists sell off their block-holding shares to minor shareholders in the stock markets, entrepreneurs will emerge as largest shareholders.

22 Earlier studies of the impact of venture capital on the IPO firm performance, which were mainly carried out by using the US data did not deal with the difference of the ownership of venture capitalists as an important factor that may affect the IPO firm performance. It seems that this is because those empirical studies were conducted in the US, in which entrepreneurial firms mainly receive funding from independent venture capital companies that are not affiliated with other large institutions.

23 These two hypotheses about the market condition originated from Kroszner and Rajan (1994).

24 Universal banks are in general defined as banks that are by regulation permitted to and are able to perform the full range of financial services: commercial and investment banking, securities trading, insurance brokerage and other financial activities under one roof.

25 This public outcry finally led to the legislation of the Glass-Steagall Act of 1933 that barred commercial banks that were members of the Federal Reserve System and their affiliated institutions from holding, trading, or underwriting corporate securities (Roe, 1994).

26 However, by using German IPO data, Klein and Zoeller (2003) show that IPOs underwritten by German universal-banks are correlated with higher underpricing, which can be shown as evidence of conflict of interest that universal banks may incur.

27 Their working definition of "relational financing" is as follows: relational financing is a type of financing in which the financier is expected to make additional financing in a class of uncontractible states in the expectation of future rents over time. They refer to types of financing that are not relational as "arm's length" financing.

28 The average initial day-return of venture capital-backed companies (8.43 per cent) was higher than that of non-venture capital-backed companies (7.47 per cent).

29 In this multi-regression testing model, they controlled for issue size, underwriter quality and the standard deviation of post-issue share prices, which acts as a proxy variable for the *ex ante* uncertainty encircling the company.

30 These differences are statistically significant at the 0.01 level by t-statistics.

31 The initial return of VC-backed IPOs was 13.5 per cent, compared with 10.1 per cent of non-VC-backed IPOs.

32 They investigate the long-run underperformance of IPOs in a sample of 934 venture-capital-backed IPOs from 1972–1992 and 3,407 non-venture-capital-backed IPOs from 1975–1992. The market index-adjusted five-year buy-and-hold-return (BAHR) of VC-backed firms was –20.7 per cent, compared with – 49.3 of non-VC-backed IPOs.

33 Initial return of VC-backed firms was 10 per cent, compared with 13 per cent of non-VC-backed firms. Three-year cumulative return was 25.7 per cent for VC-backed-firms, while non-VC-backed recorded 12.3 per cent.

34 The initial return is calculated as the difference between offer price and the closing price of the sixth day of trading in their research. The mean initial returns were 9.5 per cent and 9.4 per cent for VC-backed IPOs and non-VC-backed IPOs, respectively.

35 The twenty-four month CAARs of VC-backed group is 0.14 per cent, while that of non-VC-backed group is – 3.11 per cent. The thirty-six CAARs' are – 5.9 per cent and – 11.6 per cent for both groups, respectively.

36 The underpricing of VC-backed IPOs was 52.4 per cent, while that of non-VC-backed IPOs was 48.4 per cent. Since this empirical research was carried out for the samples of Germany's Neuer Markt that was launched for the financing of innovative growth companies in 1997, these high initial returns of both groups reflect the fact that they were affected by the "hot" market situation.

37 The eighteen-month abnormal BAHR of VC-backed IPO was 18.9 per cent, compared with 7.3 per cent of non-VC-backed IPOs.

38 For the sample of Japanese venture-backed IPOs (210 firms) and other IPOs (246 firms), they found that the initial return for venture backing was 19.2 per cent, while that of other IPOs was 12.7 per cent.

39 The adjusted BAHR of VC-backed groups and non-VC-backed groups were – 29.8 per cent and – 27.0 per cent, respectively.

40 The initial return of VC-backed IPOs was 16.5 per cent, compared with 14.5 per cent of non-VC-backed IPOs. The stock price growth rates after six month were – 2.5 per cent and 2.7 per cent for VC-backed firms and non-VC-backed firms, respectively.

41 Following the definition of stock market-based system and bank-based system in sub-section 3.7.1, the Korean financial system is closer to bank-based system

where a few local banks provide more than half of the national financing to the business, even though the size of banks are not as big as that of German and Japanese banks. Given the dramatic growth of the stock market in recent years, Korean financial system is a hybrid of bank-based and stock market-based system. More often than not, it is called 'emerging market' (Smith and Chun, 2003).

42 The excess initial return is calculated as the difference between the offer price and the closing price on the first day that did not hit the daily upper price limit that exists in Korean stock markets and is interpreted as underpricing. The excess initial return of venture firm (209 firms) was 167.2 per cent, compared with 108.1 per cent of non-venture firms (138 firms). This excess initial return will be used for calculating the underpricing in this book, so will be explained in detail in Chapter 4.

43 Kim and Park (2002) did not compare the initial returns between VC-backed firms and non-VC-backed firms. Instead, they used the concept of 'Venture Business', which is a special legal category of firms in Korea, to divide IPO samples. 'Venture Business' includes four types of SMEs under the under 'the 1997 Special Measures Law for Fostering Venture Businesses' and is provided legal assistance such as tax benefit. A firm backed by venture capital can be qualified as a 'Venture Business' by applying for it. In KOSDAQ, a firm that is not designated as a 'Venture Business' is classified into 'General business'. In this book, I will not analyse the difference of IPO firm performance by this category, because the government granted too many firms the title of 'Venture Business' to promote the growth of high-tech SMEs, thus the 'Venture Business' has been criticised as not reflecting the authentic quality equal to high-tech SMEs.

44 The underpricing of the IPOs where any underwriter had shareholdings in the firms through venture capital subsidiary was 10.3 per cent, while that of the IPOs where no underwriter had shareholdings in the firms through venture capital subsidiary was 9.1 per cent. The five-year adjusted BAHR of the IPOs of both cases were 20.5 per cent and 25.9 per cent, respectively. Gompers and Lerner find that certification of underwriters exists, though. The initial returns were affected only by underwriter reputation, with more prestigious underwriters being linked to less underpricing and positive long-term performance.

45 The initial two-day return of IPOs when lead underwriters had ownership in the venture capital subsidiary was 50.5 per cent, compared with 61.5 per cent when no lead underwriters had ownership in the venture capital subsidiary.

46 When venture capitalists are affiliated with an investment bank, initial returns on average were 7.4 per cent, while otherwise initial returns were 15.0 per cent.

47 Initial returns (9.3 per cent) when venture capitalists were underwritten by investment banks' affiliates were higher than those (7.4 per cent) when venture capitalists were only affiliated with investment banks.

48 The 36 months CAR (33.25 per cent) for IPOs backed by venture capitalists who were underwritten by investment bank affiliates was much higher than those (−3.71 per cent) for IPOs backed by venture capitalists who were affiliated with investment banks, but were not sponsored by them. Moreover, when venture capitalists were not affiliated with any investment banks, their long-term performances were worse than both the above cases.

49 The underpricing of bank-affiliated VC-backed IPO was 84.2 per cent, which was significantly higher than 39.6 per cent of other VC-backed IPOs. The eighteen-month abnormal BAHRs were 10.3 per cent and 18.2 per cent, respectively.

50 The average initial return of IPOs backed by securities-companies-affiliated VCs was 20.6 per cent

51 Singapore can be called as a 'neutral market' in venture capital research in that independent and financial institution-affiliated VCs are equally distributed in the

financial system, unlike the US and the UK where independent VCs dominate venture capital industry or Germany and Japan where financial institutions-affiliated VCs dominate venture capital industry. (Wang, Wang et al.,2002).

52 The underpricing of independent VCs-backed IPO was 20.7 per cent, while that of financial institutions-affiliated VC-backed IPO was 33.4 per cent. Two-year abnormal returns were 47.4 per cent and –3.5 per cent, respectively.

4　Data and methodology[1]

4.1　Overview

To test the hypotheses, I need various types of variables that will be covered in the univariate and multivariate analysis. In a nutshell, I will measure underpricing and long-term market performance by stock price returns and use them as dependent variables in the univariate and multivariate analysis, as will be explained in detail below. In the univariate analysis, the underpricing and the long-term performance will be compared by t-test and non-parametric tests in terms of various types of IPOs firms (VC-backing, hot market situation, age, market capitalisation, industry). In the multivariate analysis, I implement a regression analysis of the underpricing and long-term performance for the all IPO firms, IPO firms that were listed in hot-market period and IPO firms that were listed in cold-market period, respectively. In doing this, I will employ a range of dummy variables representing VC-backing, the reputation of VCs, the ownership structure of VCs and the reputation of underwriter and auditor as independent variables, and diverse control variables that will be used as proxies for ex-ante uncertainty, high-tech industry and the hot market situation.

　　Before conducting this empirical analysis, I, in this chapter, introduce the data and methods that will be used to test our hypotheses. As specified at the beginning of the book, the empirical subject of our research is the IPOs on KOSDAQ market during the period of 1999–2001. I therefore collected all the IPO and performances data of all 372 firms newly listed in KOSDAQ in this period, about half of which are backed by venture capital companies.

　　　　In Section 4.2, I describe our data sources in detail. Some issues relating to sample selection will be also covered in this section. In Section 4.3, I deal with the methods I will use in our empirical study. I explain the concepts and definitions of "stock market performance" in terms of underpricing and long-term performance, which will be used as dependent variables in the univariate and multivariate analysis. After that, I set out the specification of the multivariate regression model I carry out in Chapter 6 and 7. I describe, in particular, the independent variables that represent VC-backing, the reputation of VC-backing, the different organisational types of VC-backing and the reputation of underwriter and auditor, and several control variables that will be used as proxies of firm characteristics and stock market situation. I specify five multivariate regression models that I implement in order to test our hypotheses.

4.2 Data construction

4.2.1 Data collection and sources

I collected the large volume of data required from diverse sources. First, all the IPO data of 372 going-public firms are based on the IPO prospectus which they report to Korean FSS (Financial Supervisory Service)[2] prior to IPO for the purpose of getting the approval for being listed in KOSDAQ. The IPO prospectuses include all the basic data associated with IPO such as volume of market capitalisation, gross spreads, costs of underwriting, name of underwriter etc., along with the history, business and operation of the IPO firms.[3] The ownership of the IPO firms at the time of IPO is available from these prospectuses, where I also extracted the information on VC-backing for the firm: names of venture capital companies that participated in the ownership and the volume (and percentage) of shares they own. IPO firms must report the identity and the shareholdings of venture capitalists (and other large shareholders[4]) if they hold 5 per cent and more of the total shares at IPO.[5] For this book, FSS arranged in addition for securities companies (underwriters) and auditors in operation in Korea to report their turnover and the number of underwriting and auditing activities, respectively, for the period of 1998–2000, and provided us with the summarised data, which were greatly helpful to calculate their market shares in Korean IPO market that were used to build up the reputation indicators of these organisations.

Daily stock prices of each firm, including both IPO firms and their matched firms were offered by Tong-Yang Securities Co. which shares the daily stock prices of every firm listed in KSE and KOSDAQ with other financial institutions through the electrical network operated by KIS (Korea Information Service). The IPO offering price of each IPO firm and daily KOSDAQ index were supplied by KOSDAQ. The Korean Stock Exchange provides us with daily KOSPI (Korea Stock Price Index) data. Yearly financial statements were supplied by Tong-Yang Securities Co, too.

The IPO numbers in each year in KOSDAQ and KSE were found in the annual report published by KSDA (Korea Securities Dealers Association) and KOSDAQ website (www.kosdaq.or.kr). Information on the institutional identity of each venture capital company, i.e., the parenting investor of the venture capital company was provided by KVCA (Korean Venture Capital Association). Two-digit Korean Industry Classification (KIC) codes that classified the 372 firms into various industry groups were found in the website of Ministry of Commerce, Industry and Energy (www.mocie.go.kr).

The dataset was collected as in the most comprehensive way as possible to analyse Korean IPOs in this period and represents a major research input. I describe in detail the variables derived and their use in the following section of this chapter.

4.2.2 Selection issues

There are at least two potential issues regarding sources of bias in the collected data that may happen in our empirical analysis.

First, considering only IPO firms in the empirical analysis has the obvious limitation of ignoring other firms that realised venture capital investment by M&A or other exit routes. VC-backed IPO firms tend to be mainly among the most successful ones since venture capitalists tend to bring highly qualified firms to IPO to achieve abnormal returns and build-up their reputation (Gompers, 1995). As a result, the impact of VC-backing on performance might be overestimated by looking only at the firms that were exited by IPO (Rindermann, 2002). However, this potential bias toward the selection of the most successful firms into our sample may also apply to the non-VC-backed IPOs in our sample.

Second, I treat the VC-backing as an exogenous variable that is randomly distributed. However, it may represent an endogenous choice between entrepreneurs and venture capitalists (Rindermann, 2003). All entrepreneurs do not want venture capital financing and not all of them receive it even though they want it. The endogenous preference for the eventual exit from the entrepreneurs might lead to a non-random distribution of VC-backed IPOs. Hence, the difference in the types of entrepreneurs and their preference for the venture capital funding to other kinds of financing might introduce a selectivity bias (Lee and Wahal, 2002). The preference of venture capitalists to concentrate in the specific types of firms and industries might also be reflected in both firm and IPO characteristics, such as the size and age of firms (Gompers and Lerner, 2001; Lee and Wahal, 2002). To capture high-tech industry and other selection effects which may happen due to the endogenous preferences of venture capitalists for specific types of firms and industries, the multivariate analysis employs control variables (for example age and size), and specifically schemed dummy variable for the high-tech industries of the IPO firms.

4.3 Methodology

4.3.1 Initial return

To estimate the effect of underpricing, initial returns will be calculated. Initial returns are generally calculated as price change from the offering price to the first day closing price of IPO stock[6] (Barry, Muscarella et al.,1990; Megginson and Weiss, 1991).

However, the closing price on the first day is not an appropriate measure for calculating initial returns in our KOSDAQ samples, because the KOSDAQ regulated daily price movements with a band of plus and minus 12 per cent, and in many IPOs the closing price of the first-day trading reaches the upper limit and often keeps on rising by hitting the daily limit several days in a row with a small volume of trading, until a large trading occurs (Kim and Park, 2002, Berkman and Lee, 2002). In addition, the price band for the first-day trading is widened upward from plus 12 per cent to 100 per cent from 25 July 2000. Therefore, instead of using the first-day return as initial return (underpricing), I use another method in order to calculate the initial return, in a way analogous to the method that was suggested by Kim and Park (2002).[7]

Initial return is calculated as the difference between the offer price and the closing price on the first day that the IPO stock did not hit the daily upper limit.[8] I then adjust that by the movement in the KOSDAQ index[9] between the first day of trading and the first day that the IPO stock did not hit the daily upper limit. Accordingly, the initial return is defined as

$$IR_{it} = \frac{P_{it} - P_{i0}}{P_{i0}} - \frac{KQ_{it} - KQ_{i0}}{KQ_{i0}}$$

Where P_{i0} is the offer price of an IPO firm i, P_{it} is the closing price on the first day that the IPO firm did not hit the daily upper limit, KQ_{i0} is the KOSDAQ index on the first day of the IPO stock trading, and KQ_{it} is the KOSDAQ index on the first day that the IPO firm did not hit the daily upper limit. I adjust initial return by KOSDAQ index because our return is calculated over several days from the first-day of trading, following the suggestion of Kim and Park (2002).

4.3.2 Buy-and-hold abnormal return (BHAR)[10,11]

I will use buy-and-hold abnormal return (BHAR) in order to estimate the effect of the long-term performance.

According to Ritter (1991) and Barber and Lyon (1997), the buy-and-hold return of an IPO stock is defined as[12]

$$R_{iT} = \left[\prod_{t=UnderpricingDay}^{T} (1 + r_{it}) - 1 \right]$$

Where T is 252 days[13] (one-year) or 504 days (two-year)[14] and r_{it} is the firm i's return on day t. Thus the one-year (twelve-month) buy-and-hold return spans from the first day that the IPO firm did not hit the upper limit to 252 days, and two-year (twenty-four month) buy-and-hold return spans from the first day that the IPO firm did not hit the upper limit to 504 days.

The mean buy-and-hold return[15] is computed as

$$R_T = \frac{1}{N} \left[\sum_{i=1}^{N} R_{it} \right]$$

Where N is the number of the firms.

The benchmark-adjusted buy-and-hold abnormal return is (BHAR) is calculated by subtracting the buy-and-hold return of the benchmark from the raw buy-and-hold return of an IPO stock.

$$BHAR = \frac{1}{N} \sum_{i=1}^{N} \left[\left(\prod_{t=UnderpricingDay}^{T} (1 + R_{it}) \right) - \left(\prod_{t=UnderpricingDay}^{T} (1 + R_{i(benchmark),t}) \right) \right]$$

Where $R_{i(benchmark),t}$ is calculated in the identical way to R_{it}. Alternative benchmarks are discussed in Section 4.3.4 below.

A positive (negative) value of BHAR indicates that IPOs outperform (underperform) returns of specified benchmark firms.[16]

4.3.3 Benchmark

Studies of IPO firms' long-term performances have used diverse benchmarks to adjust the raw BHARs. This is because researchers want to know IPO firms' performances relative to other portfolio and control firms. This concern in the relative long-term performances is related to the fact that the choice of trading strategy that is carried out in order to get abnormal return is implicit in the measurement of long-term performance (Brav, Geczy et al.,2000). Brav, Geczy et al. state that when the returns of IPO firms are associated with pervasive and measurable sources of economic risk, or firm characteristics help determine expected returns, the sample returns must be adjusted by matching with those on benchmarks whose economic risk or return-determining characteristics are similar to the target group. They quote Fama (1970), who points out that any performances tests must have notion of what 'normal' returns are.

A lot of questions were raised regarding benchmark issues in measurement of long-term performances. Several researchers have documented that the measurement of long-term performance adjusted by benchmark has an impact on both the degree of abnormal returns and the size and statistical significance (Barber and Lyon, 1997; Kothari and Warner, 1997; Fama, 1998; Lyon, Barber et al.,1999; Brav, 2000; Loughran and Ritter, 2000; Brav, Geczy et al.,2000).

As is shows in Table 4.1 below, various types of benchmarks were used in order to adjust raw return. Market index, other reference portfolios return and control

Table 4.1 Summary of benchmarks used in previous research of IPO long-term performances

Authors	Abnormal returns	Return benchmark
Ritter (1991)	CAR	Market Index
	BHAR	Size/industry matched firm
		Size portfolio
Loughran and Ritter (1995)	BHAR	Market Index
	Fama and French three factor model[17]	Size matched firm
Barber and Lyon (1997)	CAR	Size portfolios
	BHAR	Book-to-market portfolios
	Fama and French three factor model	Size/book-to-market portfolios
		Market Index
		Size-matched firm
		Book-to-market matched firm
		Size/book-to-market matched firm

Authors	Abnormal returns	Return benchmark
Brav, Geczy et al. (2000)	BHAR	Market Index Size/book-to-market portfolio Size/book-to-market/ momentum portfolio
Brav and Gompers (1997)	BHAR Fama and French three factor model	Market Index Size/book-to-market portfolio Industry Portfolio
Fama and French (1993)	Fama and French three factor model	
Rosa, Velayuthen et al. (2003)	BHAR Fama and French three factor model	Market Index Size portfolio Book-to-market portfolio
Cai and Wei (1997)	BHAR	Market Index Industry portfolio Size portfolio Market-to-book portfolio Size/Market-to-book portfolio Book assets/industry portfolio
Kim, Krinsky et al. (1995)	BHAR	Market Index Industry Index Size/Industry matched firm
Gompers and Lerner (1999)	BHAR	Size/book-to-market portfolio
Carter, Dark et al. (1998)	BHAR	Market Index
Carter and Manaster (1990)	CAR	Market Index
Hamao, Parker et al. (2000)	BHAR	Size/Industry matched firm
Espenlaub, Garrett et al. (1999)	CAR	Market Index

firm return were used as benchmarks in the seminal study of Ritter (1991) and the following other long-term performance studies.

In order to increase the robustness of our analysis, I use five benchmarks[18]: two market indexes [KOSDAQ index (KOSDAQ) and KSE index (KSE)], two matched-firm benchmarks [size-and-industry-matched firm (SIMF) and size-and-book-to-market-ratio-matched-firm (SBMF)], and a matched portfolio benchmark [size-and-book-to-market-ratio-matched-portfolio (SBMP)]. Each benchmark BHAR is used to adjust raw BHAR, as discussed in Section 4.3.2. Our research does not aim to clarify the statistical meaning of each benchmark, but rather to differentiate the long-term performances between VC-backing and non-VC-backing groups.

KOSDAQ index should be included first because our samples firms were brought to IPO in the KOSDAQ market. KSE index is included to detect if there is any difference when raw BHARs are compared to another market index in addition to the KOSDAQ index.

Size-and-industry-matched-firm (SIMF) approach was included because it was one of the frequently used benchmarks in the long-term performance literature. Ritter (1991) suggested the SIMF approach. I identify SIMF in the following way. First, I find the KOSDAQ-listed and KSE-listed firms[19] in the same industry (measured as the same two-digit KIC codes). Second, I match an IPO firm to a control firm with the closest size (measured by market capitalisation at the time of IPO) among the same industry target firms.

Researchers focusing on long-term performance tend to use both size-and-book-to-market-matched-firm (SBMF) approach and size-and-book-to-market-matched-portfolio (SBMP) approach, hence our inclusion of these benchmarks (Barber and Lyon 1997; Brav, Geczy et al.,2000).

I identify SBMF, following the three steps suggested by Barber and Lyon (1997).[20] First, I find all firms, out of KOSDAQ-listed and KSE-listed firms, with a market value of equity (measured by market capitalisation at the time of IPO) between 70 per cent and 130 per cent of the market value of equity of an IPO firm. Second, from this set of firms, I select a firm with the book-to-market ratio closest to that of the IPO firm.

I also identify SBMP, following the method used by Brav, Geczy et al. (2000). Size and book-to-market portfolios are created as follows. To create size (measured by market capitalisation) quintile breakpoints, only KSE stocks[21] were divided equally into five size groups. And to generate book-to-market ratio[22] quintile breakpoints, the KSE stocks were divided equally into five book-to-market ratio groups. I then formed 25 (5 × 5) size and book-to-market portfolios by intersecting the portfolio breakpoints and allocating all KOSDAQ firms into these portfolios. An IPO firm is matched with a size and book-to-market portfolio, and benchmark portfolios are reformed each quarter.[23]

4.3.4 Univariate tests

Our univariate empirical analysis aims to compare initial return and benchmark-adjusted long-term performance, the results of which will be documented in Chapters 6 and 7, respectively. In addition, in Chapter 5, I also compare other features of IPO firms between VC-backing IPO firms and non-VC-backing IPO firms for the purpose of understanding major characteristics of KOSDAQ IPO firms.

Univariate analyses are conducted in two ways. First, I compare means by the t-test[24] for the two independent groups of VC-backed and non-VC backed IPOs. And then I compare ranks of means by Mann-Whitney Test[25] for the two independent VC-backing and non-VC backing groups. When I compare the underpricing and the long-term performance among four sub-groups of VC-backed and non-VC-backed IPOs, according to VCs' institutional affiliation (bank-affiliated, security company-affiliated, other institution-affiliated and non-VC-backed), I use the Kruskal-Wallis test.

While the Mann-Whitney test is for two independent samples, the Kruskal-Wallis test is a non-parametric test used to compare more-than-two independent

(k) groups of sampled data. This test is implemented in the way analogous to the analysis of the Mann-Whitney test. However, while the Kruskal-Wallis test is designed to detect the mean difference among k *groups on the whole*, if and only such a difference is found among k groups, I use the following procedure to determine which *pairs* of the samples differ (Conover, 1980). I can say that the sample i and j seem to be different if the following inequality is satisfied:

$$\left| \frac{R_i}{n_i} - \frac{R_j}{n_j} \right| \rangle \; t_{1-(\alpha/2)} \left(S^2 \frac{N-1-T}{N-k} \right)^{\frac{1}{2}} \left(\frac{1}{n_i} + \frac{1}{n_j} \right)^{\frac{1}{2}} \tag{1}$$

Where R_i and R_j are the rank sums of the two samples, n_i and n_j are the sample size of the two samples, $t_{1-(\alpha-2)}$ is the $(1 - \alpha/2)$ quantile of the t distribution with N-k degrees of freedom, α is the significance level, N is the number of total observations, k is the number of the total samples, X_{ij} is the ith observation of jth sample, S^2 comes from the Equation (2) below and T comes from the Equation (3) below.

$$S^2 = \frac{1}{N-1} \left(\sum_{allranks} R(X_{ij})^2 - N \frac{(N+1)^2}{4} \right) \tag{2}$$

$$T = \frac{1}{S^2} \left(\sum_{i=1}^{k} \frac{R_i^2}{n_i} - \frac{N(N+1)^2}{4} \right) \tag{3}$$

4.3.5 Multiple regression

I implement multiple regressions in order to understand how stock market performances are affected by venture capital factors, when other factors are taken into account. Multiple regression explains which of the independent variables is of most or least important in explaining variance in dependent variables and how much of the variance in dependent variables can be explain when the independent variables are taken together (Walsh, 1990).

I attempt to understand the relationship between stock market returns as dependent variables and diverse independent variables representing the venture capital, underwriter and auditor factors and other variables used to control for other effects such as ex-ante uncertainty, high-tech industry and the hot market situation.

4.3.5.1 VC-Backing and its reputation

To assess whether VC-backing has a specific impact on the performances of IPOs, I introduce a dummy variable (*VC*) which take the value of 1 when an IPO firm is backed by venture capital and 0 when it is not.[26] VC-backing is confirmed in the IPO prospectuses when, at least, a venture capital company invests in the IPO firm by 5 per cent and more. Entering a dummy variable representing venture capital backing in this way is used in many studies (Barry et al., 1990; Megginson, 1991; Espenlaub et al., 1996; Hamao et al., 2000). This variable representing VC-backing (*VC*) is expected to show positive coefficients in long-term performances regressions and negative coefficients in underpricing regressions.

As I discussed in Chapter 3, there may be differences in the quality of VC-backing and the reputation of venture capitalist. These differences may be reflected in the representation of board of directors (Barry, Muscarella et al.,1990), pre- and post-issue equity shares owned by venture capitalists (Field and Hanka, 2000), the number of venture capitalists having equity position in the IPO firm (Gompers, 1995), the age of lead venture capitalist at the time of IPO (Gompers, 1996) or dummy variable representing the Big VCs holding a greater market share of IPOs (Beatty, 1989).[27]

In this empirical analysis, I design two dummy variables representing the quality and reputation of venture capitalist. A dummy variable (*VCk*) has the value of 1 when Korean Technology Bank (KTB) backs IPOs as a lead venture capitalist. KTB is the most frequently appearing venture capitalist in the ownership section of IPO prospectus. I also include a dummy variable (*VC3*) representing the "Big Three" venture capital companies [KTB, Korean Technology Investment (KTI), Korean Development Bank Capital (KDBC)] whose IPO market shares are greater than other venture capital companies. When these three venture capital companies back an IPO firm as lead venture capitalists, the dummy variable (*VC3*) takes the value of 1. KTB, KTI and KDBC are considered as the major big three venture capitalists to distinguish themselves from other venture capital companies in their capability and occupy the majority of VC-backed IPOs as the lead venture capitalists in our sample. If these monitoring proxies are linked to the quality and reputation of venture capitalist, a positive sign of the coefficients in the multiple regressions on the long-term performance (initial return) is expected, and a negative impact on the initial returns is expected.

4.3.5.2 *Institutional difference of venture capital*

I devise three mutually exclusive dummy variables that take the value of 1 if the lead venture capitalist of an IPO firm is affiliated with bank (*VCbank*), securities company (*VCsecu*), or other companies or individuals (*VCetc*),[28] respectively (Hamao, Parker et al.,2000). Furthermore, in order to capture the effect of direct bank ownership and other financial institutions ownership in an IPO firm, a dummy variable (*Bank*) that takes on the value of 1 when banks have shareholdings of going-public firms at IPO and a dummy variable (*Secu*) that takes on the value of 1 when security companies have ownership in the IPO firm are introduced (Hamao, Parker et al., 2000). I expect that if bank-affiliated venture capital (*VCbank*) and banking ownership (*Bank*) takes a positive impact on the underpricing and long-term performances, a positive sign of the coefficients in the multiple regressions on the long-term performance will be shown and a negative sign of the regression coefficients on the underpricing. In the cases of securities company-affiliated venture capitalist (*VCsecu*) and security companies ownership (*Secu*), signs of the coefficients in the regressions will be expected as the opposite of those of bank-affiliated venture capital.

4.3.5.3 *Reputation of underwriter and auditor*

In line with the previous studies on IPO performances, our empirical analysis includes a variable regarding the reputation of the underwriter and auditor. Carter and Manaster (1990) and Carter et al. (1998) account for the reputation of underwriter by using a classification methodology that is based on their relative positions in the Tombstone of an offering. They construct a measure of underwriter reputation from the stock offering "tombstone"[29] in the US newspapers announcements, from which underwriters' relative reputation was placed. By distributing 10 to 1 points by the order of underwriter appearance in the tombstone, the authors make a ten-tier reputation measure and differentiate the underwriters' prestige. Megginson and Weiss (1990) measures the ranking of each underwriter according to the relative market share, which is determined by dividing the underwriter's total amount of underwriting (measured as the offer price times the number of shares of an IPO firm times the number of the IPO firms) by the industry's total. Johnson and Miller (1988) also developed a four-tier underwriter reputation measurement[30] in a similar way that Carter and Manaster ranked underwriters. As for the reputation of auditors, Beatty (1989) proposes "Big Eight" audit firms in US as prestigious auditors that larger and less risky IPO firms clients tend to hire, constructing a dummy variable that equals to 1 when auditor firms belong to that category.

In order to classify highly reputable underwriters (auditors) from less reputable underwriters (auditors), I borrow the concepts of the underwriter and auditor reputation from Megginson and Weiss (1990) and Beatty (1989) by constructing two dummy variables: a variable representing highly reputable "Big Three" underwriters (*Und3*) and highly reputable "Big Three" auditors (*Aud3*) whose value is set equal to 1.[31] The underwriter and auditor reputation coefficients of the underpricing regressions will be expected to show negative signs, compared with the positive signs for the long-term performance regressions.

4.3.5.4 *Control variables*

To avoid model specification errors due to omitted variables, the multiple regressions employ control variables representing firm characteristics[32] and stock market condition.

To control for size effects, I employ the natural logarithm of market capitalisation at the time of IPO[33] (*LMC*) (Gompers and Lerner, 1999; Wang, Wang et al.,2002). In a similar way, to control for book-to-market effect, I employ the book-to-market ratio at the time of IPO[34] (*Bmr*) (Hamao, Packer et al.,2000). Other control variables such as the natural logarithm of firm age (*Lage*) (Kutsuna, Cowling et al.,2000), shareholdings of CEO and their related persons at IPO time (*ShCEO*) (Ljungqvist and Wilhelm, 2003) are also included. These variables control for the ex-ante uncertainty of the IPO firms. These control variables are expected to have a negative relationship with underpricing and positive relationship with the long-term performance. Additionally, a dummy variable (*Hi-Tech*) which equals to 1 if IPO firms belong to high-tech industry and 0 if in other industries is included to control for industry effects.[35] This high-tech variable is expected to have a positive relationship with underpricing and negative relationship with long-term performance. The long-run prediction is negative, because high-tech firms, including the internet-oriented firms, are hypothesised to experience the same sharp declines when the dot.com bubble ended in March 2000 as happened in the USA (Arosio, Giudici et al.,2000).

To capture stock market effects, I employ three variables. The number of all IPOs in KOSDAQ on the last month prior to an IPO (*NumIPO*), the average of daily KOSDAQ index on the last month prior to an IPO (*Kqindex*), and the monthly proportionate change of the average of the daily KOSDAQ index between the second last month and the last month prior to an IPO (*Kqchange*) to capture hot market effects, market index performance, and monthly change of market index, respectively (Arosio, Giudici et al.,2000; Loughran and Ritter, 2002). These variables are expected to have a positive relationship with underpricing and a negative relationship with the long-term performance. In other words, IPO firms will show very high initial returns when they come to stock market in the hot-market period, but these firms are likely to suffer from the sharp decline afterwards in the long run. Along with these variables of stock market situation, I include underpricing (*UP*) in the long-term performance regressions in order to capture the underpricing effects on the long-term performance. As was argued by Shiller (1990), the IPO firms that went through the high initial returns at the initial stage of IPOs are expected to worse performance in the long run.

For the regressions on the initial returns, all control variables are included in the regressions. In analysing long-run returns, when KOSDAQ-index-adjusted returns are used as dependent variables, the control variables used as proxies of stock market situation (*NumIPO, Kqindex, Kqchange*) were removed, because the KOSDAQ-index-adjusted returns already reflect the market-index adjustment factor. For the similar reason, when SIMF-adjusted BHARs are employed, the variables controlling size (*LMC*) and industry (*Hi-Tech*) were dropped out of the regressions, because the returns already control for these two effects. In a similar way, the control variables representing size (*LMC*) and book-to-market ratio (*Bmr*) are removed from the regressions when SBMP-adjusted BHARs are used in the regression models.

4.3.5.5 Regression models

I construct five regression models in two regimes to test the hypothesis derived from the literature review in Chapter 3. One type of regime includes all the IPO firms for the regression, whereas another regime contains VC-backed IPOs only. I regress independent dummy and control variables against underpricing (initial returns) and long-term performance (twenty-four month BHARs). The regressions on underpricing and long-term performance are conducted for three time periods: all IPOs from April 1999 to September 2001; IPOs in the hot market from April 1999 to March 2000; IPOs in the cold market from April 2000 to September 2001. Since the KOSDAQ was heavily affected by the hot market situation from late 1999 to early 2000 in line with the worldwide internet or high-technology bubble, it is likely that the stock market returns show different patterns in the hot and cold-market period. This distinction of the samples into hot and cold-market period provides us with a testing ground to investigate whether our hypotheses turn out to equally work in both periods and will reveal whether or not our whole sample results are affected by aggregation bias. Table 4.2 shows the summary of model specifications in the multiple regressions I employ in this analysis in Chapters 6 and 7 for initial returns and long-run returns, respectively.

Table 4.2 Summary of model specifications in multiple regression

	Model 1	*Model 2*	*Model 3*	*Model 4*	*Model 5*
	Panel A: regression for all sample firms				
Hypotheses	**H1a, H1b**	**H1a, H1b**	**H3a, H3b H4a, H4b**	**H3a, H3b H4a, H4b**	**H5a, H5b H6a, H6b**
Variables					
Lage	– (IR) + (BHAR)	– (IR) + (BHAR)	– (IR) + (BHAR)	– (IR) + (BHAR)	– (IR) + (BHAR)
LMC	– (IR) + (BHAR)	– (IR) + (BHAR)	– (IR) + (BHAR)	– (IR) + (BHAR)	– (IR) + (BHAR)
Bmr	– (IR) + (BHAR)	– (IR) + (BHAR)	– (IR) + (BHAR)	– (IR) + (BHAR)	– (IR) + (BHAR)
ShCEO	– (IR) + (BHAR)	– (IR) + (BHAR)	– (IR) + (BHAR)	– (IR) + (BHAR)	– (IR) + (BHAR)
Hi-Tech	+ (IR) – (BHAR)	+ (IR) – (BHAR)	+ (IR) – (BHAR)	+ (IR) – (BHAR)	+ (IR) – (BHAR)
NumIPO	+ (IR) – (BHAR)	+ (IR) – (BHAR)	+ (IR) – (BHAR)	+ (IR) – (BHAR)	+ (IR) – (BHAR)
Kqindex	+ (IR) – (BHAR)	+ (IR) – (BHAR)	+ (IR) – (BHAR)	+ (IR) – (BHAR)	+ (IR) – (BHAR)
Kqchange	+ (IR) – (BHAR)	+ (IR) – (BHAR)	+ (IR) – (BHAR)	+ (IR) – (BHAR)	+ (IR) – (BHAR)
UP	– (BHAR)	– (BHAR)	– (BHAR)	– (BHAR)	– (BHAR)
VC	– (IR) + (BHAR)	– (IR) + (BHAR)			– (IR) + (BHAR)
VCbank			– (IR) + (BHAR)	– (IR) + (BHAR)	
VCsecu			+ (IR) – (BHAR)	+ (IR) – (BHAR)	
VCetc			– (IR) + (BHAR)	– (IR) + (BHAR)	
Bank		– (IR) + (BHAR)		– (IR) + (BHAR)	

(Continued)

Table 4.2 (Continued)

	Model 1	Model 2	Model 3	Model 4	Model 5
Secu		+ (IR) – (BHAR)			
Und3					– (IR) + (BHAR)
Aud3					– (IR) + (BHAR)

Panel B: Regression for VC-Backed Firms Only					
Hypotheses	H2a, H2b	H2a, H2b	H3a, H3b H4a, H4b	H3a, H3b H4a, H4b	H5a, H5b H6a, H6b
Variables					
Lage	– (IR) + (BHAR)	– (IR) + (BHAR)	– (IR) + (BHAR)	– (IR) + (BHAR)	– (IR) + (BHAR)
LMC	– (IR) + (BHAR)	– (IR) + (BHAR)	– (IR) + (BHAR)	– (IR) + (BHAR)	– (IR) + (BHAR)
Bmr	– (IR) + (BHAR)	– (IR) + (BHAR)	– (IR) + (BHAR)	– (IR) + (BHAR)	– (IR) + (BHAR)
ShCEO	– (IR) + (BHAR)	– (IR) + (BHAR)	– (IR) + (BHAR)	– (IR) + (BHAR)	– (IR) + (BHAR)
Hi-Tech	+ (IR) – (BHAR)	+ (IR) – (BHAR)	+ (IR) – (BHAR)	+ (IR) – (BHAR)	+ (IR) – (BHAR)
NumIPO	+ (IR) – (BHAR)	+ (IR) – (BHAR)	+ (IR) – (BHAR)	+ (IR) – (BHAR)	+ (IR) – (BHAR)
Kqindex	+ (IR) – (BHAR)	+ (IR) – (BHAR)	+ (IR) – (BHAR)	+ (IR) – (BHAR)	+ (IR) – (BHAR)
Kqchange	+ (IR) – (BHAR)	+ (IR) – (BHAR)	+ (IR) – (BHAR)	+ (IR) – (BHAR)	+ (IR) – (BHAR)
UP	– (BHAR)	– (BHAR)	– (BHAR)	– (BHAR)	– (BHAR)
VCk	– (IR) + (BHAR)				
VC3		– (IR) + (BHAR)			– (IR) + (BHAR)
VCbank			– (IR) + (BHAR)	– (IR) + (BHAR)	
VCsecu			+ (IR) – (BHAR)	+ (IR) – (BHAR)	
VCetc			– (IR) + (BHAR)	– (IR) + (BHAR)	
Bank		– (IR) + (BHAR)		– (IR) + (BHAR)	
Secu		+ (IR) – (BHAR)			
Und3					– (IR) + (BHAR)
Aud3					– (IR) + (BHAR)

Note: Regressions on initial returns and BHARs are based on the model specifications below. All the regressions employ the venture capital indicators and control variables as specified above. + and – in each cell indicates the expected positive or negative sign of the coefficient. The definition of the variables is appended in the Glossary at the end of the book.

The five regression models in the two regimes test our hypotheses derived from Chapter 3. Model 1 tests for the impact of VC-backing (*VC*). Model 2 tests for impact of VC-backing (*VC*) in the first regime which includes all the IPO firms for the regression, and for the impact of the reputation of VC-backing (*VCk* and *VC3*) in the second regime which includes VC-backed firms only. Model 3 and 4 test for the institutional affiliation of VC (*VCbank* and *VCsecu*). Model 5 tests for the reputation of underwriter and auditor (*Und3* and *Aud3*) along with the VC-backing (in the first regime) and the reputation of VC-backing (in the second regime). Each of the five regression is estimated with a constant term and the variables controlling respectively for the effect of IPO company characteristics (age, market capitalisation, book-to-market ratio, the shareholdings of CEO and his related persons, and the dummy variable of high-tech industry), stock market condition (number of IPOs, market index, and monthly change of market index) and underpricing.[36]

Notes

1 Parts of this chapter appeared in shorter and revised forms in Ch.26 "The Impact of Venture Capital Participation and Its Affiliation with Financial Institutions on the Long-term Performance of IPO Firm: Evidence from Korea in Hot and Cold Market Periods", by Jaeho Lee from *Oxford Handbook of Venture Capital*, edited by Cumming, Douglas (2012) and "The Hot and Cold Market Impacts on Underpricing of Certification, Reputation and Conflicts of Interest in Venture Capital Backed Korean IPO" by Jaeho Lee from *Korean Venture Management Review*, 12(4) (2009). Original parts have been used in this chapter with permission of Oxford University Press and The Korean Association of Small Business Studies, respectively.

2 FSS is the regulatory authority in charge of supervising financial institutions in Korea.

3 IPO prospectuses are available online in Korean language from FSS website (www.fss.or.kr) for the firms that were brought public since April 2000. For the firms that went public from 1999 to April 2000, I had to take a look at every prospectus whose original photocopies had been kept for disclosure in The Office of Disclosure in FSS. The IPO prospectus should have information on the following: I.1) IPO characteristics; 1.II) Investment risk to be considered; 1.III) Underwriter's opinion about the IPO firm; 1.IV) The purpose of raising fund in the stock market; 1.V) Plan to market stabilisation of the underwriter; 2.I) The summary of the IPO firm's operation; 2.II) Details of business; 2.III) Financial statements; 2.IV) Report of auditors; 2.V) Corporate governance; 2.VI) The distribution of shareholdings; 2.VII) Directors and employees; 2.VIII) Transactions with related parties; 2.IX) Supplementary reports

4 These large shareholders include personals, banks, other financial institutions and corporate venturing companies, government etc.

5 If the venture capitalists invest in the IPO firms by less than 5 per cent, they do not appear in the ownership section of IPO prospectuses. Where the venture capitalists own less than 5 per cent share of an IPO firm, the firm is classified as 'non-VC-backed' in our analysis. Holdings of less than 5 per cent may indicate that the venture capitalists are not interested in the management of the IPO firm as minor shareholders. In this case, they are considered as not contributing to the certification and the value-addition of the firm.

6 The initial return is typically calculated as the following

$$IR_1 = \frac{P_1 - P_0}{P_0}$$

Where P_1 is the first day closing price of an IPO stock and P_0 is the offering price of the IPO stock.

7 In other research, initial returns are occasionally calculated as the difference between the offer price and the closing price after some days of trading, for example, six days in Espenlaub, Garrett et al. (et al. (1999), in order to calculate the degree of underpricing that is not fully reflected in the first-day price.

8 It took 9 days on average up until 25 July 2000 that an IPO stock did not hit the daily upper limit for the first time after IPO, while it took three days on average after this date.

9 This adjustment of the underpricing by market index was suggested in Aggarwal and Rivoli (1990).

10 Barber and Lyon (1997), Brav and Gompers (2000) and Fama (1998) examine the long-term performance using BHAR and CAR (Cumulative Abnormal Return). CAR is calculated by summing benchmark-adjusted monthly average returns for entire event months. There is no consensus among them as to which method should be used, however. Barber and Lyon (1997) emphasise the benefit of BHARs for considering the investors' actual experiences for investment, as the use of CARs does not adequately represent the returns obtained by an investor who holds a stock for a long period of time. The returns obtained by an investor in the long run are better approximated by the compounding monthly returns of the short run. In this book, I use BHAR as the primary estimate measuring the long-term performances of KOSDAQ IPO firms.

11 Brav (2000) states that the series of long-run returns are not independent each other, because the returns tend to be correlated around a specific time point. He states that this correlation of returns mislead to a poor specification of the statistical tests. Fama (1998) and Mitchell and Stafford (2000) point out that the BHARs across the sample may be subject to cross-sectional dependence due to the presence of overlapping returns. Fama (1998) and Lyon, Barber et al. (et al. (1999) state that the use of methods that take into account time series of returns eliminate the problem of cross-sectional correlation between the firms. Consequently, Fama (1998), Lyon, Barber et al. (et al. (1999), and Conn, Cosh et al. (2003) recommend using calendar time portfolio technique to overcome this problem. In an unreported analysis, I calculated calendar time abnormal returns (CTARs) of IPO firms, which showed the similar pattern of significant difference using univariate tests between different types of IPOs that were compared in Chapter 7, but did not show significant coefficients in multivariate regressions.

12 In other research, including Ritter (1991), BHAR is calculated from the first-day of trading. However, considering the fact that the first-day closing price does not reflect the underpricing fully due to the daily price change limit in KOSDAQ, I used the closing price on the first day that an IPO firm did not hit the upper price limit as the starting day for calculating BHAR. Doukas and Gonenc (2003), by similar reasoning, used the third-day closing price as the starting day of BHAR.

13 Considering that KOSDAQ is open five days a week, from Monday to Friday, a month is generally counted as 21 days, with a year being counted up as 252 days. This method of counting long-term days comes from Ritter (1991).

14 While much research deals with BHARs up to 36 months (three years) or 60 months (five years) after the IPO date, our research limits the time period of long-term performances to one year (12 month) and two years (24 months). Although the maximum period of our long-term performance measurement is two years,

other studies indicate that long-term performance is well specified by the end of year two (Rosa, Velayuthen et al 2003; Lee, Taylor et al.,1996) and the end of year one (Aggarwal and Rivoli, 1990).

15 Loughran and Ritter (2000) show that the choice of the method of weighting stock market returns across the samples is a relevant question. If the research interest lies in quantifying the change in the average wealth of the investor as a consequence of a certain event, the correct method would be value-weighting. However, if the interest is focused on the implications of potential stock market mispricing, equal-weighting would be more adequate. I use equal-weighting method by averaging BHARs across the samples.

16 For reference, following Ritter (1991), I also report wealth relative (WR) that is defined as follows:

$$WR = \frac{1 + \frac{1}{N}\left[\sum_{i=1}^{N} R_{it}\right]}{1 + \frac{1}{N}\left[\sum_{i=1}^{N} R_{i(benchmark)t}\right]}$$ A WR of greater than 1.0 is interpreted that IPOs

outperform a benchmark; a WR of less than 1.0 indicates that IPOs underperforms. Thus, when a BHAR is positive, its WR is more than 1.0, and when a BAHR is negative, its WR is less than 1.0.

17 Fama and French (1993) and Fama(1998) recommended to use Fama-French three-factor models as an alternative approach to long-term performances calculated by event studies (such as BHAR). Fama-French model is specified as follows.

$$R(t) - RF(t) = a + bRMRF(t) + sSMB(t) + hHML(t) + e(t)$$

R(t) denotes the abnormal return of an asset or portfolio. RMRF is the value-weighted market return on KOSDAQ firms (RM) minus the risk free rate (RF). SMB (small minus big) is the difference each month between the return on small firms an big firms. HML (high minus low) is the difference each month between the return on a portfolio of high book-to-market ratio stocks and the return on a portfolio of low book-to-market ratio stocks. The long-term performance of the firms is measured as the intercept of this regression. In an unreported analysis, we calculated the long-term performance given by Fama and French model, but this model does not seem to calculate meaningful results from the KOSDAQ IPO data. However, the RMRF, SMB and HML yielded significant coefficients as expected in the model originally.

18 The researchers generally agree that abnormal returns calculated by using reference portfolios cause three statistical biases. Barber and Lyon (1997) sum up the biases: (1) *new listing bias,*which arises because in event studies of long-term abnormal returns, abnormal firms generally have a long-event history of returns, while firms that constitute the index or reference portfolio typically include new IPO firms that begin trading subsequent to the event month; (2) *rebalancing bias,* which arises because the compound returns of a reference portfolio, such as an equally weighted market index, are typically calculated assuming periodic (generally monthly) rebalancing, while the returns of sample firms are compounded without rebalancing; and (3) *skewness bias,* which arises because long-term abnormal returns are positively skewed.

19 Because the KOSDAQ-listed firms are not enough to match all the IPO firms, I included the KSE-listed firms for the target firms, too. In principle, an IPO is matched with a control firm only once.

20 Barber and Lyon (1997) state that the control firm approach that matches an IPO firm with a firm with a similar size and book-to-market value produces well specified statistical tests in all situations they considered. Besides, they find significant biases in the statistical tests when the abnormal returns are estimated using a portfolio as a benchmark, for example, a market index. Brav, Geczy et al. (2000) also show that abnormal returns of long-term performances fade away when they match sample firms with other firms by size and book-to-market characteristics, thus suggesting that abnormal returns of previous studies arose from the mis-specification of long-term performance returns. However, Ritter and Welch (2002) argue that, while the selection of control firm has an impact on the calculation of long-term performances, the seasonal effect such as the hot issue market has more profound impact on the long-term performance.

21 Brav, Geczy et al. (2000) use only New York Stock Exchange (NYSE) stocks to create size and book-to-market ratio quintile breakpoints. This approach is based on Fama and French (1995), who use only NYSE stocks to generate the breakpoints to make sure that the firms are well scattered across the portfolios.

22 Book-to-market ratio is calculated by dividing the book value by market capitalisation at a certain time. I define book value as common equity value and market capitalisation as the number of shares times the stock price.

23 I present a detailed description on the raw, benchmark and adjusted BHARs in Chapter 7. All the benchmark returns show the decreasing pattern from the first day of IPO to 24 months, except for SBMP. The underperformance of KOSDAQ benchmark is more severe than KSE, SIMF, and SBMF. This poorer performance of KOSDAQ benchmark suggests the considerable decline of KOSDAQ index after March 2000, when the second-tier stock markets began to shrink globally. The outperformance of SBMP suggests that the new listing firms in the matched portfolios or quarterly rebalancing method to reform the portfolio might affect the SBMP returns, as suggested by Barber and Lyon (1997).

24 The t-test is used to test a hypothesis about a mean and about the differences between two means. The t-test formulae require normal distribution of data and differ according to whether variances of the two subsamples are equal or not (Walsh, 1990).

25 The Mann-Whitney test is a non-parametric test used to compare two independent groups of sampled data. Unlike the parametric t-test, this non-parametric test makes no assumptions about the distribution of the data such as normality. This test is an alternative to the independent group t-test, when the assumption of normality or equality of variance is not met. This, like many non-parametric tests, uses the ranks of the data rather than their raw values to calculate the statistic. Since this test does not make a distribution assumption, it is not as powerful as the t-test. (Conover, 1980)

26 VC-backing is confirmed in the IPO prospectuses when, at least, a venture capital company invests in the IPO firm by 5 per cent and more.

27 In a separate analysis not reported here, I carried out estimations of our performance equation using the shareholdings held by VC, VC age, and VC size. I found that they were not significantly related to underpricing and long-term performance. In the results below, I follow Beatty's (1989) approach in which the reputation of auditors was represented in value of the Big-Eight group dummy variable that took the value of 1 and others that took the value of 0.

28 I have no hypothesis on this dummy variable representing other institutions or personals-affiliated VCs, but I expect that the coefficients of this dummy variable will be minus (in underpricing regressions) and plus (in long-term performance regressions), following the general discussion in the role of venture capitalists. However, it is expected that other institution-affiliated VCs will show less (more)

positive impact on the underpricing and the long-term performance than bank-affiliated VCs (security company-affiliated VCs), thus leading to more (less) underpricing coefficients and worse (better) long-term performance coefficients, compared with those of bank-affiliated VCs (security company-affiliated VCs).

29 The lead underwriter's name appears as the very first one from the left at the top of the tombstone in US newspaper announcements.

30 A rank of three, the most prestigious level, is assigned to each underwriter identified as a member of the "bulge bracket", a two is assigned to those considered part of the "major bracket", and a one is assigned to underwriters in the "sub-major bracket". All other underwriters are assigned zero. The "bulge bracket" is, for example, a group of investment banks that have occupied a leading role in high-quality securities underwriting, such as Morgan Stanley, First Boston and Salomon Brothers.

31 The big three underwriters and auditors occupy the majority of market share, respectively. The big three underwriters are LG Investment and Security, Daishin Securities and Samsung Securities Co. and the big three auditors are Samil Accounting Co., Ahn Kwon & Co. and Anjin Deloitte Touche Tohmatsu. Dummy variables are based on the relative market share of underwriters and auditors, respectively. The market share of an underwriter is estimated by dividing the whole gross spreads of the IPO firms that it sponsored by the sum of gross spreads of all the IPO firms. The auditor market share is estimated by the turnover of each auditor for an IPO firm from 1998–2000 divided by the sum of turnover of all auditors during the same period.

32 The control variables that I employ in the multivariate regressions are drawn from the sections of "industry distribution", "firm characteristics" and "ownership structure" of IPO firms which will be presented in detail in Chapter 5. In an unreported analysis, I employed the variables of "sources of funds" and "financial and operating performance" in the regressions, and found that they were insignificantly related to underpricing and long-term performance.

33 I define market capitalisation as the multiplication of offer price and number of shares outstanding.

34 I define book-to-market ratio as the proportion of book value of equity to market capitalisation at the time of IPO.

35 The classification of high-tech industry and non-high-tech industry follows that in Loughran and Ritter (2000). The high-tech industries include Other Machinery and Equipment (KIC 29), Computers and Office Machinery (30) Electrical Machinery and Apparatuses (31) Electronic Components, Radio, Television (32) Medical, Precision and Optical Instruments (33), Computer and Related Activities (72).

36 The control variable of underpricing is employed in long-term performance regressions only.

5 The characteristics of IPO firms on KOSDAQ 1999–2001[1]

5.1 Overview

In this chapter, I describe the main characteristics of our IPO samples. First, in Section 5.2, I describe the time pattern of IPO debuts and the distribution of IPOs between VC-backed and non-VC-backed IPOs group. I present the number of IPOs for each month on KOSDAQ from April 1999 to September 2001 and show how the monthly trend of IPOs is related to the KOSDAQ and KSE index. In Section 5.3, I describe the industrial distribution of IPOs and the industrial pattern of VC-backed and non-VC-backed IPOs. In Section 5.4, I present summary data on the characteristics of IPOs, distinguished by again between VC and non-VC backed IPOs. The data cover firm age, market capitalisation, book-to-market ratio, gross proceeds, underwriting costs, age of CEO, and number of employees. In Section 5.5, I account for the ownership structure of IPO samples: how many shares are on average held by CEO, CEO's family, board of directors, venture capitalists, corporate venturing institutions, banks, and security companies. In Section 5.6, I set out the financing patterns of IPO firms: funding from banks, financial institutions, and capital markets. In Section 5.7, I present the figures of financial statements such as total assets, book value of equity and turnover, and various ratios regarding financial and operating performances. Section 5.8 briefly compares the characteristics of KOSDAQ IPO firms with that of other main countries' data. Section 5.8 provides a summary conclusion of our main findings.

5.2 Trend of IPO

Our sample consists of 372 IPOs that took place in KOSDAQ during the period of 1999 – 2001. As can be seen in Table 5.1, 94 IPOs occurred in 1999, 172 in 2000, and 106 in 2001. Over this period, the number of firms listed in KOSDAQ dramatically increased. At the end of 1999, there were 453 firms in KOSDAQ, but the number of listed firms increased to 608 at 2000 year-end and 721 at 2001 year-end, showing 34.2 per cent and 18.5 per cent rise each year, respectively.

Table 5.1 Number of VC-backed and non-VC-backed IPOs by year on KOSDAQ and number of firms on KOSDAQ and KSE

	KOSDAQ	KSE	VC-backed IPO	Non-VC-backed IPO	All IPOs
1999	453	725	49	45	94
2000	608	704	78	94	172
2001	721	689	46	60	106

Source: KSDA (2002) and KOSDAQ website (www.kosdaq.or.kr).

Note: The total number of firms listed in KOSDAQ and KSE contains mutual funds. The information on VC-backed and non-VC-backed IPOs was found by the author from the ownership structure section in the IPO prospectuses. An IPO firm, which has any venture capitalist holding 5 per cent or more of the shareholdings in the ownership structure section, is considered as a VC-backed firm.

Table 5.2 The per cent distribution of VC-backed and non-VC-backed IPOs by year

Year	VC	Non-VC	All
1999	52.1	47.9	100.0
2000	43.6	56.4	100.0
2001	41.5	58.5	100.0

Source: Author's own calculations

On the other hand, the KSE IPO market remained stagnant in the same period. The total number of KSE firms had been slightly decreasing from 725 in 1999 to 689 in 2001. From 1999 to 2001, very few firms went to KSE for the purpose of going public, but all the firms that had been planning to put themselves in public stock markets seem to come to KOSDAQ, which laid down less strict standards on a firm's listing than KSE. KOSDAQ was utilised as a conduit that facilitated the IPOs of high-tech firms and other SMEs, who became willing to list their shares due to relaxed requirements for IPOs (KSDA, 2002).

Tables 5.1 and 5.2 show that VC-backed IPOs account for more than 40 per cent of total IPOs each year from 1999 to 2001, although their share fell by 10 per cent between 1999 and 2001. Figure 5.1 shows the monthly number of IPOs in KOSDAQ. There is considerable volatility. IPOs peaked in December 1999 and decreased in January and February 2000. The IPO market was hot enough to attract more than 20 firms in July 2000, February 2001, July 2001, and August 2001.

I can see from Figure 5.1 that the number of IPOs each month is more volatile than, but broadly consistent with, the trend of KOSDAQ and KSE index generally. Even though the monthly averaged KOSDAQ index reached the highest point in March 2000, three months after KOSDAQ recorded the highest number of IPOs in December 1999, higher monthly number of IPOs generally coincides with the increasing values of the KOSDAQ index and the KSE index. The figure

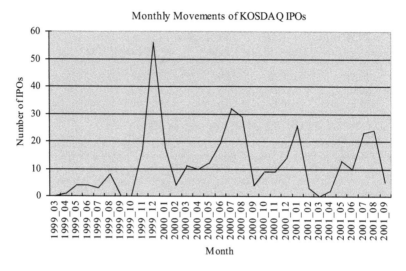

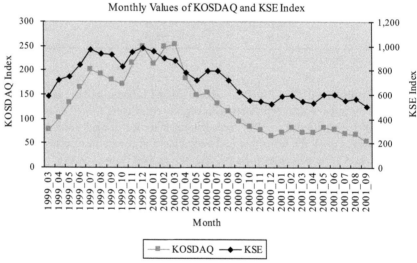

Figure 5.1 Monthly movements in KOSDAQ IPOs and the KOSDAQ and KSE stock market indices

Source: KOSDAQ (www.kosdaq.or.kr) and KSE (www.kse.or.kr)

also shows that the KOSDAQ market index had been more volatile than KSE from March 1999 to September 2001.

It seems that going-public firms wanted to take advantage of the "windows of opportunity" by timing the IPOs when the KOSDAQ market index was significantly rising in late 1999, as suggested by Aggarwal and Rivoli (1990) and Lowry and Schwert (2002). However, while the number of IPOs peaked in December 1999, the number of IPOs sharply declined in January and February 2000 which predated the sharp decline of market index in March 2001. After that, the number of IPOs tends to increase when KOSDAQ index is going up. It is interesting that, while the KOSDAQ index continued to decline after March 2000 and did not recover to the previous highest level, firms continued to make their debut in KOSDAQ. In fact, 235 firms (63 per cent in our sample) were taken public between May 2000 and September 2001.

5.3 Industry distribution

Table 5.3 shows the industry distribution of IPO firms. Like other international over-the-counter-stock markets, KOSDAQ attracted a lot of high-tech firms. When the IPO firms were classified by the two-digit KIC codes, the top three high-tech industries occupy almost 50 per cent out of whole sample. "Electric components, radio, television and communication" industry amounts to 71 IPOs (19.1 per cent), "Computer and related activities" industry 70 IPOs (18.8 per cent) and "Other machinery and equipment manufacturing" industry 45 IPOs (12.1 per cent). There industries are closely related to computer, multimedia and internet hardware/software products that led the development of "new economy" throughout 1990s.

The top three high-tech industries are followed by the other industries such as "Chemical and chemical products" industry (29 IPOs), "Electrical machinery" industry (17 IPOs), "Wholesale trade" industry (17 IPOs), "Medical and optical instruments" industry (15 IPOs), and "Computer and office machinery" industry (14 IPOs). It seems that the traditional industries such as construction (6 IPOs) and textiles (4 IPOs) did not take a major role in KOSDAQ IPOs. This industry classification of KOSDAQ IPO firms clearly shows that KOSDAQ has focussed on financing high-tech firms (KSDA, 2001).

Table 5.3 also shows that VC-backed IPOs are concentrated in the high-tech industries. Even though VC-backed IPOs are less than majority (173 IPOs, 46 per cent out of 372 sample firms) on the whole, they exceeded non-VC-backed IPOs in the top two high-tech industries. VC-backed IPOs represent 46 IPOs (26.6 per cent out of VC-backed IPOs) in "Electric components, radio, television and communication manufacturing" industry. For "Computer and related activities" industry, VC-backed IPOs amounts to 42 IPOs (24.3 per cent out of VC-backed IPOs). This implies that venture capitalists explicitly show a clear preference in high-tech firms and tend to concentrate on some narrow set of industries (Hellmann and Puri, 2000).[2]

Other major industries in which VC-backed IPOs are more prevalent than non-VC-backed IPOs are "Computer and office machinery manufacturing" industry (10 IPOs), "Medical and optical instruments" industry (10 IPOs), "Research and Development" industry (2 IPOs) and "Retail trade" industries industry (2 IPOs).

Table 5.3 Industry distribution of KOSDAQ IPO firms 1999–2001

KIC	Industry	Total		VC		Non-VC	
		No	%	No	%	No	%
32	Manufacture of Electronic Components, Radio, Television	71	(19.1)	46	(26.6)	25	(12.6)
72	Computer and Related Activities	70	(18.8)	42	(24.3)	28	(14.1)
29	Manufacture of Other Machinery and Equipment	45	(12.1)	20	(11.6)	25	(12.6)
24	Manufacture of Chemicals and Chemical Products	29	(7.8)	11	(6.4)	18	(9.0)
51	Wholesale Trade and Commission Trade	18	(4.8)	5	(2.9)	13	(6.5)
31	Manufacture of Electrical Machinery and Apparatuses	17	(4.6)	5	(2.9)	12	(6.0)
33	Manufacture of Medical, Precision and Optical Instruments	15	(4.0)	10	(5.8)	5	(2.5)
30	Manufacture of Computers and Office Machinery	14	(3.8)	10	(5.8)	4	(2.0)
28	Manufacture of Fabricated Metal Products	10	(2.7)	1	(0.6)	9	(4.5)
88	Other Recreational, Cultural and Sporting Activities	10	(2.7)	4	(2.3)	6	(3.0)
64	Post and Telecommunications	9	(2.4)	3	(1.7)	6	(3.0)
22	Publishing, Printing and Reproduction of Recorded Media	6	(1.6)	2	(1.2)	4	(2.0)
34	Manufacture of Motor Vehicles, Trailers and Semitrailers	6	(1.6)	2	(1.2)	4	(2.0)
45	General Construction	6	(1.6)	1	(0.6)	5	(2.5)
15	Manufacture of Food Products and Beverages	5	(1.3)	0	(0.0)	5	(2.5)
18	Manufacture of Sewn Wearing Apparel and Fur Articles	5	(1.3)	1	(0.6)	4	(2.0)
75	Business Support Services	5	(1.3)	1	(0.6)	4	(2.0)
17	Manufacture of Textiles, Except Sewn Wearing apparel	4	(1.1)	1	(0.6)	3	(1.5)
21	Manufacture of Pulp, Paper and Paper Products	3	(0.8)	0	(0.0)	3	(1.5)
27	Manufacture of Basic Metals	3	(0.8)	1	(0.6)	2	(1.0)
73	Research and Development	3	(0.8)	2	(1.2)	1	(0.5)
	Other industries *	18	(4.8)	5	(2.9)	13	(6.5)
	Total	372	(100.0)	173	(100.0)	199	(100.0)

Source: IPO prospectuses (industry information); Ministry of Commerce, Industry and Energy (www.mocie.go.kr) website (KIC code).

*) We grouped all industries with fewer than three samples into a group called "other industries". These include Manufacture of Rubber and Plastic Products (25), Retail Trade (52), Supporting and Auxiliary Transport Activities (63), Real Estate Activities (70), Motion Picture, Broadcasting and Performing Arts Industries (87), Tanning and Dressing of Leather, Manufacture of Luggage and Footwear (19), Manufacture of Other Non-metallic Mineral Products (26), Manufacture of Furniture (36), Hotels and Restaurants (55), Land Transport (60), Air Transport (62), Professional, Scientific and Technical Services (74), Education (80).

5.4 IPO characteristics

Table 5.4 provides a detailed analysis of the characteristics of the IPO firms grouped by VC-backed and non-VC-backed status.

A comparison of the size and age of the firms shows that VC-backed IPOs are smaller and younger than those of non-VC-backed IPOs. Age of firm[3] of VC-backed IPOs is, on average, 8.2 years, whereas that of non-VC-backed IPOs is 12.8, with the difference being significant at 1 per cent level under both the parametric and non-parametric tests.[4]

Average market capitalisation volume, which is the multiplication of offer price and number of shares outstanding, of VC-backed IPOs (50.4 BW[5]) is significantly lower than that of non-VC-backed IPOs (100.2 BW). Gross spread, which is the total amount of the money an IPO firm receives by selling the shares, also shows a significant difference at 10 per cent level by Mann-Whitney test: 10.6 BW for VC-backed IPOs and 16.7 BW for non-VC-backed IPOs. Total costs for underwriting is lower for VC-backed IPOs (411.7 MW) than for non-VC-backed IPOs (416.7 MW), which is significant at 10 per cent level by Mann-Whitney test. The data in the table suggest that the difference of underwriting is caused by the underwriting fees that are paid to underwriters, rather than miscellaneous fees such as legal, auditing, printing costs etc. However, the percentage of underwriting costs to gross proceeds is rather higher for VC-backed IPOs (7.1 per cent) than for non-VC-backed IPOs (6.9 per cent) at 10 per cent level by the Mann-Whitney test. While the gross spreads received by VC-backed firms on average are only two-thirds as large as those received by non-VC-backed firms, VC-backed firms seem to pay relatively higher costs of underwriting.

Table 5.4 also shows that CEOs of VC-backed firms are on average younger than the counterpart of non-VC-backed firms. (47.7 years vs 53.0 years) and that the members of board of directors, including CEOs, are less paid than those of non-VC-backed firms are (37.2 MW vs 43.4 MW). These differences are significance at 1 per cent using both the t-test and Mann-Whitney test. For the size of board of directors, VC-backed firms on average have 6.3 members while non-VC-backed firms have 6.9 members, both of which are different at 5 per cent level using the T-test. VC-backed firms also had significantly less employees (105.0) than non-VC-backed firms (246.4). However, the yearly salary that is paid to employees, excluding board of directors, does not show significant difference between the groups.

The book-to-market ratio, which is calculated as the proportion of book value of equity at the last year before IPO to the market capitalisation volume at the time of IPO, shows that VC-backed IPOs recorded a significantly lower book-to-market ratio (0.187) than non-VC-backed IPOs (0.450). This indicates that the market capitalisation of VC-backed IPOs increased more than the book value of equity, compared with the case of non-VC-backed IPOs. The offer price between VC-backed IPOs (11,457.9 Won) and non-VC-backed IPOs (11,811.3) does not show a significant difference.

Table 5.4 Selected characteristics of VC-backed and non-VC-backed IPOs on KOSDAQ 1999–2001

	VC-Backed IPOs' Mean Median	Non VC-Backed IPOs' Mean Median	T-statistics by t-test	Z-scores by Mann-Whitney test
Age of firm (Year)	8.2	12.8	–5.70***	–5.90***
	6.7	*10.7*		
Offer Price (Won)	11,457.9	11,811.3	–0.24	–0.73
	5,500.0	*8,000.0*		
Market capitalisation volume (BW)	50.4	100.2	–1.28	–2.15**
	30.1	*20.0*		
Book-to-market Ratio	0.2	0.5	–5.68***	–7.33***
	0.1	*0.3*		
Gross proceeds (BW)	10.6	16.7	–1.59	–1.93*
	7.0	*5.2*		
Underwriting fees (MW)	368.8	374.3	0.11	–1.78*
	261.7	*210.0*		
Miscellaneous fees (MW)	41.1	42.3	0.28	–0.47
	29.2	*32.3*		
Total costs for underwriting (MW)	411.7	416.7	–0.10	–1.66*
	305.4	*247.0*		
Ratio of underwriting costs to gross proceeds (per cent)	7.1	6.9	0.04	–1.69*
	4.2	*4.5*		
Age of CEO (Year)	47.7	53.0	–5.55***	–5.33***
	46.4	*53.2*		
Number of board of directors	6.3	6.9	–2.14**	–0.80
	6.0	*6.0*		
Yearly salary per each board of director (MW)	37.2	43.4	2.86***	–2.70***
	35.0	*39.8*		
Number of employees	105.0	246.4	–3.63***	–4.99***
	77.0	*115.0*		
Yearly Salary per each employee (MW)	16.6	16.9	0.39	–0.01
	15.8	*16.0*		

Source: IPO prospectuses and financial data provided by Korean Information System

Note: BW and MW indicate billion Won and million Won (Korean currency), respectively. Exchange rate of Won to British pounds is roughly W2,000 / £1 over recent years. Asterisks denote significance at the level of 1 per cent (***), 5 per cent (**), and 10 per cent (*).

From the IPO characteristics of Table 5.4, it can be generally said that VC-backed firms are younger and smaller than non-VC-backed firms. This difference in size and firm age between two groups shows the tendency of venture capital investment into small and medium enterprises (Brewer, 1996).

5.5 Ownership structure

Table 5.5 analyses the ownership structure of IPOs at IPO. The IPO prospectuses of KOSDAQ IPO firms that provided an identity of major shareholders having more than 5 per cent of total shares was used to classify the shareholders into seven ownership groups, as specified in the table (CEO, CEO's family, board of directors, venture capitalist, corporate venturing corporations, bank, security company).

The average shareholdings of the CEO is similar between VC-backed IPOs (32.2 per cent) and non-VC-backed IPOs (31.8 per cent). Average shareholdings of board of directors do not differ significantly between VC-backed IPOs (7.8 per cent) and non-VC-backed IPOs (9.7 per cent). However, the average shareholdings of the CEO's family show significant differences (6.1 per cent for VC-backed IPOs, 13.0 per cent for non-VC-backed IPOs). The sum of shareholdings of CEO and their related persons[6] (family and board of directors) shows

Table 5.5 Ownership structure of IPO firms on KOSDAQ 1999–2001

	VC-Backed IPOs' Mean Median	Non VC-Backed IPOs' Mean Median	T-statistics by t-test	Z-scores by Mann-Whitney test
Shareholdings of CEO (%)	32.2	31.9	0.18	−0.65
	32.8	*31.7*		
Shareholding of CEO's family (%)	6.1	13.0	−4.60***	−3.13***
	1.4	*5.7*		
Shareholdings of board of directors (BoD) (%)	7.8	9.7	−1.35	−0.86
	4.2	*2.3*		
Shareholdings of CEO and their related persons (%) (CEO+ family + BoD)	46.2	54.4	−3.05***	−3.41***
	48.0	*57.1*		
Shareholding of corporate venturing institutions (%)	5.2	14.0	−4.00***	−3.74***
	0.0	*0.0*		
Shareholding of venture capitalists (%)	15.1	0.0	26.06***	−18.00***
	13.5	*0.0*		
Shareholding of banks (%)	1.3	0.7	1.25	−2.11**
	0.0	*0.0*		
Shareholding of security companies (%)	1.6	2.2	−0.88	−0.16
	0.0	*0.0*		

Source: Author's own calculations based on IPO prospectuses

Note: Asterisks denote statistical significance at the level of 1 per cent (***), 5 per cent (**), and 10 per cent (*).

that there is a significant difference between VC-backed IPOs (46.2 per cent) and non-VC-backed IPOs (54.4 per cent).

The average shareholding of VCs in VC-backed firms is 15.1 per cent. This figure is quite low, especially compared with the average holding of US venture capitalist at IPO (36.6 per cent), as shown in Megginson and Weiss (1991). While corporate venturing companies accounted for only 5.2 per cent of total shareholdings of VC-backed IPOs on average, they explain 14.0 per cent of those of non-VC-backed IPOs. This difference is significant at 1 per cent level. It is also shown that banks have average shareholdings of 1.3 per cent for VC-backed firms and 0.7 per cent for non-VC-backed firms. Security companies have 1.6 per cent for VC-backed firms and 2.2 per cent for non-VC-backed firms. While the shareholdings held by banks are significantly different between VC-backed and non-VC-backed groups at 5 per cent level by Mann-Whitney test, those held by security companies are not significantly different between the groups.

Given the life cycle of the financing of entrepreneurial firms that were mentioned in Chapter 2, venture capitalists filled the equity gap of VC-backed firms when they had suffered from insufficient funding from insiders such as family and parenting companies (various types of corporate venturing companies) (Berger and Udell, 1998).

5.6 Sources of funds

Table 5.6 exhibits the sources of funds of VC-backed and non-VC-backed firms at the last year before IPO. VC-backed firms seem to rely less on securing loans from banks and financial institutions.[7]

Looking at absolute values first, I see that the funding from banks for VC-backed firms at the end of last year before IPO is on an average 3.8 BW, compared that for non-VC-backed firms is 16.1 BW. The funding from financial institutions as a whole, including banks, also shows a big difference between two groups: 4.3 BW for VC-backed firms vs 47.1 BW for non-VC-backed firms. VC-backed firms raised 1.9 BW on average by issuing bonds and additional shares in capital markets during the last year before IPO, while non-VC-backed firms raised 18.1 BW which is almost ten times the amount raised by VC-backed firms. Each of these differences is significant at the 5 per cent level using the non-parametric test. The lack of significance on a parametric basis suggests some extreme values in the variables within each group.

When I calculate relative size of funding from financial institutions and capital markets by dividing the absolute volume of funding size by total asset of the same period, the significant differences tend to disappear. For the VC-backed firms, the proportion of funding from banks to total assets is 19.5 per cent, while that of non-VC-backed firms is 18.9. The proportions of funding from financial institutions to total asset are 23.1 per cent and 22.1 per cent for VC-backed and non-VC-backed firms, respectively. Neither of these difference is statistically significant. However, the proportion of funding from capital markets to total asset shows that VC-backed firms raised relatively more money in capital markets (24.2 per cent)

Table 5.6 Sources of funds

	VC-Backed IPOs' Mean Median	Non VC-Backed IPOs' Mean Median	T-statistics by t-test	Z-scores by Mann-Whitney test
Loans from banks (BW)	3.8	16.1	−1.41	−1.98**
	1.5	*2.5*		
: Proportion to total asset (%)	19.5	18.9	0.25	−0.45
	14.1	*14.4*		
Loans from all financial institutions, including banks (BW)	4.3	47.1	−1.07	−2.05**
	1.8	*2.8*		
: Proportion to total asset (%)	23.1	22.1	0.40	−1.05
	19.6	*16.9*		
Funding from capital markets (BW)	1.9	18.1	−1.40	−1.99**
(corporate bonds and equity)	*0.8*	*0.2*		
: Proportion to total asset (%)	24.2	20.8	0.47	−2.27**
	11.1	*5.1*		

Source: IPO prospectuses

Note: BW and MW indicate billion Won and million Won (Korean currency), respectively. Exchange rate of won to British pounds is roughly W2,000 / £1 over the recent years. Asterisks denote significance at the level of 1% (***), 5% (**), and 10% (*).

than non-VC-backed firms (20.8 per cent). The difference is significant at 5 per cent level by Mann-Whitney test.

5.7 Financial and operating performance

In Table 5.7, I show various types of financial and operating performance of IPO firms during the last year before IPO. Financial ratios in the Table 5.7 are calculated as follows: (1) Leverage and Liquidity Ratios: Debt-equity ratio = long-term debt, that is, debenture + long-term borrowings/equity; Current ratio = current asset/current liabilities; Quick ratio = quick asset/current liabilities; Operating cash flows to maturing obligations = operating cash flows/current liabilities; (2) Efficiency Ratios: Sales-to-assets ratio = turnover/total assets, Return on capital employed = ordinary income/long-term capital employed, R&D Intensity = R&D costs/total assets, Advertisements intensity = sales & administration costs/total assets; (3) Profitability Ratios: Net income margin = net income/ turnover; Return on Asset = ordinary income/total asset, Operating income margin: operating income/turnover, Earning per share = net income/number of shares outstanding

Table 5.7 Operating performances of IPO firms

	VC-Backed Mean Median	Non VC-Backed Mean Median	T-statistics by t-test	Z-scores by Mann-Whitney test
Panel A: Major Figures from Financial Statements				
Total assets (BW)	17.5	78.4	−2.31**	−4.51***
	12.8	18.1		
Total liabilities (BW)	9.0	54.7	−1.98**	−3.76***
	6.1	8.5		
Book value of Equity (BW)	8.2	23.6	−3.21***	−4.65***
	5.6	8.6		
Turnover (BW)	22.1	67.0	−3.08***	−4.23
	13.9	20.3		
Net Income (BW)	1.8	−0.2	1.35	−2.73***
	1.2	1.6		
Net Cash Flow (BW)	1.0	−1.5	0.81	−0.80
	0.4	0.3		
Panel B: Leverage and Liquidity Ratios				
Debt-equity ratio (%)	291.8	27.4	1.08	−1.01
	14.3	10.5		
Current ratio (%)	264.3	219.7	1.69*	−2.76***
	183.2	152.7		
Quick ratio (%)	219.0	185.4	1.30	−1.84*
	140.8	122.5		
Net Cash Flows/Total assets (%)	6.1	4.0	1.534	−0.859
	3.1	2.2		
Panel C: Efficiency Ratios				
Sales-to-assets ratio (%)	127.6	129.3	−0.201	−0.276
	113.4	116.8		
Return on capital employed (%)	23.6	21.9	0.81	−1.04
	21.3	19.7		
R&D intensity (%)	6.0	2.6	5.22***	−5.37***
	3.3	0.4		
Advertisements intensity (%)	18.9	19.1	−0.10	−0.08
	14.0	14.4		
Panel D: Profitability Ratios				
Net income margin (%)	7.8	8.2	−0.21	−1.21
	8.4	7.6		
Return on asset (%)	11.0	10.0	0.980	−1.479
	10.1	8.3		
Operating income margin (%)	11.1	7.4	0.78	−1.39
	11.9	10.6		
Earning per share (W)	2,835.9	3,989.8	−1.35	−1.22
	1,445.5	1,937.5		

Source: Author's own calculations based on the data provided by Korean Information System

Note: MW in Panel A and Panel C indicates million Won (Korean currency). Exchange rate of won to British pounds is roughly W2,000 / £1 over the recent years. Asterisks denote significance levels at 1% (***), 5% (**), and 10% (*).

In Panel A, I show the size of total assets, total liabilities and the book value of equity from balance sheets, turnover and net income from income statements, and the net cash flow from cash flow statements. As was clearly shown from market capitalisation in Table 5.4, VC-backed firms are smaller in size than non-VC-backed firms. Mean of total assets of VC-backed IPOs is 17.5 BW while that of non-VC-backed IPOs is 78.3 BW. Mean of total liabilities (book value of equity) of VC-backed IPO is 9.0 BW (8.2 BW) while that of non-VC-backed is 54.7 BW (23.6 BW). The difference of total assets, total liabilities and the value of equity is significant at 1 per cent and 5 per cent level. While turnover of VC-backed firms recorded 22.1 BW on average, just one-third as much as that of non-VC-backed firms, net income of VC-backed firms was 1.8 BW, compared with − 0.2 BW of non-VC-backed firms. It is also seen that VC-backed firms had positive net cash flow (1.0 BW), compared with negative net cash flow (− 1.5 BW) of non-VC-backed firms.[8] However, the median of net income of VC-backed firms (1,171.9 MW) was lower than that of non-VC-backed firms (1,594.6 MW). Median cash flows are positive for both groups: 410.0 MW for VC-backed firms vs 338.8 MW for non-VC-backed firms. The difference of turnover and net income is significant at 1 per cent level, but net cash flow is not significantly different between the two groups.

In Panel B, I show the leverage and liquidity ratios which measures financial position of the IPO firms. The ratios show that VC-backed firms were in a better short-term financial position. The current ratio of VC-backed firms was on average 264.3 per cent, compared with 219.7 per cent of non-VC-backed firms. The quick ratio also shows that VC-backed firms had more liquid assets that could readily be turned into cash in order to pay back current liabilities than non-VC-backed firms: 219.0 per cent for VC-backed firms vs 185.4 per cent for non-VC-backed firms. The difference of current ratio between the two groups is significant at 10 per cent level by T-test and at 1 per cent level by Mann-Whitney test. The quick ratio is also different at 10 per cent level by Mann-Whitney test. However, debt-equity ratio, which is related to ability to meet long-term liabilities, was not significant different between the two groups.

Panel C shows efficiency ratios that judge how efficiently a firm is using its investment in assets. The sales-to-asset ratio and return on capital employed are not significantly different between VC-backed and non-VC-backed firms. It is shown that VC-backed firms expended higher proportion of their assets in R&D activities. R&D intensity of VC-backed firms is 6.0 per cent, compared with 2.6 per cent of non-VC-backed firms. This result is consistent with the finding in the study by Jain and Kini (2000) who found that more VC-backed firms belonged to the category of R&D intensity above industry average. However, the table shows that VC-backed firms spent a similar portion of their assets in advertisement activities as did non-VC-backed firms. The difference of advertisement intensity is not significantly different between the two groups.

Panel D shows the profitability ratios that measure the operating performance of a firm. VC-backed firms and non-VC-backed firms do not present any significant differences in profitability ratios. Net income margin of VC-backed firms was 7.8 per cent, compared with 8.2 per cent of non-VC-backed firms. Return on asset (11.0 per cent vs 10.0 per cent), Operating income margin (11.1 per cent vs 7.4 per cent) and Earning per share (2,835.9 Won vs 3,989.8 Won) were not significantly different between VC-backed firms and non-VC-backed firms.

5.8 Comparison with other major countries

Table 5.8 briefly compares the IPO characteristics (market capitalisation, age, high-tech industry ratio and VC ownership) of KOSDAQ IPO firms with that of other major four countries' data. The data for each country are based on different sample periods. Our aim is to use these data to compare the difference of VC-backed and non-VC-backed IPOs. There are changes across time in the countries, but the averages presented here are reasonable reflections of persistent country differences.

Table 5.8 Comparison of KOSDAQ data with other major countries

	US		UK		Germany		Japan		Korea	
	VC	Non-VC	VC	Non-VC	VC	Non-VC	VC	Non-VC	VC	Non-VC
Market capitalisation (Million $)	92.7 [1]	55.7 [1]	120.4 [2]	198.9 [2]	221.4 [3]	301.8 [3]	41.0*) [4]	52.8*) [4]	38.1	75.8
Age (Years)	6.0 [5]	12.2 [6]	9.8 [7]	11.6 [7]	10.5 [8]	11.5 [8]	33.2 [9]	36.8 [9]	8.2	12.8
High-tech Industry (%)	45.0 [10]	33.0 [10]	77.1 [11]	85.2 [11]	85.0 [12]	88.5 [12]	33.4 [13]	21.1 [13]	76.9	49.7
VC ownership (%)	34.3 [14]	-	21.3 [15]	-	40.3 [16]	-	6.7 [17]	-	15.1	-

Sources: 1) Brau, Brown et al. (2004) (sample period: 1990–1996); 2) Espenlaub, Garrett et al. (1999) (sample period: 1992–1995); 3) Kraus and Burghof (2003) (sample period: 1997–2001); 4) Hamao, Packer et al. (2000) (sample period: 1989–1995); 5) Megginson and Weiss (1991) (sample period: 1983–1987); 6) Gompers (1996) (sample period: 1978–1987) Rindermann (2003) (sample period: 1996–1999); 8) Franzke (2003) (sample period: 1997–2002); 9) Hamao, Packer et al. (2000) (sample period: 1989–1995); 10) Brau, Brown et al. (2004) (sample period: 1990–1996); 11) Rindermann (2003) (sample period: 1996–1999); 12) Kraus and Burghof (2003) (sample period: 1997–2001); 13) Suzuki (2003) (sample period: 1996–2000); 14) Barry Muscarella et al. (1990) (sample period: 1978–1987); 15) Espenlaub, Garrett et al. (1999) (sample period: 1992–1995); 16) Franzke (2003) (sample period: 1997–2002); 17) Kutsuna (2002) (sample period: 1995–1996)

Notes: Market capitalisation of each country (except for the US) was converted to US dollar by the exchange rate at the year-end of the sample period when each market capitalisation was calculated. (*The Japanese data are gross spreads, which are generally considerably smaller than market capitalisation volume). Age is the years from the establishment date to IPO date. The ratio of high-tech industry was calculated by the author, based on the Loughran and Ritter (2000)'s high-tech industry classification, as discussed in Chapter 4. (High-tech industry ratio of US was calculated by the original authors). VC ownership is the percentage of VC shareholding of total shares at the time of IPO. The values are simple averages of the studies reviewed.

It appears that the average market capitalisation of the other countries' stock markets was generally bigger than that of KOSDAQ. It is also seen that, as in the case of KOSDAQ, VC-backed IPOs are generally smaller than non-VC-backed IPOs. A notable exception is the US case (USD 92.7 million vs USD 55.7 million).[9] I find that the market capitalisation of German IPOs (USD 221.4 million vs USD 301.8 million) considerably exceeded that of IPOs in other countries.

The table also shows that in every country venture capitalists brought younger firms to IPO market, compared with non-VC-backed IPOs. It took less time for VC-backed firms to get listed after they were founded than non-VC-backed firms. It is shown that the average age of the US VC-backed firms (6.0 years) was lower than that of KOSDAQ VC-backed firms (8.2 years), followed by the UK (9.8 years), Germany (10.5 years) and Japan (33.2 years).

It is observed that the proportion of high-tech firms is higher for VC-backed IPOs than for non-VC-backed IPOs in three countries: US (45.0 per cent vs 33.05), Japan (33.4 per cent vs 21.1 per cent) and Korea (76.9 per cent vs 49.7 per cent). In the UK and Germany, high-tech firms explain more than half of VC-backed and non-VC-backed IPOs, respectively. However, the proportion of high-tech firms is lower for VC-backed IPOs than for non-VC-backed IPOs (UK: 77.1 per cent vs 85.2 per cent, Germany: 85.0 per cent vs 88.5 per cent).

At the time of IPO, venture capitalists own considerable amount of shares of IPO firms. The Japanese VC ownership is less than 10 per cent on average, but in other countries, venture capitalists hold more than 10 per cent of total shares of IPO firms at IPO. German venture capitalists are shown to have 40.3 per cent of IPO shares, followed by the US (34.3 per cent) and the UK (21.3 per cent). The VC-ownership of KOSDAQ IPOs (15.1 per cent) is relatively lower than Germany, the US and the UK, but is higher than Japan.

One noteworthy implication of this comparison is that the Korean case generally follows a similar pattern with that of other major countries. It is possible to argue on the basis that the results of KOSDAQ case can be compared with those from other countries.

5.9 Summary of the chapter

I have presented a description of the characteristics of our IPO sample firms in this chapter. It was shown, in Section 2, that the number of firms listed in KOSDAQ dramatically increased from 1999 to 2001. Like other international secondary stock markets, KOSDAQ attracted a lot of high-technology firms. The top three high-tech industries of electrical components, computer and related activities and other machinery manufacturing account for almost half of the whole sample (Section 5.3).

From the comparison of IPO characteristics between VC-backed firms and non-VC-backed firms in Section 5.4, I find that VC-backed firms are significantly younger and smaller than non-VC-backed firms. This difference in size and firm age between VC-backed and non-VC-backed IPOs clearly shows the tendency of venture capital investment to focus on SME and early stage firms (Brewer et al., 1996).

In Section 5.5, it was shown that VC-backed firms have fewer shareholdings by CEO's family and corporate venturing institutions than non-VC-backed firms do. It can be argued that venture capitalists filled the equity gap of VC-backed firms when they could not secure sufficient funding from insiders such as family and parenting companies, or/and that the original owners of VC-backed firms were more willing to see their ownership diluted either to foster growth or capitalise on their early investments by selling a portion of their equity (Berger and Udell, 1998).

Section 5.6 shows that VC-backed firms did not receive as much funding from banks and other financial institutions, and did not issue as much bonds and shares in the capital markets, as non-VC-backed firms did. However, the differences were small when normalised by the size of the firms, so that there is not clear evidence of capital market rationing for these VC-backed firms.

In Section 5.7, I presented the financial and operating performances of IPO firms. VC-backed firms are smaller in total assets and turnover than non-VC-backed firms are. It was found that VC-backed firms were in a better short-term financial position, and they invested a higher proportion of their assets in R&D activities. I did not find any significant differences in profitability ratios.

In Section 5.8, I briefly compare the IPO characteristics of KOSDAQ IPO firms with that of other major countries' data. I could see that that IPO characteristics of KOSDAQ IPO firms was generally similar with that of other major countries. VC-backed IPOs was generally smaller than non-VC-backed IPOs, except for the US. In every country, venture capitalists brought IPO firms earlier than other non-VC-backed IPOs. The proportion of high-tech firms is higher for VC-backed IPOs than for non-VC-backed IPOs in three countries (the US, Japan and Korea). In the UK and Germany, high-tech firms explain more than half of VC-backed and non-VC-backed IPOs, but the proportion of high-tech firms is lower for VC-backed IPOs than for non-VC-backed IPOs. At the time of IPO, venture capitalists own considerable amount of shares of IPO firms in each country.

Notes

1 IPO characteristics of VC-backed and non-VC-backed companies and related descriptions in this chapter appeared in rearranged forms in Ch.26 "The Impact of Venture Capital Participation and Its Affiliation with Financial Institutions on the Long-term Performance of IPO Firm: Evidence from Korea in Hot and Cold Market Periods" by Jaeho Lee from *Oxford Handbook of Venture Capital*, edited by Cumming, Douglas (2012) and "The Hot and Cold Market Impacts on Underpricing of Certification, Reputation and Conflicts of Interest in Venture Capital Backed Korean IPO" by Jaeho Lee from *Korean Venture Management Review*, 12(4) (2009). Original parts have been used in this chapter with permission of Oxford University Press and The Korean Association of Small Business Studies, respectively.
2 However, I can also see that VC-backed IPOs occur at least once in two thirds of industries (23 industries out of the whole 35 industries)
3 Age of firms is the years from the establishment date to IPO date.

4 This difference of firm age between VC-backed and non-VC-backed firms may be evidence of another kind of "grandstanding" which were documented by Gompers (1996) and Barnes and Mccarthy (2002). Venture capitalists might bring younger firms to stock market to build up their reputation and make it feasible to raise venture capital commitment from outside investors.

5 BW: Billion Won, MW: Million Won.

6 Commercial Law in Korea states that CEO's family and board of directors are classified as "persons that have special relationship with CEO".

7 These other financial institutions include "merchant banking corporations" and "mutual savings banks".

8 Median cash flow are positive for both groups: 410.0 MW for VC-backed firms vs 338.8 MW for non-VC-backed firms.

9 This may reflect the particular sample period for the US. I could not find studies covering later periods in terms of VC-backed and non-VC-backed IPOs.

6 Underpricing

6.1 Overview

In this chapter, I present the results of a univariate and a multivariate analysis of underpricing. As explained in Chapter 4, I adopted a new method to calculate underpricing to allow for the institutional features of the Korean stock market. This method is based on calculating the difference between the offer price and the closing price on the first day that did not hit the daily upper limit. This chapter documents various types of analysis that were carried out on this newly formed underpricing measurement.

Section 6.2 aims to compare underpricing across different classifications of IPOs; VC-backed and non-VC-backed; hot and cold issue market; age (young and old), market capitalisation (small and big), and industry (high-tech and non-high-tech), respectively. In this section, hypothesis H1a (the impact of VC-backing on underpricing) is tested. Section 6.3 extends the analysis of Section 6.2 by comparing underpricing between VC-backed IPOs and non-VC-backed IPO cross-classified by hot issue market, age, market capitalisation and industry. In this section, hypothesis H1a is also tested. Section 6.4 compares the underpricing by the institutional type of VC-backing: bank-affiliated, security company-affiliated, other institution-affiliated and non-VC-backed. This comparison of underpricing by the institutional type of VC-backing is also cross-classified by hot issue market, age, market capitalisation, and industry. In this section, hypothesis H3a (the impact of bank-affiliated VC-backing on underpricing) and H4a (the impact of security company-affiliated VC-backing on underpricing) are tested. In section 6.5, I compare the underpricing between hot market and cold market cross-classified by venture-capital-backing, age, market capitalisation and industry. In section 6.6, I report the result of multiple regressions on underpricing. Multiple regressions were carried out for IPOs in the whole sample period, IPOs in the hot market and IPOs in the cold market, respectively. Each of our hypothesis is tested in this section.

6.2 Underpricing by the different types of IPOs

Table 6.1 compares the underpricing (or initial returns) between different groups of firms. The underpricing for VC-backed IPOs is significantly higher (2.02) than non-VC-backed IPOs (1.49) during the whole period.[1]

Table 6.1 Underpricing by different types of IPOs on KOSDAQ 1999–2001

	Mean	Median	Mean	Median	T-statistics by t-test	Z-scores by Mann-Whitney test
(A) Venture-capital-backing						
	VC-backed		Non-VC-backed			
Underpricing	2.02	1.19	1.49	1.00	2.15**	−1.79*
(No. IPOs)	(173)		(199)			
(B) Hot Market Issue						
	Hot Market		Cold Market			
Underpricing	2.80	2.14	1.19	0.89	6.54***	−6.20***
(No. IPOs)	(127)		(245)			
(C) Age						
	Young		Old			
Underpricing	2.05	1.23	1.43	1.00	2.50**	−2.45**
(No. IPOs)	(186)		(186)			
(D) Market Capitalisation						
	Small		Big			
Underpricing	1.98	1.36	1.50	0.82	1.96*	−4.15***
(No. IPOs)	(186)		(186)			
(E) Industry						
	High-tech		Non-high-tech			
Underpricing	1.77	1.07	1.70	1.00	0.28	−0.01
(No. IPOs)	(232)		(140)			

Source: Korean Information System, IPO prospectuses

Notes: KOSDAQ IPO samples are divided into two groups respectively as: (1) VC-backed Firms (when any venture capitalist owns 5% or more of total shares of an IPO firm) and Non-VC-backed Firms; (2) Hot Market issue (when an IPO was listed in KOSDAQ in the period up to March 2000) and Cold Market issue (after March 2000); (3) Young firms (when the age of firm is equal to or less than the median value, 9.6 years) and Old firms; (4) Small firms (when the market capitalisation calculated as the offer price multiplied by the number of shares is equal to or less than the median value, 2.4 billion Won) and Big firms; (5) High-tech firms (which include Other Machinery and Equipment (KIC 29), Computers and Office Machinery (30) Electrical Machinery and Apparatuses (31) Electronic Components, Radio, Television (32) Medical, Precision and Optical Instruments (33), and Computer and Related Activities (72) as was defined in Chapter 4) and Non-high-tech firms. These different types of groupings apply to the remaining parts of the chapter. Asterisks denote significance levels at the level 1% (***), 5% (**), and 10% (*).

This comparison of underpricing between VC-backed and non-VC-backed IPOs is relevant for testing our hypothesis H1a. The impact of VC-backing is expected to result in less underpricing. This comparison rejects the hypothesis. Venture capitalists did not reduce the degree of underpricing as certifying agents who could lessen the information asymmetry between investors and issuers. Rather, given our discussion in the literature review, IPOs backed by venture capitalists seem to be recognised as more risky and uncertain by investors, who thus appear to require a higher risk premium on the issue. This result of more underpricing by VC-backed IPOs is consistent with the findings in Francis and Hasan (2001) and Smart and Zutter (2000), both of who used the US data in the 1990s. I will come back to the underpricing by VC-backing in hot and cold market in Section 6.3 and Section 6.5.

Table 6.1 also shows that IPO firms brought to the stock market in the hot issue period (up until March 2000) recorded higher initial returns (2.80) on average than those (1.19) in the cold issue market (after March 2000). The difference of initial returns between the two periods is significant at 1 per cent level. This result clearly shows that initial returns are closely correlated with market conditions, as argued in Ibbotson, Sindelar et al. (1994) and Lowry and Schwert (2002). Market conditions seem to influence the initial returns in the bank-based Korean system much as in other stock markets.

The initial returns of young firms (2.05) are statistically significantly higher those than of old firms (1.43). This is consistent with the view that investors require a greater risk premium[2] for young firms that generally have more uncertain prospects than old firms. This finding is consistent with the difference of underpricing between small and big firms. The average initial return of the small market capitalisation group (1.98) turns out to be statistically significantly higher than that of large market capitalisation group (1.50). This evidence also appears to show that investors demand a higher risk premium on the IPOs of small firms that are recognised as more uncertain and risky than big firms.

There is no significant difference in initial returns for high-tech and non-high-tech companies. The underpricing of the high-tech industry group is 1.77, compared with 1.70 for the non-high-tech group. This is an interesting result, because high-tech stocks (especially relating to information and communication technology) showed higher initial return than non-high-tech stocks in late 1990s and the first quarter of 2000 (Schultz and Zaman, 2001) in the US. However, I shall see later in this chapter that the initial return of high-tech and non-high-tech groups shows a difference when the samples are compared in hot and cold market. It seems that the pooling of the samples across the whole sample period affects the calculation of average initial returns between high-tech and non-high-tech groups.

6.3   Underpricing by VC-backed and non-VC-backed IPOs

In this section, I display a bivariate analysis of underpricing by VC-backed IPOs and non-VC-backed IPOs respectively cross-classified by hot market, age, market capitalisation and industry.

Table 6.2 shows that the initial returns of VC-backed firms and non-VC-backed firms are statistically significantly higher in the hot market than in the cold market, for young firms than old firms, and for small firms than for big firms. However, the difference of initial returns is not significant for high-tech and non-high-tech groups.

Table 6.2 IPO Underpricing by VC-backing and non-VC-backing classified by state of the market, age, market capitalisation, and industry on KOSDAQ 1999–2001

	Mean	Median	Mean	Median	T-statistics by t-test	Z-scores by Mann-Whitney test
Panel A: Hot Market Issue						
	Hot market		Cold market			
VC-backing	3.61	2.38	1.11	0.76	6.51***	−6.73***
(No. IPOs)	(63)		(110)			
Non-VC-backing	2.00	1.34	1.25	1.00	2.48**	−2.07**
(No. IPOs)	(64)		(135)			
T-statistics[1]	2.84***		−0.74			
Z-scores[2]	−3.50***		−0.84			
Panel B: Age						
	Young		Old			
VC-backing	2.37	1.22	1.41	1.07	2.25**	−1.30
(No. IPOs)	(111)		(62)			
Non-VC-backing	1.58	1.24	1.44	0.93	0.44	−1.68*
(No. IPOs)	(75)		(124)			
T-statistics	2.01**		−0.10			
Z-scores	−0.79		−1.07			
Panel C: Market Capitalisation						
	Small		Big			
VC-backing	2.42	1.84	1.77	0.93	1.55	−3.59***
(No. IPOs)	(67)		(106)			
Non-VC-backing	1.73	1.20	1.14	0.61	2.03**	−2.97***
(No. IPOs)	(119)		(80)			
T-statistics	2.07**		1.70*			
Z-scores	−2.51**		−1.54			
Panel D: Industry						
	High-tech		Non-high-tech			
VC-backing	1.93	1.19	2.34	1.17	−0.84	−1.22
(No. IPOs)	(133)		(40)			
Non-VC-backing	1.55	1.02	1.44	0.98	0.38	−0.39
(No. IPOs)	(99)		(100)			
T-statistics	1.17		2.15**			
Z-scores	−0.78		−2.15**			

Source: Korean Information System, IPO prospectuses

Note 1) T-statistics by t – test between VC-backing and non-VC-backing for each different type of IPOs

Note 2) Z-scores by Mann-Whitney test between VC-backing and non-VC-backing for each different type of IPOs

Asterisks denote significance levels at the level of 1% (***), 5% (**), and 10% (*).

Note 3) Panel A of this table and related description appeared in "The Hot and Cold Market Impacts on Underpricing of Certification, Reputation and Conflicts of Interest in Venture Capital Backed Korean IPO" by Jaeho Lee from "Korean Venture Management Review", 12(4) (2009) and has been re-used in this chapter by permission of The Korean Association of Small Business Studies.

Panel A shows that the initial return of VC-backed firms is statistically significantly higher in the hot market (3.61) than in the cold market (1.11). Although the initial return of non-VC-backed firms is also higher in hot market (2.00) than in cold market (1.25), the difference of the initial returns is not as severe as in the case of VC-backed firms. But, the difference is still significant at 5 per cent level. This tendency for the initial return to be higher in the hot market regardless of VC-backing clearly shows that the high initial returns of the whole sample in KOSDAQ might be driven by the overreaction of investors in the hot market (Kim and Park, 2002). This suggests that the rejection of hypothesis H1a in the previous section is driven by the hot period result. In the cold market, there is little difference in the initial returns and, in fact, the non-VC backed IPOs have slightly higher underpricing than VC-backed IPOs.

In Panel B, young firms show higher returns than old firms in both VC-backed and non-VC-backed IPOs. The initial return of young firms in VC-backing group is 2.37, compared with 1.41 of old firms in the same group. The difference of the initial returns is significant at 5 per cent level using the t-test. For non-VC-backed firms, the difference of initial returns between young firms (1.58) and old firms (1.44) is no less acute than the case of VC-backed firms, but the difference is only significant at 10 per cent level using Mann-Whitney test. In Panel C, small firms present statistically significantly higher underpricing than large firms for both VC-backed and non-VC-backed firms. VC-backed small firms recorded 2.42 while VC-backed big firms recorded 1.77 and the difference of initial returns between two groups is significant at 1 per cent level using Mann-Whitney test. Non-VC-backed firm also show the difference of initial returns between small firms (1.73) and big firms (1.14), which is significant at 5 per cent level by t-test and 1 per cent level by Mann-Whitney test.

Panel D shows that the average initial return of high-tech firms in VC-backing group is 1.93, compared with 2.34 of non-high-tech firms in the same group. For non-VC-backing group, the mean initial return of high-tech firms is 1.55, while that of non-high-tech firms is 1.44. However, high-tech firms do not provide evidence of significantly higher underpricing than non-high-tech firm for both VC-backed and non-VC-backed groups.

Table 6.2 also shows a significant difference between VC-backed and non-VC-backed IPOs across rows in each panel. It is found that the initial returns of VC-backed IPOs are significantly higher than those of non-VC-backed IPOs in the hot market, for young firms, for small firms, for big firms and for non-high-tech firms. The initial returns of VC-backed IPOs are higher than those of non-VC-backed IPOs for high-tech firms, but the difference is not significant. However, in the cold market and old firms group, VC-backed IPOs show lower underpricing than non-VC-backed IPOs. The difference of initial returns in these two cases is not significant, though.

The comparison of underpricing by VC-backing and non-VC-backing with the different types of IPOs across columns shows that the significantly higher returns are found in hot market, young firms group and small firms group. The difference of initial return in these three groups is higher for VC-backed

IPOs than for non-VC-backed IPOs. The comparison of underpricing across rows also exhibits that VC-backed IPOs show significantly higher initial returns in each of the different groups of IPOs. This analysis shows that VC-backed IPOs were related to higher underpricing in the KOSDAQ IPOs over the period 1999–2001 as a whole, thus rejecting our hypothesis H1a (the impact of VC-backing on underpricing). However, the higher underpricing of VC-backed IPOs seems to fade away in the cold market, which prompts a research question on the role of VC-backing in the hot and cold-market period, respectively.

6.4 Underpricing by types of institutional affiliation of VC-backing

Table 6.3 exhibits the initial returns according to the types of institutional affiliation of VC-backing: bank-affiliated VC-backed IPOs, security company-affiliated VC-backed IPOs, other institution-affiliated VC-backed IPOs (excluding bank-affiliated and security company-affiliated) and non-VC-backed IPOs. As explained in Chapter 3, this classification is based on the kind of institution identified as the parent company of a venture capitalist that participated in the shareholding of an IPO firm as a lead venture capitalist. The initial returns are compared among these four groups for total firms, the firms brought to the stock market in the hot-market period and the firms listed in the cold-market period, respectively. The purpose of comparing the initial returns among these the above four groups according to the institutional difference is to test hypothesis H3a (the impact of bank-affiliated VC-backing on underpricing) and H4a (the impact of security company-affiliated VC-backing on underpricing). The IPOs backed by the bank-affiliated VCs are expected to show less underpricing, while those backed by the security company-affiliated VCs will show more underpricing.

Table 6.3 shows that the initial return of the bank-affiliated group is 2.33, followed by 2.06 of the other institution-affiliated, 1.49 for the non-VC-backed and 1.29 for the security company-affiliated group. I thus find that, contrary to the Hypotheses 3a and 4a, the bank-affiliated VC IPOs show the highest underpricing, and security company-affiliated VCs show the lowest. The difference of the initial returns is significant only between other institution-affiliated VC and non-VC-backed, which does not provide evidence in support of our hypothesis H3a and H4a.

I also find that in the hot market the difference of initial returns among the institutional affiliation VC groups follows the same pattern of the whole IPO sample.

It is found that in the hot market the underpricing of the bank-affiliated is significantly higher than other three groups of IPOs. This finding rejects the H3a. However, in the cold market, I find that IPOs backed by the bank-affiliated VC recorded the lowest underpricing (0.72) among the four groups, while those backed by the security company-affiliated VC showed the second highest

Table 6.3 Underpricing by institutional type of VC-backing on KOSDAQ 1999–2001

	Bank-affiliated VC		Security Company-affiliated VC		Other Institution-affiliated VC		Non-VC-backed		Significance[1]
	Mean	Median	Mean	Median	Mean	Median	Mean	Median	
(A) Total									
Underpricing (No. IPOs)	(a) 2.33 (32)	1.26	(b) 1.29 (19)	1.19	(c) 2.06 (122)	1.15	(d) 1.49 (199)	1.00	c>d at 10%
(B) Hot Market									
Underpricing (No. IPOs)	(e) 4.68 (13)	4.43	(f) 1.48 (5)	2.00	(g) 3.54 (45)	2.38	(h) 2.00 (64)	1.34	e>f at 5% e>g at 10% e>h at 1% g>h at 1%
(C) Cold Market									
Underpricing (No. IPOs)	(i) 0.72 (19)	0.58	(j) 1.22 (14)	0.86	(k) 1.19 (77)	0.89	(l) 1.25 (135)	1.00	
Significance[2]	1) e>i at 1%				g>k at 1%		h>l at 5%		

Source: Korean Information System, IPO prospectuses

Note 1) Significance of mean difference between groups by Kruskal-Wallis test

Note 2) Significance of mean difference between hot and cold markets for each group by Mann-Whitney test

underpricing (1.22). In the cold market I find no statistically significant difference which is also inconsistent with our hypotheses 3a and 4a. Furthermore, the comparison of initial returns across rows between hot and cold markets shows that the different institutional types of VC-backing showed significantly higher underpricing in the hot market than in the cold market generally.

Table 6.4 compares the initial returns of IPOs backed by bank-affiliated VC, security company-affiliated VC and other institution-affiliated VC cross-classified

Table 6.4 underpricing by institutional type of VC-backing with the age, size, and industry of IPOs and the hotness of the market on KOSDAQ 1999–2001

	Mean	Median	Mean	Median	T-statistics by t-test	Z-scores by Mann-Whitney test
(A) Hot Market Issue						
	Hot market		Cold market			
Banks-affiliated VC (a)	4.68	*4.43*	0.72	*0.58*	5.64***	−4.28***
(No. IPOs)	(13)		(19)			
Security Co.-affiliated VC (b)	1.48	*2.00*	1.22	*0.86*	0.39	−0.88
(No. IPOs)	(5)		(14)			
Other Institu.-affiliated VC I	3.54	*2.38*	1.19	*0.89*	4.78***	−5.14***
(No. IPOs)	(45)		(77)			
Significance[1]	a > b at 5% a > c at 10% level		-			
(B) Age						
	Young		Old			
Banks-affiliated VC (d)	2.54	*1.06*	2.01	*1.42*	0.53	−0.40
(No. IPOs)	(19)		(13)			
Security Co.-affiliated VC I	1.41	*1.19*	0.85	*0.66*	0.77	−0.65
(No. IPOs)	(15)		(4)			
Other Institu.- affiliated VC (f)	2.51	*1.25*	1.29	*0.98*	2.32**	−1.80*
(No. IPOs)	(77)		(45)			
Significance	-		-			
I Market Capitalisation						
	Small		Big			
Banks-affiliated VC (g)	2.85	*1.73*	1.80	*0.50*	1.08	−2.11**
(No. IPOs)	(16)		(16)			
Security Co.-affiliated VC (h)	2.30	*1.67*	1.10	*1.10*	1.56	−0.39
(No. IPOs)	(3)		(16)			
Other Institu.- affiliated VC (i)	2.29	*1.85*	1.91	*0.93*	0.72	−2.74***
(No. IPOs)	(48)		(74)			
Significance	-		-			

(Continued)

Table 6.4 (Continued)

	Mean	Median	Mean	Median	T-statistics by t-test	Z-scores by Mann-Whitney test
(D) Industry						
	High-tech		Non-high-tech			
Banks-affiliated VC (j)	2.29	1.26	2.56	1.92	−0.19	−0.74
(No. IPOs)	(28)		(4)			
Security Co.-affiliated VC (k)	1.44	1.20	0.72	0.43	1.02	−1.05
(No. IPOs)	(15)		(4)			
Other Institu.- affiliated VC (l)	1.90	1.11	2.51	1.21	−1.05	−1.56
(No. IPOs)	(90)		(32)			
Significance	-		l > k at 10%			

Note 1) Significance of mean difference between groups by Kruskal-Wallis test
Asterisks denote significance levels at the level 1% (***), 5% (**), and 10% (*).

by hot market issue, age, market capitalisation, and industry. It is shown that the IPOs backed by three different organisations of VCs all show higher underpricing in the hot market than in the cold market. The initial return of bank-affiliated case in the hot market is 4.68, compared with 0.72 in the cold market. The security company-affiliated case shows the underpricing of 1.48 in the hot market and 1.22 in the cold market. The other institution-affiliated VC shows the underpricing of 3.54 in the hot market, compared with 1.19 in the cold market. The difference of the initial returns is significant for bank-affiliated and other institution-affiliated at 1 per cent level.[3]

When the IPO firms were divided into age groups, other institution-affiliated VC shows a significant higher underpricing for young firms (2.51) compared with old firms (1.29). Bank-affiliated VC shows higher initial return for young firms (2.54) than old firms (2.01) and security company-affiliated VC also exhibit higher underpricing for young firms (1.41) than old firms (0.85), but the difference of the initial returns for both types of IPOs with young and old firms is not significant. The initial return of young firms is significantly higher than that of old firms in the case of other institution-affiliated VCs. For market capitalisation groups, the underpricing is higher for small firms than big firms in all three cases. The difference of the initial returns is, however, not statistically significant for the security company-affiliated group. There is no difference between high-tech and non-high-tech sectors grouped by three different organisations of VCs.

Furthermore, the comparison of initial returns across rows in each panel seems to show that the difference of initial returns among bank-affiliated, security company-affiliated and other institution-affiliated is not significant for each different types of IPOs, except for the hot market issue and non-high-tech group.

6.5 Underpricing in hot and cold markets with the different types of IPOs

This section compares the initial returns of IPOs in the hot and the cold markets cross-classified by age, size, and industry.[4]

Table 6.5 shows that young firms show significantly higher return than old firms in the hot market. The initial return of young firms is 3.85, compared with 2.00 of old firms. This might be evidence that in the hot market investors required more risk premium on the young firms or the overreaction of investors pulled up the initial prices of young firms. There is no significant difference of initial return between young firms (1.29) and old firms (1.07) in the cold market.

Table 6.5 Underpricing for IPOs cross-classified by VC-backing, age, size, and industry sector in the hot and cold markets on KOSDAQ 1999–2001

	Mean	*Median*	*Mean*	*Median*	*T-statistics by t-test*	*Z-scores by Mann-Whitney test*
(A) Age						
	Young		Old			
Hot Market	3.85	*2.86*	2.00	*1.49*	3.26***	−3.66***
(No. IPOs)	(55)		(72)			
Cold Market	1.29	*0.94*	1.07	*0.78*	1.16	−1.14
(No. IPOs)	(131)		(114)			
T-statistics[1]	6.69***		3.10***			
Z-scores[2]	−6.06***		−3.20***			
(B) Market Capitalisation						
	Small		Big			
Hot Market	2.48	*1.91*	3.35	*2.17*	−1.43	−1.06
(No. IPOs)	(80)		(47)			
Cold Market	1.60	*1.28*	0.88	*0.51*	3.96***	−5.06***
(No. IPOs)	(106)		(139)			
T-statistics	2.74***		6.41***			
Z-scores	−2.16**		−6.21***			
(C) Industry						
	High-tech		Non-high-tech			
Hot Market	3.62	*2.42*	1.89	*1.06*	3.06***	−4.07***
(No. IPOs)	(67)		(60)			
Cold Market	1.55	*0.66*	1.01	*1.00*	2.73***	−2.48**
(No. IPOs)	(80)		(165)			
T-statistics	8.38***		0.87			
Z-scores	−7.85***		−0.36			

Source: Korean Information System, IPO prospectuses

Note 1) T-statistics by t – test between hot and cold markets for each different type of IPOs
Note 2) Z-scores by Mann-Whitney test between hot and cold markets for each different type of IPOs
Asterisks denote significance levels at the level of 1% (***), 5% (**), and 10% (*).

Big firms show insignificantly higher underpricing (3.35) than small firms (2.48) in the hot market. However, in the cold market, the small firms show significantly higher underpricing than big firms. This clearly shows that in the cold market an IPO firm with large size can reduce ex-ante uncertainty on its business operation, and thus investors require less underpricing (Megginson and Weiss, 1991). This effect is lost in the hot market.

I find the significant difference of initial returns between high-tech and non-high-tech groups in both hot and cold markets. In the hot market, high-tech firms show the initial return of 3.62, while non-high-tech firms show 1.89. The difference of these initial returns is significant at 1 per cent level. In the cold market, the degree of initial returns dropped considerably, but the initial return of high-tech group (1.55) is still significantly higher than non-high-tech group (1.01) at 1 per cent level. This could imply that investors demand a greater risk premium on the investment in the high-tech firms.

Furthermore, the comparisons of the initial returns across rows in each panel show that, in almost all of cases, the initial returns are significantly higher in the hot market than in the cold market. Only one category, non-high-tech group, does not show the significant difference between hot market and cold market issue, although in this case hot market issue shows a higher underpricing than cold market issue. It seems to be evident that KOSDAQ IPOs in our sample period make different initial returns in the hot and cold-market period, regardless of the different types of IPOs.

6.6 Multivariate regression analysis of underpricing[5]

So far I have considered univariate and bivariate analyses of underpricing. In this section, I begin our multivariate analysis. The analysis addresses each of the groups of hypotheses I have set out. It follows the structure set out at the end of Chapter 4, which indicated the structure of regression analysis proposed and the expected coefficients sign patterns. In each table in this section, I adopt the format set out in Chapter 4. Each table contains five regressions.

Model 1 tests for the impact of VC-backing (H1a) by including a dummy variable *VC* taking the value of 1 for VC-backed IPOs. *VC* is expected to show negative sign.

Model 2, in the first regime (which includes all sample firms), tests for the impact of VC-backing (H1a) by including *VC* and, in the second regime (which includes VC-backed firms only), tests for the impact of the reputation of VC-backing (H2a) by including dummy variables *VCk* and *VC3* which take the value of 1, when KTB and the big three venture capitalists respectively (KTB, KTI, and KDBC) back IPOs as lead venture capitalists, respectively. *VCk* and *VC3* are expected to show negative signs.

Model 3 and 4 test for the impact of institutional affiliation of VC (H3a and H4a) by including dummy variables *VCbank* and *VCsecu* which take the value of 1, when bank-affiliated VCs and security company-affiliated VCs back IPOs as lead venture capitalists, respectively. *VCbank* is expected to have negative coefficients and *VCsecu* to have positive coefficients.

Model 5 tests for the impact of reputation of underwriter and auditor (H5a and H6a) by including dummy variables *Und3* and *Aud3* which take the value of 1, when big three underwriters and big three auditors are involved with the IPO process and the auditing, respectively. *Und3* and *Aud3* are expected to show negative coefficients. Model 5 also tests for the impact of VC-backing (in the first regime) (H1a) and the reputation of VC-backing (in the second regime) (H2a).

Each of the five regressions is estimated with a constant term and eight variables controlling respectively for the effect of IPO company characteristics (age, market capitalisation, book-to-market ratio, the shareholdings of CEO and his related persons, and high-tech industry) and stock market condition (number of IPOs, market index, and monthly change of market index).

6.6.1 Regression analysis of underpricing for all IPOs

Panel A of Table 6.6 shows that market capitalisation (*LMC*), the book-to-market ratio (*Bmr*), and the shareholding of CEO and his related persons (*ShCEO*) are negatively related to underpricing at 1 per cent or 5 per cent level for all five models. This result is evidence that market capitalisation, the relative size of book value of equity to first-day market capitalisation and the shareholdings of CEO and his related persons functioned positively in reducing underpricing by alleviating *ex-ante* uncertainty of IPO firms.

This negative relationship of market capitalisation is not consistent with the finding in Gompers (1996) and Gompers and Lerner (1999). The negative relationship of the book-to-market ratio is consistent with the finding in Hamao, Packer et al. (2000). The negative coefficients of CEO and his related persons on underpricing are consistent with the finding in Ljungqvist and Wilhelm (2003). Panel A also shows that stock market conditions are closely related to underpricing. The number of IPOs in the last month before an IPO firm gets listed (*NumIPO*) has a negative relationship with underpricing. This is consistent with the demand for IPO stocks being satisfied by a higher supply of shares (Arosio, Giudici et al.,2000). The market index at the last month before an IPO firm get listed (*Kqindex*) and monthly change of market index (*Kqchange*), which is calculated as the difference between the KOSDAQ index of the second last month and that of the last month before an IPO firm comes to listing, have a positive relationship with underpricing. All coefficients in Panel A for these two variables are significant at 1 per cent level. Underpricing seems, therefore, to be positively related to the market index and the monthly change of market index.

In Panel B, which provides estimates based on VC-backed firms only, the significantly negative relationship of the market capitalisation, the book-to-market ratio and the shareholdings of CEO and his related persons with underpricing disappears, but age of firm (*Lage*) comes up as having a negative relationship with underpricing at 5 per cent or 10 per cent level for all five model specifications. This is consistent with our expectation that the older companies will reduce the degree of underpricing by alleviating the information asymmetry problems (Megginson and Weiss, 1991). Panel B also shows that the market index is positively

Table 6.6 Regression on underpricing for all IPOs

	Model 1		Model 2		Model 3		Model 4		Model 5	
Panel A: Regressions for All Sample Firms										
Intercept	7.54	(3.28)***	7.77	(3.27)***	7.18	(3.03)***	7.27	(3.06)***	7.22	(3.11)***
Lage	-0.21	(-1.21)	-0.25	(-1.45)	-0.22	(-1.26)	-0.24	(-1.36)	-0.20	(-1.15)**
LMC	-0.21	(-2.28)**	-0.22	(-2.31)**	-0.19	(-2.02)**	-0.20	(-2.07)**	-0.19	(-2.05)
Bmr	-0.57	(-2.89)***	-0.56	(-2.92)***	-0.56	(-2.85)***	-0.56	(-2.87)***	-0.50	(-2.60)***
ShCEO	-1.50	(-2.64)***	-1.25	(-2.16)**	-1.51	(-2.60)***	-1.39	(-2.38)**	-1.57	(-2.81)***
Hi-Tech	0.13	(0.50)	0.11	(0.42)	0.13	(0.51)	0.11	(0.43)	0.13	(0.51)
NumIPO	-0.04	(-3.12)***	-0.04	(-3.09)***	-0.04	(-3.13)***	-0.04	(-3.13)***	-0.04	(-3.11)***
kqindex	0.01	(4.84)***	0.01	(4.60)***	0.01	(4.79)***	0.01	(4.69)***	0.01	(4.86)***
Kqchange	3.79	(3.25)***	3.89	(3.33)***	3.93	(3.31)***	4.00	(3.38)***	3.81	(3.26)***
VC	-0.12	(-0.47)	-0.10	(-0.45)					-0.11	(-0.44)
VCbank					-0.12	(-0.29)	-0.15	(-0.36)		
VCsecu					-0.81	(-1.91)*	-0.77	(-1.79)*		
VCetc					-0.01	(-0.04)	-0.02	(-0.08)		
Bank			0.47	(1.21)			0.46	(1.19)		
Secu			0.26	(0.59)						
Und3									-0.25	(-0.83)
Aud3									-0.19	(-0.91)
AdjustedR	0.25		0.25		0.25		0.26		0.25	
Prob > F	0.00		0.00		0.00		0.00		0.00	
No. IPOs	372		372		372		372		372	

Panel B: Regressions for VC–backed Firms Only

	(1)	(2)	(3)	(4)	(5)
Intercept	9.03 (1.73)*	9.51 (1.84)*	8.13 (1.43)	8.25 (1.44)	9.32 (1.75)*
Lage	-0.46 (-1.86)*	-0.55 (-1.98)**	-0.51 (-1.94)*	-0.55 (-2.09)**	-0.50 (-1.85)*
LMC	-0.27 (-1.34)	-0.29 (-1.47)	-0.25 (-1.19)	-0.25 (-1.20)	-0.27 (-1.31)
Bmr	-1.73 (-1.52)	-1.73 (-1.51)	-1.74 (-1.57)	-1.68 (-1.50)	-1.69 (-1.50)
ShCEO	-1.51 (-1.24)	-1.21 (-0.85)	-1.60 (-1.27)	-1.40 (-1.03)	-1.60 (-1.37)
Hi-Tech	-0.08 (-0.16)	-0.07 (-0.13)	-0.10 (-0.19)	-0.09 (-0.18)	-0.13 (-0.24)
NumIPO	-0.03 (-1.61)	-0.03 (-1.58)	-0.03 (-1.61)	-0.03 (-1.63)	-0.03 (-1.65)
kqindex	0.02 (3.39)***	0.02 (3.46)***	0.02 (3.45)***	0.02 (3.48)***	0.02 (3.52)***
Kqchange	4.29 (2.46)**	4.26 (2.46)**	4.48 (2.50)**	4.48 (2.49)**	4.23 (2.42)**
VCk	-0.31 (-0.87)				
VC3		0.01 (0.01)	0.53 (0.91)	0.47 (0.82)	-0.01 (-0.03)
VCbank			0.73 (1.42)	0.69 (1.29)	
VCetc				0.32 (0.68)	
Bank		0.37 (0.81)			
Secu		0.12 (0.22)			
Und3					0.04 (0.07)
Aud3					-0.39 (-1.13)
AdjustedR	0.33	0.33	0.34	0.34	0.33
Prob > F	0.00	0.00	0.00	0.00	0.00
No.IPOs	173	173	173	173	173

Note: This table reports regression coefficients of underpricing of IPOs on various independent variables. The definition of independent variables is same with that of Table 4.5. T-statistics in the parentheses are heteroskedasicity consistent. VCsecu in Panel B was dropped in the regressions. Asterisks beside t-statistics *, **, *** denote significance at 10%, 5%, 1% level, respectively.

related to underpricing at 1 per cent level and that the monthly change of market index has a positive relationship with underpricing at 5 per cent level, as was the case for the sample as a whole.

In terms of our hypotheses using each of the five models, I find that, in Panel A for the whole sample, Model 1 and 2 show that there is no effect for VC-backing. Model 2 also shows that the shareholdings of banks (*Bank*) and security companies (*Secu*) in addition to VC-backing have no impact on R-square and produce insignificant coefficients on those variables. In model 3 which tests for the impact of different types of institutional ownership of VC-backing, the result is generally insignificant, although in keeping with our univariate results I found significantly negative coefficients for security company-affiliated VC (*VCsecu*) at 10 per cent level. This result is repeated in Model 4. These significantly minus coefficients of security company-affiliated VC (*VCsecu*) reject our hypothesis H4a (more underpricing by the backing of security company-affiliated VCs). There is no evidence of less underpricing by bank-affiliated VCs in Model 3 and Model 4, thus showing no support for the hypothesis H3a. Finally, Model 5, which tests for the impact of underwriter and auditor reputation, yields insignificant results. Panel B reveals that, for the VC-backed firms, there is no significant evidence of the impact of VC-backing, the reputation of VC-backing, the institutional affiliation of VC-backing and the reputation of underwriter and auditors, respectively.

The multivariate regression on the underpricing for the samples in the whole period does not provide evidence in support of our hypothesis H1a, H2a, H3a, H4a, H5a and H6a. Rather, the coefficients results in the Model 3 and 4 of Panel A suggest that security company-affiliated VCs are related to less underpricing, thus rejecting the hypothesis H4a.

6.6.2 Regression analysis of underpricing for IPOs in hot market

So far I have analysed the data over the whole period 1999–2001. Now I turn to the regression results for the IPOs in the hot-market period.

Table 6.7 shows the coefficients results of underpricing of IPO firms in the hot-market period. The coefficient signs of control variables in Table 6.7 are generally consistent with those of Table 6.6. The age of the firm (*Lage*) has a significantly negative relationship with underpricing in Panel A. The book-to-market ration (*Bmr*) is also negative related with underpricing in the Model 1 of Panel B at 10 per cent level. The shareholdings of CEO and his related persons (*ShCEO*) also turns out to be negatively related to underpricing in three models of Panel A. This result is consistent with our expectation that these variables may act as alleviating uncertainty of the IPO firms, thus contributing to the reduction of the underpricing.

A noteworthy result in this table is that the dummy variable indicating high-tech industry has a significantly positive relationship with underpricing at 5 per cent or 10 per cent level in all models of Panel A and at 10 per cent level in Model 1 of Panel B. These positive signs of coefficients are consistent with our expectation. The investors are likely to require a higher risk premium on high-tech firms.

Table 6.7 Regression on underpricing for the IPOs in hot market

	Model 1		Model 2		Model 3		Model 4		Model 5	
Panel A: Regressions for All Sample Firms										
Intercept	-0.40	(-0.10)	-0.13	(-0.03)	-3.58	(-0.85)	-3.45	(-0.81)	-1.59	(-0.39)
Lage	-0.86	(-2.06)**	-0.89	(-2.22)**	-0.72	(-1.72)*	-0.74	(-1.79)*	-0.78	(-1.87)*
LMC	-0.01	(-0.06)	-0.03	(-0.25)	0.08	(0.62)	0.07	(0.51)	0.04	(0.34)
Bmr	0.23	(0.80)	0.24	(0.84)	0.27	(0.92)	0.27	(0.91)	0.43	(1.39)
ShCEO	-2.60	(-1.82)*	-1.94	(-1.36)	-2.57	(-1.77)*	-2.32	(-1.55)	-2.78	(-1.88)*
Hi-Tech	0.98	(2.03)**	0.95	(1.85)*	1.06	(2.09)**	1.01	(1.96)*	1.03	(2.03)**
NumIPO	-0.05	(-2.24)**	-0.05	(-2.17)**	-0.06	(-2.43)**	-0.06	(-2.44)**	-0.05	(-2.24)**
kqindex	0.03	(2.39)**	0.03	(2.23)**	0.03	(2.58)***	0.04	(2.58)**	0.03	(2.53)**
Kqchange	7.86	(3.37)***	7.80	(3.28)***	8.86	(3.44)***	8.76	(3.31)***	7.73	(3.49)***
VC	0.44	(0.62)	0.49	(0.74)					0.44	(0.60)
VCbank					0.87	(0.83)	0.80	(0.77)		
VCsecu					-2.90	(-2.99)***	-2.79	(-2.73)***		
VCetc					0.80	(1.05)	0.80	(1.04)		
Bank			1.30	(1.43)			1.11	(1.22)		
Secu			0.58	(0.50)						
Und3									-0.53	(-0.71)
Aud3									-0.64	(-1.31)
AdjustedR	0.29		0.30		0.33		0.34		0.30	
Prob> F	0.00		0.00		0.00		0.00		0.00	
No. IPOs	372		372		372		372		372	

(Continued)

Table 6.7 (Continued)

	Model 1		Model 2		Model 3		Model 4		Model 5	
Panel B: Regressions for VC-backed Firms Only										
Intercept	-5.44	(-0.63)	-4.34	(-0.49)	-12.12	(-1.45)	-14.95	(-1.56)	-5.62	(-0.65)
Lage	-0.63	(-0.70)	-1.17	(-1.43)	-1.15	(-1.25)	-1.25	(-1.44)	-0.86	(-0.89)
LMC	-0.01	(-0.05)	-0.08	(-0.29)	0.21	(0.73)	0.16	(0.52)	-0.03	(-0.09)
Bwr	-5.30	(-1.79)*	-3.75	(-1.26)	-1.01	(-0.36)	-1.03	(-0.38)	-4.01	(-1.47)
ShCEO	-3.10	(-1.30)	-2.44	(-0.83)	-3.84	(-1.66)	-3.20	(-1.29)	-3.62	(-1.46)
Hi-Tech	1.34	(1.68)*	1.25	(1.66)	1.09	(1.51)	1.16	(1.65)	1.11	(1.44)
NumIPO	-0.07	(-1.74)*	-0.08	(-1.71)*	-0.09	(-1.98)*	-0.09	(-1.96)*	-0.08	(-1.83)*
Kqindex	0.06	(1.92)*	0.07	(1.87)*	0.08	(2.33)**	0.08	(2.28)**	0.07	(2.13)**
Kqchange	2.57	(0.85)	2.98	(0.94)	6.58	(1.66)	6.16	(1.46)	2.94	(0.89)
VCk	-1.36	(-1.59)								
VC3			-0.20	(-0.18)					-0.41	(-0.38)
VCbank					-3.82	(-3.21)***	3.51	(2.69)***		
VCsecu					0.06	(0.06)				
VCetc							3.68	(2.21)**		
Bank			1.67	(1.64)			1.20	(1.02)		
Secu			-0.08	(-0.07)						
Und3									0.21	(0.19)
Aud3									-1.01	(-0.91)
AdjustedR	0.35		0.34		0.39		0.40		0.34	
Prob> F	0.01		0.00		0.00		0.00		0.02	
. IPOs	173		173		173		173		173	

Note: This table reports regression coefficients of underpricing of IPOs on various independent variables. The definition of independent variables is same with that of Table 4.5. T-statistics in the parentheses are heteroskedasicity consistent. *VCbank* in Model 3 of Panel B and *VCsecu* in Model 4 of Panel B were dropped in the regressions. Asterisks beside t-statistics *, **, *** denote significance at 10%, 5%, 1% level, respectively.

However, since the high-tech effect was insignificant for the period as a whole in Table 6.6, the results here might be evidence that high-tech firms were hugely affected by the hot market sentiment on the high-tech stocks that listed in the late 1990s and 2000.

The control variables regarding the stock market situation show significant coefficients in almost all of the model specifications. The number of IPOs (*NumIPO*) has a positive relationship with underpricing at 5 per cent level in all models of Panel A and at 10 per cent level in all models of Panel B. This is a clear evidence that when the stock market is " watered down" by the high number of IPOs, the initial return of IPO firms tends to go down. The market index (*Kqindex*) is positively related to underpricing at 5 per cent level in all models of Panel A and 5 per cent or 10 per cent level in all models of Panel B. The monthly change of market index (*Kqchange*) turned out to have a profound impact on the underpricing in the hot market. The coefficients of monthly change of market index range from 7.73 to 8.86 in all models of Panel A at 1 per cent level. Even though the significance disappears in Panel B, probably due to the interaction of the variables in the regression procedures, the coefficients of monthly change of market index in Panel B ranges from 2.57 to 6.58. These coefficients are higher than for the period as a whole, suggesting that the initial returns are correlated to the movement of stock market trend (Ibbotson, Sindelar et al.,1994) and even more strongly connected with the hot-market period.

Panel A shows that the coefficients of our hypotheses indicators are generally consistent with those of the regressions for the samples in the whole period. In Model 3 and 4, the impact of security company-affiliated VC (*VCsecu*) is even stronger than in the period as a whole. None of the other variables included to test our hypotheses in Models 1, 2, and 5 is significant in the hot period as was the case for the period as a whole. Panel B shows that within the VC-backed group there is a significantly negative coefficient for security company-affiliated VC (*VCsecu*) in Model 3 and a significantly positive coefficient for bank-affiliated VC (*VCbank*) in Model 4. It is not clear that the reduction of underpricing produced by backing of security company-affiliated VCs may be caused by their certification for the IPO firm. Equally it may indicate that IPOs backed by security company-affiliated VC were not as highly evaluated by investors in the hot-market period. The positive relationship of bank-affiliated VC with the underpricing may imply that the IPOs backed by bank-affiliated VC attracted over-reactive investors in the hot market situation. The positive coefficient of bank-affiliated VCs and the negative coefficient of security company-affiliated VCs indicate that I must reject hypotheses H3a and H4a, which expect that bank-affiliated VCs will show negative relationship with underpricing and security company-affiliated VCs positive relationship with underpricing.

6.6.3 Regression analysis of underpricing for IPOs in cold market

In Table 6.8, the regression results for the cold market are presented.

The control variables relating to IPO characteristics show a consistent sign of coefficients with the cases of the hot market. The market capitalisation (*LMC*)

Table 6.8 Regression on underpricing for the IPOs in cold market

	Model 1		Model 2		Model 3		Model 4		Model 5	
Panel A: Regressions for All Sample Firms										
Intercept	14.28	(4.15)***	14.23	(4.10)***	14.64	(4.26)***	14.62	(4.25)***	14.22	(4.21)***
Lage	−0.05	(−0.40)	−0.04	(−0.29)	−0.04	(−0.27)	−0.03	(−0.23)	−0.02	(−0.18)
LMC	−0.52	(−3.56)***	−0.52	(−3.52)***	−0.54	(−3.67)***	−0.54	(−3.67)***	−0.52	(−3.59)***
Bmr	0.08	(0.20)	0.09	(0.22)	0.07	(0.16)	0.07	(0.18)	0.07	(0.17)
SbCEO	−0.56	(−1.32)	−0.61	(−1.34)	−0.58	(−1.40)	−0.61	(−1.44)	−0.70	(−1.66)*
Hi–Tech	−0.14	(−0.67)	−0.13	(−0.62)	−0.14	(−0.67)	−0.14	(−0.64)	−0.16	(−0.76)
NumIPO	−0.06	(−6.20)***	−0.06	(−6.14)***	−0.06	(−6.22)***	−0.06	(−6.18)***	−0.07	(−6.25)***
kqindex	0.02	(3.50)***	0.02	(3.43)***	0.02	(3.59)***	0.02	(3.57)***	0.02	(3.52)***
Kqchange	1.76	(2.17)**	1.70	(2.04)**	1.61	(1.96)*	1.57	(1.88)*	1.65	(1.97)**
VC	−0.19	(−1.11)	−0.19	(−1.07)					−0.17	(−0.99)
VCbank					−0.73	(−3.35)***	−0.72	(−3.34)***		
VCsecu					0.19	(0.50)	0.19	(0.49)		
VCetc					−0.12	(−0.64)	−0.12	(−0.61)		
Bank			−0.14	(−0.52)			−0.10	(−0.37)		
Secu			−0.04	(−0.17)						
Und3									−0.35	(−1.76)*
Aud3									0.18	(1.11)
AdjustedR	0.32		0.32		0.34		0.34		0.33	
Prob> F	0.00		0.00		0.00		0.00		0.00	
No.IPOs	372		372		372		372		372	

Panel B: Regressions for VC–backed Firms Only

	(1)	(2)	(3)	(4)	(5)
Intercept	23.36 (3.41)***	23.09 (3.35)***	23.97 (3.77)***	24.04 (3.80)***	22.48 (3.16)***
Lage	-0.01 (-0.06)	0.06 (0.33)	0.06 (0.39)	0.11 (0.64)	0.01 (0.05)
LMC	-0.85 (-3.22)***	-0.83 (-3.16)***	-0.90 (-3.63)***	-0.90 (-3.64)***	-0.80 (-2.93)***
Bmr	-1.89 (-2.49)**	-1.82 (-2.35)**	-1.95 (-2.86)***	-2.00 (-2.92)***	-1.65 (-2.05)**
SbCEO	-1.21 (-1.31)	-1.49 (-1.42)	-1.40 (-1.57)	-1.65 (-1.69)*	-1.30 (-1.37)
Hi–Tech	-0.97 (-2.20)**	-0.95 (-2.11)**	-0.97 (-2.33)**	-0.97 (-2.31)**	-0.99 (-2.20)**
NumIPO	-0.05 (-4.37)***	-0.05 (-4.26)***	-0.05 (-4.59)***	-0.05 (-4.49)***	-0.05 (-4.51)***
kqindex	0.01 (3.09)***	0.01 (3.00)***	0.01 (3.57)***	0.01 (3.56)***	0.01 (2.81)***
Kqchange	2.23 (2.09)**	2.05 (1.93)*	1.79 (1.67)*	1.69 (1.56)	2.11 (1.96)*
VClk	0.11 (0.39)				
VC3		-0.14 (-0.60)			-0.17 (-0.71)
VCsecu			1.08 (2.39)**	1.03 (2.35)**	
VCetc			0.73 (2.94)***	0.72 (2.96)***	
Bank	-0.44 (-1.58)			-0.37 (-1.57)	
Secu	0.02 (0.07)				
Und3					-0.13 (-0.50)
Aud3					-0.09 (-0.47)
AdjustedR	0.45	0.46	0.50	0.50	0.45
Prob> F	0.00	0.00	0.00	0.00	0.00
No. IPOs	173	173	173	173	173

Note: This table reports regression coefficients of underpricing of IPOs on various independent variables. The definition of independent variables is same with that of Table 4.5. T-statistics in the parentheses are heteroskedasicity consistent. *VCbank* in Panel B was dropped in the regressions. Asterisks beside t-statistics *, **, *** denote significance at 10%, 5%, 1% level, respectively.

has a significantly negative relationship with underpricing in all models of Panel A and Panel B at 1 per cent level. The book-to-market ratios (*Bmr*) are also negatively related to underpricing at 1 per cent or 5 per cent level in all models of Panel B. The shareholding of CEO and this related persons (*ShCEO*) is significant in Model 5 of Panel A. A noteworthy result is that the high-tech firms (*Hi-Tech*) had a negative impact on underpricing in the cold market. In all models of panel B, the coefficients of high-tech industry are negative at 5 per cent level. This may imply that the revised opinion on the high-tech firms after the crash of high-tech stock boom led to weak price reactions after IPO. The stock market situation seems to influence the degree of underpricing in the cold market consistently in the same way that it did in the hot market. The Number of IPOs (*NumIPO*) has a significantly negative relationship with underpricing in all the models of Panel A and Panel B at 1 per cent level. The Market index (*Kqindex*) and Monthly change of market index (*Kqchange*) have a significantly positive relationship with underpricing, too. However, the impact of monthly change of market index on underpricing is lower in the cold market, compared with the hot market, since the coefficients of monthly change of market index are reduced considerably, although they are still significant.

The coefficients on our hypotheses indicators in the cold-market period are in striking contrast with those of the whole sample and the hot-market period. While, as in the cases of the regression for the samples for the whole period and the hot-market period, there is no evidence in support of the VC-backing and the reputation of VC-backing (hypotheses H1a and H2a), the coefficient results of the institutional affiliation of VC-backing show significant evidence in support of the hypothesis H3a and H4a. Model 3 and Model 4 of Panel A shows that the bank-affiliated VC has a significantly negative relationship with underpricing at 1 per cent level.

However, security company-affiliated VC shows significantly positive relationship with underpricing in Models 3 and 4 of Panel B at 5 per cent level. Other institution-affiliated VC shows positive, but not as high as security company-affiliated, coefficients in Models 3 and 4 of Panel B. This clearly shows that bank-affiliated VC played a role in certifying IPO firms, thus lessening the extent of underpricing. The higher significantly positive coefficients of security company-affiliated VC may be evidence that security company-affiliated VC may incur the conflict of interest between issuing firms and investors, so that the investors require more risk premium on the purchase of the shares (Gompers and Lerner, 1999; Hamao, Packer et al.,2000). These results clearly support the impact of underpricing by bank-affiliated VCs (H3a) and the impact of security company-affiliated VCs (H4a). Furthermore, Model 5 of Panel A also finds evidence that the reputation of underwriter (*Und3*) leads to less underpricing at 10 per cent level, thus supporting the hypothesis H5a.

The conflicting results of institutional affiliation of VC-backing in the hot market and the cold market are interesting.[6] It seems that, in the hot market where the demand for shares exceeds the supply of shares, overreaction of investors tends to lean towards the IPO stocks. In this case, regardless IPO shares pricing, investors may pull up the prices of IPO stocks at the initial period, especially if they are considered as a good target for the investment. However, in the cold market where the demand of shares is likely to be not enough to purchase all the shares, issuing firms should allow for underpricing to occur in order to attract investors by assuring a high initial return (Rock, 1986; Ritter, 1998). However, the reputable financial player that reduces the information asymmetry between issuer and investor can alleviate the degree of underpricing (Carter and Manaster, 1990). Therefore, the significantly negative relationship of bank-affiliated VC with underpricing in the cold market may show that the bank-affiliated VC was recognised as certifying the IPO firm by reducing information asymmetry problems. On the other hand, the significantly positive relationship of security company-affiliated VC with underpricing in the cold market may indicate that the security company-affiliated VC may incur the conflict of interest due to the possibility that they may overprice an IPO firm. However, I can see that in the hot market the underpricing based on the information asymmetry and the certifying agent does not realise in the pattern I expect in the cold market. IPO stocks backed by more reputable financial players are likely to be evaluated highly by investors at the initial stage of IPOs, thus with prices of the IPO firms rising sharply for a short period after IPO.

It seems that the cold market fits our hypotheses relating to information asymmetry and the certifying role of the financial agents but the hot market does not. Loughran and Ritter (2002) argued the underpricing theory relating to information asymmetry and the certifying role of financial agents is for the period 1980s when the stock market return did not experience as enormous initial returns as in the late 1990s and early 2000. I find that our underpricing hypotheses based on the traditional information asymmetries theories were rejected in the whole period and the hot-market period, but worked well in the cold-market period, thus in line with Loughran and Ritter (2002)'s argument.

6.7 Summary of the chapter

In this chapter, I presented the results of univariate, bivariate and multivariate analyses of underpricing.

Section 6.2 compared the underpricing between different types of IPO firms. The underpricing of VC-backed IPO is significantly higher than that of non-VC-backed IPO throughout the whole sample period. This difference rejects the H1a, contrary to our expectation that venture capitalists will reduce the extent of underpricing as a financial agent who certifies the VC-backed IPO firms. This result is not consistent in the finding of Megginson and Weiss (1991) who found a decrease of underpricing for the IPOs when venture capitalists participated in the ownership of the firms. However, our results is consistent with the findings in Francis and Hasan (2001) and Smart and Zutter (2000), both of which used US data of hot market in late 1990s. Section 6.2 also shows that the IPO firm brought to KOSDAQ in the hot issue market recorded significantly higher initial returns than those in the cold issue market. This result obviously shows that the initial returns are closely correlated with market conditions (Ibbotson, Sindelar et al., 1994; Lowry and Schwert, 2002). Further analysis of underpricing based on the groups divided by age and market capitalisation shows that the initial returns of young and small firms are significantly higher than those that of old and big firms, respectively. However, I do not find any significant difference of initial returns for high-tech and non-high-tech groups.

More detailed analysis of underpricing by VC-backed IPOs and non-VC-backed IPOs respectively on their relationship with other types of IPOs in the Section 6.3 generally confirms the results that were found in Section 6.2. However, I find that the difference of underpricing in the hot and cold market is insignificant for the non-VC-backed cases, even though the initial return of VC-backing is significantly higher for hot market issues than for cold market issues.

Section 6.4 exhibits the initial returns according to the institutional affiliation of VC-backing and non-VC-backed IPOs. I showed that the initial return of the bank-affiliated VC is higher than the other groups, although the difference is not significant. However, in the hot market, the IPOs backed by bank-affiliated VC experiences significantly higher underpricing, while the IPOs backed by security company-affiliated VC shows significantly lower underpricing. This result is contradictory to our hypotheses H3a and H4a, which expects that the bank-affiliated case will show less underpricing and the security company-affiliated will show higher underpricing. However, in the cold market, the bank-affiliated VC shows the lowest underpricing, compared with the second highest underpricing of security company-affiliated VC, although the differences of initial returns among the groups is insignificant. This section shows that the underpricing rank shown by bank-affiliated VC and security company-affiliated VC is reversed in the hot and cold market. This finding may imply that the hypothesis linked to financial agency that certifies the IPO firms who are suffering from the information asymmetry is relevant in the cold market situation, but not in the hot market situation (Loughran and Ritter, 2002). Further analysis of underpricing by the institutional difference of VC-backing and non-VC-backed IPOs respectively on their relationship with other types of IPOs generally confirms the results that were found in Section 6.2.

Section 6.5 displays the initial returns of IPOs in the hot market and in the cold market across different types of IPOs. I find that in the hot market VC-backed IPO recorded a significantly higher initial return than non-VC-backed IPOs. However, there is not a significant difference in initial returns between VC-backed-IPOs and non-VC-backed in the cold market. Furthermore, the young firms show significantly higher return than the old firms in the hot market and the small firms show significantly higher underpricing than big firms in the cold market. In addition, I find a significant difference of initial returns between high-tech and non-high-tech groups when they are examined in relation to hot and cold market. In both the hot market and the cold market, the initial returns of high-tech firms are significantly higher than those of non-high-tech firms, consistent with other studies (e.g. Schultz and Zaman, 2001). This effect of market overreaction to the high-tech stocks still existed in the cold-market period.

Section 6.6 reports a regression analysis of underpricing. The results of regressions for the IPOs throughout the whole sample period show that there is little evidence in support our Hypotheses. The significantly negative coefficients of security company-affiliated VC rejects the H4a, contrary to our expectation that security company-affiliated VC may cause conflict of interests between issuer and investors, thus leading to more underpricing (Gompers and Lerner, 1999; Hamao, Packer et al., 2000). The results show that it is the firm characteristics and the stock market situation that has greater relationship with underpricing of KOSDAQ IPO firms. Section 6.6 also shows the results of an analysis of underpricing in the hot-market period. The analysis finds that there is little evidence supporting our hypotheses. Rather, the coefficients of bank-affiliated VC and the security company-affiliated VC present the opposite signs to those expected for the H3a and H4a. It is shown that security company-affiliated VCs reduce the underpricing most, compared with bank-affiliated VCs and other institution-affiliated VCs. The coefficients and signs of firm characteristics and stock market situation in the hot-market period are generally consistent with those of regressions for the whole period. Section 6.6 finally reports the coefficients of underpricing of IPO firms in the cold market. I do not find significant evidence in support of the H1a and H2a in the regression results. However, the dummy variables relating to the institutional difference of VC-backing and the reputation of underwriter show evidence in support of the H3a and the H4a. The bank-affiliated VCs have a significantly negative relationship with underpricing, while the security company-affiliated VC shows a significantly positive relationship with underpricing. The higher underpricing of security company-affiliated VC is consistent with the finding in the Gompers and Lerner (1999). The reduction of underpricing by reputable underwriter is also consistent with the finding in Carter and Manaster (1990) and Carter, Dark et al. (1998). However our analysis shows that these predicted relationships did not survive in the hot-market period.

Notes

1 Note that, in this table and the remainder of the book, underpricing and long-term performance are reported as absolute proportional change with two decimal points, not as per centages.
2 Actually, I could not separate an underpricing into a risk premium required by investors and an excess demand return that occurred in the hot market. I need to work out a model to split up these two different factors of underpricing, which comprises a potential research question.
3 In interpreting the results for the security company-affiliated VCs, it is important to note that there are only 19 cases of security company-affiliated VCs. So I are dealing with small sample sizes. Our non-parametric test is still robust in these circumstances (Conover, 1980).
4 Cross-classification by state of the market and VC-backing is removed in this section, because this part is already discussed in Section 6.3.
5 Parts of multivariate analysis in this chapter were extended to another analysis in "The Hot and Cold Market Impacts on Underpricing of Certification, Reputation and Conflicts of Interest in Venture Capital Backed Korean IPO" by Jaeho Lee from *Korean Venture Management Review*, 12(4) (2009) with different results.

6 Actually, the coefficients of the dummy variables relating to VC-backing and the reputation of VC-backing had a tendency to show contradictory results in the hot market and the cold market, even though the coefficients are not significant. The coefficient of VC-backing (*VC*) was positive in the hot market, but negative in the cold market. On the contrary, the coefficient of the reputation of VC-backing (VCk) was negative in the hot market, but positive in the cold market. However, another variable relating to the reputation of VC-backing (*VC3*) is negative in both the hot and cold market. The coefficients of underwriter and auditor reputation (*Und3* and *Aud3*) are not consistently opposite in the hot and cold market unlike those of VC-backing and the reputation of VC-backing.

7 Long-term performance

7.1 Overview

This chapter presents the results of univariate and multivariate analysis of long-term performance. Long-term performance is, as discussed in Chapter 4, measured by the buy-and-hold abnormal return (BHAR) of IPO firms, which is calculated as a difference between the closing price on the first day that did not hit the daily upper limit and the price at twelve- and twenty-four months after that.[1] The BHARs are adjusted by various types of benchmarks as has been explained in Chapter 4.[2]

Section 7.2 compares the long-term performance of IPOs, grouped by venture-capital-backing (VC-backed and non-VC-backed), hot issue market (hot and cold market), age (young and old), market capitalisation (small and big), and industry (high-tech and non-high-tech), respectively. In this section, hypothesis H1b (the impact of VC-backing on long-term performance) is tested. Section 7.3 extends the analysis of Section 7.2 by comparing the long-term performance of VC-backed IPOs and non-VC-backed IPOs separately, grouped by hot issue market, age, market capitalisation and industry. In section 7.4, I compare the long-term performance of different types of VC affiliation: bank-affiliated, security company-affiliated, other institution-affiliated and non-VC-backed. In this section, hypothesis H3b (the impact of bank-affiliated VC-backing on long-term performance) and H4b (the impact of security company-affiliated VC-backing) are tested. In section 7.5, I compare the long-term performance in hot and cold markets of IPOs grouped by venture-capital-backing, age, market capitalisation and industry. In this section, hypothesis H1b (impact of VC-backing on long-term performance) is tested. Section 7.6 documents the result of multiple regressions on long-term performance. I implemented regressions for the whole period 1999–2001, the hot-market period and the cold-market period, respectively. For each period, BHARs are adjusted by KOSDAQ, SIMF, and SBMP benchmarks. Five models are estimated in each period for all sample firms (regardless of VC-backing) and for VC-backed firms only. These models correspond to our groups of hypotheses set out in Chapter 4. In this section, all hypotheses are tested.

7.2 Long-term performance by different types of IPOs[3]

7.2.1 BHARs of VC-backed vs non-VC-Backed IPOs

In the tables which follow, I provide univariate test results measuring long-term performance of VC-backed and non-VC-backed IPOs against a variety of benchmarks as discussed in Chapter 4. To help interpretation, it is useful to begin by summarising graphically how the choice of benchmark may affect the pattern of returns. I therefore present six figures that show the graphical patterns of raw, benchmark and adjusted BHARs of VC-backed and non-VC-backed IPOs. These figures are designed to illustrate the effects of using different benchmarks. They are based on the IPOs in the hot-market period at twenty-four month as well as twelve month returns.

Figure 7.1(a) shows three charts of VC-backed IPOs. Raw return shows the decreasing pattern from the first adjusted day of IPO through twelve months to twenty-four months. While the KOSDAQ benchmark return shows the same decreasing pattern as raw return from the IPO day to twenty-four months, other benchmark returns show an almost similar (KSE, SIMF, SBMF) or increasing trend (SBMP) of return from twelve months to twenty-four months after showing a sharply decreasing pattern from the IPO day to twelve months.[4] The difference in benchmark returns tended to be bigger for the twenty-four month return than for the twelve month return. After twenty-four months, the SBMP benchmark return is the highest, while the KOSDAQ benchmark return is the lowest. The benchmark-adjusted returns after twelve- and twenty-four months show a considerable decline relative to the first IPO day, except for the KOSDAQ-adjusted BHAR. While KOSDAQ-adjusted BHARs did not change considerably between twelve and twenty-four months, other benchmark-adjusted BHARs clearly show the decreasing pattern from twelve month to twenty-four month. The KOSDAQ-adjusted BHAR shows outperformance which is larger than zero after twenty-four month, but other benchmark-adjusted BHARs are located below the zero point which indicates underperformance. The SBMP-adjusted BHAR is shown to decline most considerably from twelve month to twenty-four month. So the choice of benchmark clearly matters. Figure 7.1(b) shows three charts of non-VC-backed IPOs. The changing pattern of raw, benchmark and adjusted returns is almost same with that of VC-backed IPOs. Raw return goes down considerably by twelve and twenty-four months, compared with the first day of IPO. However, the fall in raw return between twelve months and twenty-four months is smaller than that of VC-backed IPO. While the benchmark returns show a similar pattern to VC-backed IPOs benchmarks, the difference of the returns looks greater for non-VC-backed case than VC-backed one. As a result, KOSDAQ-adjusted BHAR increased from twelve month to twenty-four month due to the severe underperformance of KOSDAQ benchmark return, even though the raw return slightly declined over the same period. Because of the opposite direction of change (outperformance from twelve month to twenty-four month) of SBMP benchmark return, SBMP-adjusted BHAR shows sharp decline during the same period.

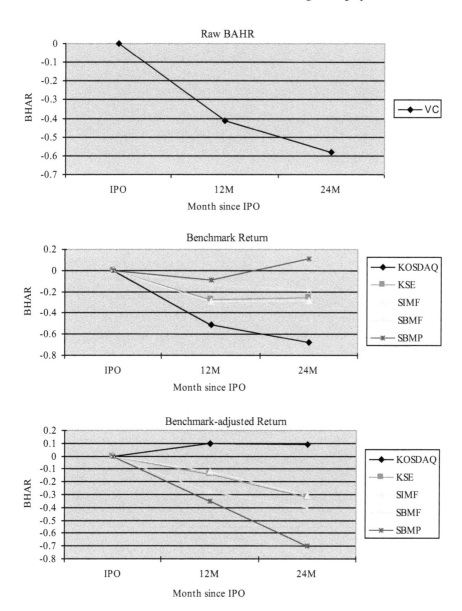

Figure 7.1(a) BHARs of VC-backed IPOs

The underperformance of the KOSDAQ benchmark throughout the period apparently reflects the sharp decline of KOSDAQ index after March 2000. While the KSE index experienced the same, it does not suffer as severe decline as KOSDAQ index, as can be seen from the higher KSE benchmark in the charts. The outperformance of SBMP benchmark relative to SIMF and SBMF benchmark

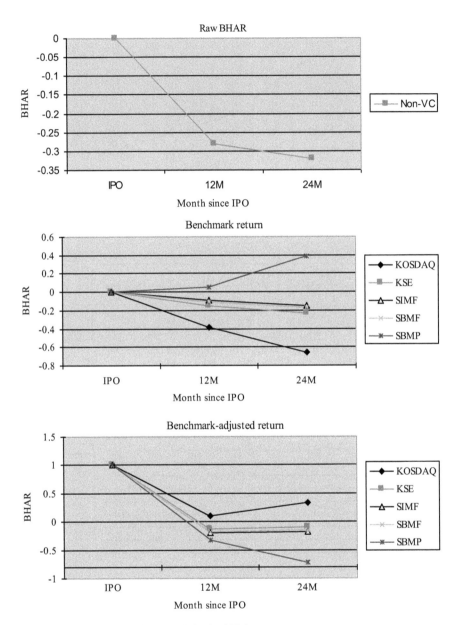

Figure 7.1(b) BHARs of non-VC-backed IPOs

reflects the fact that the method of quarterly rebalancing of the SBMP benchmark portfolio matched the IPO firms (of both VC-backing or non-VC-backing)
leads to smaller firms within benchmark in the long run, because market capitalisation of the IPO firms tended to get smaller compared with the first day of IPO.
Smaller size portfolios tended to record higher returns than bigger size portfolios

in our sample. This higher benchmark return of SBMP leads to the lower SBMP-adjusted BHAR relative to SIMF and SBMF-adjusted BHARs. SIMF and SBMF benchmarks show a rather steady pattern between twelve and twenty-four months, thus showing the less volatile change of the benchmark returns. While the IPO firms suffer from a serious decline of the stock price, theses SIMF and SBMF benchmarks seems to experience rather less changeable price movements.

The differences of benchmark returns between VC-backed and non-VC-backed IPOs are also observed in the charts. For all benchmarks, non-VC-backed IPOs show higher benchmark returns than VC-backed IPOs, which shows that benchmark returns closely followed the pattern of raw returns in which non-VC-backed IPOs outperformed VC-backed IPOs.[5]

I will get different answers depending on the benchmark chosen. From the viewpoint of investors, the KOSDAQ and KSE adjusted returns suggest if raw IPO buy-and-hold returns can beat buy-and-hold returns of market portfolio constructed by KOSDAQ- and KSE-listed firms, respectively. SIMF- and SBMF-adjusted returns indicate if raw IPO buy-and-hold returns can beat buy-and-hold-returns of a group of control firms matched by size and industry, and size and book-to-market ratio, respectively. SBMP-adjusted returns represent if raw IPO buy-and-hold return can beat buy-and-hold returns of a group of size and book-to-market matched portfolios that are rebalanced quarterly. The most robust result would be to beat all of them and the worst robust result would be to fail to beat all of them.

Now I turn to the univariate tests of long-term performance of VC-backed and non-VC-backed IPOs. Table 7.1 shows the twelve- and twenty-four-month BHARs of VC-backed and non-VC-backed IPOs. Each row of the table corresponds to a different benchmark calculation. Each row presents first the raw buy-and-hold return for VC-backed IPOs, then the benchmark return for the raw return in question, then the relevant adjusted BHAR and the wealth relative calculated as discussed in Chapter 4. Each row then continues by providing the same data for non-VC-backed IPOs. The final two columns of each row report the results of a parametric and non-parametric test of the difference between the adjusted BHARs for the VC-backed and non-VC-backed groups.

From Table 7.1, it is clearly shown that in terms of raw mean BHARs IPOs underperformed in the long run. All raw BHARs are negative. Moreover, it is shown that VC-backed firms underperformed non-VC-backed firms for raw BHARs after twelve and twenty-four months. The twelve-month raw returns of VC-backed IPOs (– 0.41) are lower than those of non-VC-backed IPOs (–0.28). The twenty-four-month raw returns of VC-backed IPOs (–0.58) also underperform those of non-VC-backed IPOs (–0.32).

BHARs adjusted by the benchmarks also show that IPOs tended to underperform after twelve and twenty-four months. Except for the KOSDAQ-adjusted BHAR, each adjusted BHAR shows that long-term performance of IPOs, irrespective of VC-backing, underperformed the benchmarks. The reason why the KOSDAQ-adjusted BHAR is positive after twelve and twenty-four months is, as I have seen, that the KOSDAQ return underperformed severely relative to other benchmarks.

Table 7.1 BHARs of VC-backed vs non-VC-backed IPOs on KOSDAQ 1999–2001

	VC-Backed IPOs				Non-VC-Backed IPOs				T-Statistics by t-test	Z-scores by Mann-Whitney Test
	Raw	Benchmark	Adjusted	(Wealth Relative)[6]	Raw	Benchmark	Adjusted	(Wealth Relative)		
Panel A: Twelve Month BHARs										
KOSDAQ	-0.41	-0.51	0.10	(1.20)	-0.28	-0.38	0.10	(1.16)	-0.02	-0.23
KSE	-0.41	-0.27	-0.14	(0.81)	-0.28	-0.15	-0.13	(0.85)	-0.15	-0.69
SIMF	-0.41	-0.29	-0.12	(0.83)	-0.28	-0.09	-0.19	(0.80)	0.58	-0.14
SBMF	-0.41	-0.13	-0.28	(0.68)	-0.28	-0.11	-0.17	(0.81)	-0.81	-1.39
SBMP	-0.43[7]	-0.09	-0.35	(0.62)	-0.27	0.05	-0.32	(0.70)	-0.28	-1.12
(No.IPOs)	(134)				(162)					
Panel B: Twenty-four Month BHARs										
KOSDAQ	-0.58	-0.68	0.09	(1.29)	-0.32	-0.66	0.33	(1.97)	-2.15**	-3.45***
KSE	-0.58	-0.26	-0.32	(0.56)	-0.32	-0.23	-0.09	(0.88)	-1.98*	-2.92***
SIMF	-0.58	-0.28	-0.31	(0.58)	-0.32	-0.15	-0.17	(0.80)	-0.81	-1.78*
SBMF	-0.58	-0.19	-0.40	(0.51)	-0.32	-0.17	-0.15	(0.82)	-1.40	-1.55
SBMP	-0.59	0.11	-0.70	(0.37)	-0.33	0.39	-0.72	(0.48)	0.16	-0.90
(No.IPOs)	(63)				(63)					

Source: Korean Information System, IPO prospectuses

Note: KOSDAQ IPO samples are grouped into VC-backed firms (when any venture capitalist owns 5% or more of total shares an IPO firm) and Non-VC-backed firms in this table. This type of grouping applies to the remaining parts of the chapter. Asterisks denote significance levels at the level 1% (***), 5% (**), and 10% (*).

For the twelve-month period, the adjusted BHARs of VC-backed IPOs are similar to non-VC-backed IPOs. None of the small differences which occur are statistically significant. On the other hand, for the twenty-four-month period, non-VC-backed IPOs show significant outperformance compared to VC-backed IPOs, when adjusted by KOSDAQ, KSE and SIMF. They show a statistically insignificant outperformance when adjusted by SBMF and SBMP.

Table 7.1 clearly shows that KOSDAQ IPO firms show poor long-term performance as was found in other studies (Ritter, 1991; Loughran and Ritter, 1995, Ritter and Welch, 2002). Therefore, it remains a puzzle why the IPOs that recorded very high initial returns at the initial stage of trading in the stock markets ended up with the poor long-term performance in the long run (Loughran and Ritter, 1995). An answer may be that the divergence of opinion between optimistic and pessimistic investors that had existed at the time of IPO disappeared in the long run (Miller, 2000) or that the IPOs, which may have been overvalued in the hot market, experienced a subsequent decline of prices (Aggarwal and Rivoli, 1990).

As I have seen, the selection of benchmarks affects the degree of long-term performance. The four positive KOSDAQ-adjusted abnormal BHARs are caused by the serious underperformance of the KOSDAQ index during the sample period.[8] While the KOSDAQ index increased sharply in the hot-market period up until March 2000, it experienced considerable decline after April 2000 and did not recover to the higher level that it reached until the end of 2001. The higher abnormal BHAR of KSE-adjusted over KOSDAQ-adjusted obviously shows that the KSE index did not decline as seriously as KOSDAQ. The control firm approach for adjusting raw returns significantly reduces the underperformance of IPO firms. The SBMP benchmark returns are uniquely among the benchmarks close to zero or positive. The positive benchmark returns of SBMP (for example, 0.11 for twenty-four month VC-backed IPOs and 0.39 for twenty-four month non-VC-backed IPOs) suggests that the size and book-to-market groups matched with IPO firms outperform other size and book-to-market groups. KOSDAQ IPO firms were concentrated in the groups of smaller sizes and lower book-to-market ratios portfolio. It seems that these smaller sizes and lower book-to-market ratio portfolio groups showed the higher return than other bigger groups and higher book-to-market ratio portfolio groups. This result is consistent with the expectation documented in Fama and French (1993).

It seems that the univariate results that I found in Table 7.1 do not support the hypothesis H1b (the impact of VC-backing on the long-term performance). The benchmark-adjusted returns are significantly higher for non-VC-backed IPOs than VC-backed IPOs. Our result is consistent with the finding in Kutsuna, Cowling et al. (2000).

7.2.2 *BHARs of hot and cold market*

Table 7.2 compares the long-term BHARs for the IPOs brought to KOSDAQ in the hot market and in the cold market. Each row of the table yields a different

Table 7.2 BHARs in hot and cold markets on KOSDAQ 1999–2001

	Hot Market				Cold Market				T-Statistics by t-test	Z-scores by Mann-Whitney Test
	Raw	Benchmark	Adjusted	(Wealth Relative)	Raw	Benchmark	Adjusted	(Wealth Relative)		
Panel A: Twelve Month BHARs										
KOSDAQ	-0.34	-0.63	0.29	(1.80)	-0.34	-0.29	-0.05	(0.93)	3.56***	-5.77***
KSE	-0.34	-0.38	0.04	(1.07)	-0.34	-0.08	-0.26	(0.71)	3.16***	-4.77***
SIMF	-0.34	-0.17	-0.17	(0.80)	-0.34	-0.20	-0.14	(0.82)	-0.21	-0.15
SBMF	-0.34	0.04	-0.38	(0.64)	-0.34	-0.24	-0.10	(0.87)	-2.16**	-2.49**
SBMP	-0.36	0.06	-0.42	(0.61)	-0.33	-0.07	-0.27	(0.72)	-1.43	-3.33***
(No.IPOs)	(127)				(169)					
Panel B: Twenty-four Month BHARs										
KOSDAQ	-0.45	-0.67	0.21	(1.64)						
KSE	-0.45	-0.25	-0.21	(0.73)						
SIMF	-0.45	-0.21	-0.24	(0.70)						
SBMF	-0.45	-0.18	-0.27	(0.67)						
SBMP	-0.46	0.25	-0.71	(0.43)						
(No.IPOs)	(126)									

Source: Korean Information System, IPO prospectuses

Note: KOSDAQ IPO samples are grouped into Hot Market issue (when an IPO was listed in KOSDAQ until March 2000) and Cold Market issue (after March 2000) in this table. This type of grouping applies to the remaining parts of the chapter. Asterisks denote significance levels at the level 1% (***), 5% (**), and 10% (*).

benchmark calculation. Each row presents first the raw buy-and-hold return for IPOs brought to KOSDAQ in the hot market, then the benchmark return for the raw return in question, then the relevant adjusted BHAR and the wealth relative. Each row then is followed by the same data for IPOs listed in the cold market. The final two columns of each row report the results of a parametric and non-parametric test of the difference between the adjusted BHARs for hot market and cold market groups.

For twelve-month BHARs, the raw returns are significantly negative and remarkably similar after twelve months for hot-market IPOs (–0.34) and for cold-market IPOs (–0.34).

For twenty-four month BHARs in hot-market IPOs, the raw return is worsening (–0.45).[9] When the raw returns are adjusted by benchmarks, abnormal returns generally show underperformance, except for the KOSDAQ-adjusted and KSE-adjusted BHARs in the hot-market period. These positive KOSDAQ and KSE adjusted BHARs are associated with the considerable decline of market indices after March 2000, as noted in Section 7.2.1. At any rate, the findings of the large underperformance of hot-market IPOs and cold-market IPOs are consistent with the poor long-term performance that are found in other studies (Ritter, 1991; Loughran and Ritter, 1995, Ritter and Welch, 2002).

Panel A shows that hot-market IPOs outperformed cold-market IPOs for two benchmarks significantly after twelve months: KOSDAQ-adjusted and KSE-adjusted. The KOSDAQ-adjusted hot market BHARs (0.29) are significantly higher than cold market BHARs (–0.05) at 1 per cent level. The KSE-adjusted hot market BHARs (0.04) are significantly higher than cold market BHARs (–0.26) at 1 per cent level. On the contrary, SBMF-adjusted and SBMP-adjusted BHARs show that cold-market IPOs outperformed hot-market IPOs significantly. The SBMF-adjusted hot market BHARs (–0.38) are significantly lower than cold market BHARs (–0.10) at 5 per cent level. SBMP-adjusted hot market BHARs (–0.42) are significantly lower than cold market BHARs (–0.27) at 1 per cent level by Mann-Whitney test. These conflicting results between KOSDAQ- and KSE-adjusted and SBMF- and SBMP-adjusted seem to occur due to the opposite change of the performance of these benchmarks in the hot and cold-market period. KOSDAQ and KSE show the higher benchmark return in the cold market than in the hot market. This seems to be caused by the decline of KOSDAQ and KSE index after March 2000, when the hot market ends and the cold market begins. SBMF and SBMP benchmark returns are higher in hot market than in cold market, which was caused by the fact that hot-market IPOs were matched with smaller size portfolios quarterly, which showed higher return than other portfolios, as their market capitalisation tends to decline, while the cold-market IPOs tended to be matched all the while with same bigger size portfolios which showed lower return than other portfolios.

Panel B shows that the twenty-four-month abnormal returns of hot-market IPOs worsened for all five benchmark-adjusted BHARs.

7.2.3 BHARs of young and old firms

Table 7.3 compares the long-term performance between young and old firms. As in Section 7.2.1 and 7.2.2, each row first provides the raw buy-and-hold return, the benchmark return and the relevant adjusted BHAR (and the wealth relative) for young and old groups. Each row then continues by providing the results of a parametric and non-parametric test of the difference between the adjusted BHARs for young and old groups, respectively.

It is shown that young firms underperform old firms after twelve and twenty-four months. The twelve-month raw BHARs are lower for young firms (–0.40) than for old firms (–0.29) and the twenty-four-month raw BHARs show lower returns for young firms (–0.59) than for old firms (–0.35).

Panel A shows that for twelve-month abnormal BHARs, young firms underperformed old firms for two benchmarks-adjusted returns. KOSDAQ-adjusted BHARs of old firms (0.13) are higher than those of young firms (0.06) significantly at 5 per cent level by Mann-Whitney test. KSE-adjusted BHARs of old firms (–0.10) are also higher than those of young firms (–0.17) significantly at 5 per cent level by Mann-Whitney test.

This outperformance of old firms over young firms is also apparent for twenty-four-month BHARs. In Panel B, KOSDAQ-adjusted BHARs of old firms (0.31) show significantly higher returns than those of young firms (0.09) at 10 per cent level by t-test and 1 per cent level by Mann-Whitney test.

KSE-adjusted BHARs of old firms (–0.11) are also significantly higher than those of young firms (–0.33) at 10 per cent level by t-test and 1 per cent level by Mann-Whitney test. SBMF-adjusted BHARs of old firms (–0.19) are significantly higher than those of young firms (–0.39) at 5 per cent level by Mann-Whitney test.

I have seen from the analysis of underpricing in Chapter 6 that young firms showed significantly more underpricing than old firms. Investors might require a higher risk premium for young firms that were generally considered as more uncertain and risky. It seems that the young firms, which were more likely to have uncertain business prospects with a shorter period of operation history, also turned out to underperform old firms in the long run.

7.2.4 BHARs of small and big firms

Table 7.4 shows the BHARs of small and big firms. Each row of the table corresponds to a different benchmark calculation. It presents the raw buy-and-hold return, the benchmark return for the raw return in question, and the relevant adjusted BHAR (and the wealth relative) for small and big firms. The final two columns of each row report the results of a parametric and non-parametric test of the difference between the adjusted BHARs for the small and big firms.

The raw BHARs are higher for small firms than for big firms. The twelve month raw BHARs of small firms are – 0.14, compared with – 0.55 of big firms.

Table 7.3 BHARs of young and old firms on KOSDAQ 1999–2001

	Young				Old				T-Statistics by t-test	Z-scores by Mann-Whitney Test
	Raw	Benchmark	Adjusted	(Wealth Relative)	Raw	Benchmark	Adjusted	(Wealth Relative)		
Panel A: Twelve Month BHARs										
KOSDAQ	−0.40	−0.46	**0.06**	(1.12)	−0.29	−0.42	**0.13**	(1.22)	−0.68	−1.97**
KSE	−0.40	−0.22	−0.17	(0.78)	−0.29	−0.20	−0.10	(0.88)	−0.79	−2.37**
SIMF	−0.40	−0.25	−0.14	(0.81)	−0.29	−0.13	−0.17	(0.81)	0.18	−1.16
SBMF	−0.40	−0.17	−0.22	(0.73)	−0.29	−0.07	−0.22	(0.76)	−0.04	−0.42
SBMP	−0.41	−0.11	−0.31	(0.66)	−0.28	0.07	−0.35	(0.67)	0.42	−0.59
(No.IPOs)	(137)				(159)					
Panel B: Twenty-four Month BHARs										
KOSDAQ	−0.59	−0.68	**0.09**	(1.28)	−0.35	−0.65	**0.31**	(1.88)	−1.91*	−3.39***
KSE	−0.59	−0.26	−0.33	(0.55)	−0.35	−0.23	−0.11	(0.85)	−1.85*	−2.87***
SIMF	−0.59	−0.35	−0.25	(0.62)	−0.35	−0.11	−0.23	(0.74)	−0.08	−1.02
SBMF	−0.59	−0.20	−0.39	(0.51)	−0.35	−0.16	−0.19	(0.78)	−1.16	−2.00**
SBMP	−0.60	0.09	−0.69	(0.37)	−0.35	0.38	−0.73	(0.47)	0.27	−0.05
(No.IPOs)	(54)				(72)					

Source: Korean Information System, IPO prospectuses

Note: KOSDAQ IPO samples are grouped into Young firms (when the age of firm is equal to or less than the median value, 9.6 years) and Old firms in this table. This type of grouping applies to the remaining parts of the chapter. Asterisks denote significance levels at the level 1% (***), 5% (**), and 10% (*).

Table 7.4 BHARs of small and big firms on KOSDAQ 1999–2001

	Raw	Benchmark	Adjusted	(Wealth Relative)	Raw	Benchmark	Adjusted	(Wealth Relative)	T-Statistics by t-test	Z-scores by Mann-Whitney Test
	Small				*Big*					
Panel A: Twelve Month BHARs										
KOSDAQ	−0.14	−0.41	**0.27**	(1.46)	−0.55	−0.47	**−0.09**	(0.84)	3.75***	−4.95***
KSE	−0.14	−0.18	**0.04**	(1.05)	−0.55	−0.24	**−0.31**	(0.59)	3.66***	−4.65***
SIMF	−0.14	−0.04	**−0.10**	(0.89)	−0.55	−0.34	**−0.21**	(0.68)	0.93	−1.51
SBMF	−0.14	0.12	**−0.26**	(0.77)	−0.55	−0.37	**−0.18**	(0.71)	−0.59	−0.29
SBMP	−0.14	0.18	**−0.31**	(0.74)	−0.57	−0.22	**−0.35**	(0.55)	0.38	−1.47
(No.IPOs)	(153)				(143)					
Panel B: Twenty-four Month BHARs										
KOSDAQ	−0.33	−0.67	**0.34**	(2.00)	−0.67	−0.67	**0.00**	(1.00)	2.92***	−3.81***
KSE	−0.33	−0.25	**−0.08**	(0.89)	−0.67	−0.24	**−0.43**	(0.44)	2.89***	−3.23***
SIMF	−0.33	−0.16	**−0.17**	(0.80)	−0.67	−0.31	**−0.35**	(0.49)	1.05	−0.65
SBMF	−0.33	0.05	**−0.37**	(0.64)	−0.67	−0.57	**−0.10**	(0.77)	−1.51	−2.33**
SBMP	−0.33	0.50	**−0.83**	(0.45)	−0.68	−0.18	**−0.50**	(0.39)	−2.18**	−2.59***
(No.IPOs)	(80)				(46)					

Source: Korean Information System, IPO prospectuses

Note: KOSDAQ IPO samples are grouped into Small firms (when the market capitalisation calculated as offer price by the number of shares is equal to or less than the median value, 2.4 billion Won) and Big firms. This type of grouping applies to the remaining parts of the chapter. Asterisks denote significance levels at the level 1% (***), 5% (**), and 10% (*).

The twenty-four month raw BHARs of small firms are – 0.33, while those of big firms are – 0.67. As was found in the previous sub-sections, the long-term returns tend to be worse over twenty-four months than over twelve month.

The KOSDAQ-adjusted BHARs of small firms (0.27) are also higher than those of big firms (–0.09). The difference of the BHARs is significant at 1 per cent level. This outperformance is also confirmed in the case of KSE-adjusted BHARs. The KSE-adjusted BHARs of small firms (0.04) are significantly higher than those of big firms (–0.31) at 1 per cent level. The other adjusted returns are insignificantly different.

Panel B also shows that the twenty-four month KOSDAQ-adjusted BHARs of small firms (0.34) are significantly higher than those of big firms (0.00) at 1 per cent level. The KSE-adjusted BHARs of small firms (–0.08) are higher than those of large firms (–0.43) significantly at 1 per cent level. A noteworthy point in Panel B is that SBMF-adjusted and SBMP-adjusted BHARs show contradictory results to the KOSDAQ-adjusted and KSE-adjusted BHARs.

SBMF-adjusted BHARs of small firms (–0.37) are significantly lower than those of big firms (–0.10) after twenty-four month. The difference of these BHARs is significant at 5 per cent level by Mann-Whitney test. The underperformance of small firms is also found when the raw returns are adjusted by SBMP. The SBMP-adjusted BHARs of small firms (–0.83) are significantly lower than those of big firms (–0.50) at 5 per cent level by t-test and 1 per cent level by Mann-Whitney Test.

The underperformance of small firms over big firms after twenty-four months for the SBMF-adjusted and SBMP-adjusted BHARs seems to be caused by the underperformance of benchmarks of big firms. The benchmark returns of small firms are 0.05 (SBMF) and 0.50 (SBMP), whereas those of big firms are – 0.57 (SBMF) and – 0.18 (SBMP). Considering the fact that the small firms raw BHARs outperformed big firms raw BHARs, the difference of the benchmark returns seem to be severe enough to result in the significant underperformance of small firm adjusted BHARs over big firm adjusted BHARs.[10]

The result of long-term outperformance of small firms over big firms is contrary to the finding of Ritter (1991), who documented that smaller offers had the worst long-term performances. DeBondt and Thaler (1987) present evidence that for low market capitalisation stocks, there is a negative relation between previous and consequent returns using holding periods of a year or more. They interpret this relation as evidence of market overreaction. However, in the KOSDAQ case, it is found that there is a positive association between small market capitalisation and outperformance.

7.2.5 BHARs of high-tech and non-high-tech firms

Table 7.5 compares the BHARs of high-tech and non-high-tech firms. Each row of the table corresponds to a different benchmark calculation. Each row presents first the raw buy-and-hold return for high-tech IPOs, then the benchmark return

Table 7.5 BHARs of high-tech and non-high-tech firms on KOSDAQ 1999–2001

	Raw	Benchmark	Adjusted	(Wealth Relative)	Raw	Benchmark	Adjusted	(Wealth Relative)	T-Statistics by t-test	Z-scores by Mann-Whitney Test
	High-Tech				Non-High-Tech					
Panel A: Twelve Month BHARs										
KOSDAQ	-0.40	-0.46	**0.06**	(1.11)	-0.26	-0.41	**0.15**	(1.26)	-0.97	-1.05
KSE	-0.40	-0.22	**-0.18**	(0.77)	-0.26	-0.19	**-0.07**	(0.91)	-1.04	-1.23
SIMF	-0.40	-0.27	**-0.13**	(0.83)	-0.26	-0.06	**-0.19**	(0.79)	0.56	-0.79
SBMF	-0.40	-0.18	**-0.22**	(0.74)	-0.26	-0.03	**-0.23**	(0.77)	0.10	-0.21
SBMP	-0.41	-0.07	**-0.34**	(0.64)	-0.25	0.07	**-0.32**	(0.70)	-0.19	-0.51
(No.IPOs)	(172)				(124)					
Panel B: Twenty-four Month BHARs										
KOSDAQ	-0.55	-0.68	**0.13**	(1.39)	-0.34	-0.65	**0.31**	(1.90)	-1.65	-3.02***
KSE	-0.55	-0.25	**-0.30**	(0.60)	-0.34	-0.24	**-0.10**	(0.87)	-1.72 *	-2.82***
SIMF	-0.55	-0.40	**-0.15**	(0.75)	-0.34	0.00	**-0.34**	(0.66)	1.16	-0.46
SBMF	-0.55	-0.21	**-0.35**	(0.57)	-0.34	-0.15	**-0.19**	(0.77)	-0.86	-1.40
SBMP	-0.56	0.14	**-0.70**	(0.39)	-0.35	0.38	**-0.73**	(0.47)	0.18	-0.34
(No.IPOs)	(67)				(59)					

Source: Korean Information System, IPO prospectuses

Note: KOSDAQ IPO samples are grouped into High-tech firms (which include Other Machinery and Equipment (KIC 29), Computers and Office Machinery (30) Electrical Machinery and Apparatuses (31) Electronic Components, Radio, Television (32) Medical, Precision and Optical Instruments (33), and Computer and Related Activities (72) as was defined in Chapter 4) and Non-high-tech firms in this table. This type of grouping applies to the remaining parts of the chapter. Asterisks denote significance levels at the level 1% (***), 5% (**), and 10% (*).

for the row in question, then the relevant adjusted BHAR and the wealth relative calculated as discussed in Chapter 4. Each row then continues by providing the same data for non-high-tech IPOs. The final two columns of each row report the results of a parametric and non-parametric test of the difference between the adjusted BHARs for high-tech and non-high-tech IPOs.

The raw returns of twelve month and twenty-four month show that high-tech firms underperformed non-high-tech firms. The raw returns of twelve-month high-tech firms are – 0.40, while those of non-high-tech firms are – 0.26. For the twenty-four month, twelve-month high-tech firms recorded – 0.55, compared with – 0.34 of non-high-tech firms.

The univariate tests in Panel A to compare the difference of adjusted BHARs between high-tech and non-high-tech groups for twelve-month returns does not find significant differences for any of the five benchmark-adjusted returns.

However, twenty-four month BHARs between high-tech and non-high-tech groups show a difference in KOSDAQ-adjusted and KSE-adjusted BHARs. The abnormal KOSDAQ-adjusted BHARs of high-tech firms are 0.13, which is significantly lower than 0.31 of non-high-tech firms at 1 per cent level by Mann-Whitney test. The BHARs adjusted by KSE also show that the difference between high-tech firms BHARs (–0.30) and non-high-tech firms BHARs (–0.10) is significant at 10 per cent level by t-test and 1 per cent level by Mann-Whitney test. However, for other benchmark-adjusted returns, no significant difference is found.

This difference of abnormal BHARs between high-tech firms and non-high-tech firms may be evidence that high-tech firms, including the information and communication technology firms, were overvalued at the time of IPO, and thus suffered from the decline of the firm performance in the long run.

Schultz and Zaman (2001) argue that the market was irrationally overpricing internet stocks in the late 1990s and managers were in a rush to make their companies public so as to seize the market share and first-mover advantages.

Even though many companies who got listed in this period experienced the large loss and did not have the explicit revenue before IPO, their stocks could come to the stock market with the name of high-tech or internet stocks and recorded the high initial returns after IPO (Hand, 2000).

However, in an industry where the firms found it difficult to survive unless they exploited the economies of scale for the operation of business, a lot of firms could not ensure that their higher level of stock prices would continue and finally ended up with a big downfall of share prices. The underperformance of high-tech firms over non-high-tech firms after twenty-four months could be evidence that KOSDAQ also experienced the same kind of dot.com bubble and the following bursting of the bubble that agitated the worldwide stock market after March 2000. This is consistent with our multivariate results of underpricing in Chapter 6. Table 6.7 showed that there was a statistically significant positive relationship between hi-tech classification and the degree of underpricing for all samples firms and VC-backed firms alone.

7.3 Long-term performance by VC-backing and non-VC-backing IPOs

Table 7.6(1) compares the long-term performance of VC-backed IPO and non-VC-backed IPOs in hot and cold market. It is shown that the VC-backed IPOs in the hot market show higher BHARs after twelve months than those in the cold market. The KOSDAQ-adjusted BHARs of hot market is 0.24, compared with the – 0.03 in the cold market. The difference of these BHARs is significant at 10 per cent level by t-test and 1 per cent level by Mann-Whitney test. This outperformance of hot-market KOSDAQ-adjusted IPOs after twelve month is also found in non-VC-backed case. The hot market KOSDAQ-adjusted BHARs of non-VC-backed are 0.35, higher than – 0.06 in the cold market. The difference is significant at 1 per cent level by t-test and Mann-Whitney test.

However, SBMP-adjusted BHARs show that the IPOs brought to market in the cold market outperform those introduced in the hot market after twelve months. The twelve-month cold market SBMP-adjusted BHARs of VC-backed IPOs (–0.28) are significantly higher than those in the hot market (–0.42) at 5 per cent level by Mann-Whitney test.

This outperformance of cold market SBMP-adjusted IPO after twelve months is also found in the non-VC-backed case. The cold-market SBMP-adjusted BHARs of non-VC-backed are – 0.26, compared with – 0.41 in the hot market. The difference is significant at 5 per cent level using the Mann-Whitney test. These conflicting results arise from the different performances of KOSDAQ and SBMP as was explained the sub-section 7.2.2. Whether the hot-market issue affected the long-term performance after twelve months depends on which counterfactual you prefer.

Table 7.6(2) compares the long-term performance of VC-backed IPOs and non-VC-backed IPOs by age. For twelve-month returns of VC-backed IPOs, old firms show a significantly higher return (0.13) than young firms (0.08) at 5 per cent level by Mann-Whitney test. Moreover the twenty-four month KOSDAQ-adjusted BHARs of non-VC-backed IPOs show that old firms (0.46) outperformed young firms (0.03) at 1 per cent level by t-test and Mann-Whitney test. This result is consistent with our finding in sub-section 7.2.3.

Table 7.6(3) clearly shows that small firms outperformed big firms after twelve month and twenty-four months for either the VC-backed or non-VC-backed case. This result is consistent with our finding in sub-section 7.2.4. Not only the raw returns of small firms are higher than those of large firms in all calculations, the adjusted returns also show that small firms outperformed large firms. The twelve-month small firms BHARs of VC-backed IPOs (0.38) are higher than those of big firms of VC-backed IPOs (–0.10). The difference is significant at 1 per cent level by t-test and Mann-Whitney test. This significant difference is also found in the KOSDAQ-adjusted BHARs of non-VC-backed IPOs. Small firms BHARs of non-VC-backed IPOs are 0.21, compared with –0.07 of big firms. The difference is significant at 5 per cent level by t-test and 1 per cent by Mann-Whitney test. Moreover, twenty-four month small firms KOSDAQ-adjusted

Table 7.6(1) BHARs by VC-backing and non-VC-backing grouped by hot- and cold- market issues on KOSDAQ 1999–2001[11]

		Hot Market				Cold Market				T-Statistics by t-test	Z-scores by Mann-Whitney Test
		Raw	Benchmark	Adjusted	(WR)	Raw	Benchmark	Adjusted	(WR)		
		12 Month									
VC	KOSDAQ	-0.42	-0.66	**0.24**	(1.70)	-0.41	**-0.38**	**-0.03**	(0.95)	1.69*	-3.94***
	SIMF	-0.42	-0.28	**-0.14**	(0.81)	-0.41	**-0.31**	**-0.10**	(0.86)	-0.29	-1.56
	SBMP	-0.46	-0.04	**-0.42**	(0.56)	-0.41	**-0.13**	**-0.28**	(0.68)	-0.86	-2.10**
	(No.IPOs)	(63)				(71)					
Non-VC	KOSDAQ	-0.26	-0.61	**0.35**	(1.88)	-0.29	**-0.23**	**-0.06**	(0.92)	3.48***	-4.38***
	SIMF	-0.26	-0.06	**-0.20**	(0.79)	-0.29	**-0.11**	**-0.18**	(0.80)	-0.10	-1.19
	SBMP	-0.26	0.15	**-0.41**	(0.65)	-0.27	**-0.02**	**-0.26**	(0.74)	-1.14	-2.47**
	(No.IPOs)	(64)				(98)					
		24 Month									
VC	KOSDAQ	-0.58	-0.68	**0.09**	(1.29)						
	SIMF	-0.58	-0.28	**-0.31**	(0.58)						
	SBMP	-0.59	0.11	**-0.70**	(0.37)						
	(No.IPOs)	(63)									
Non-VC	KOSDAQ	-0.32	-0.66	**0.33**	(1.97)						
	SIMF	-0.32	-0.15	**-0.17**	(0.80)						
	SBMP	-0.33	0.39	**-0.72**	(0.48)						
	(No.IPOs)	(63)									

Source: Korean Information System, IPO prospectuses

Note: Asterisks denote significant levels at the level of 1% (***), 5% (**), and 10% (*)

Table 7.6(2) BHARs by VC-backing and Non-VC-backing grouped by age on KOSDAQ 1999–2001

		Young				Old				T-Statistics by t-test	Z-scores by Mann-Whitney Test
		Raw	Benchmark	Adjusted	(WR)	Raw	Benchmark	Adjusted	(WR)		
		12 Month									
VC	KOSDAQ	-0.41	-0.48	0.08	(1.15)	-0.42	-0.55	0.13	(1.29)	-0.31	-2.26**
	SIMF	-0.41	-0.32	-0.09	(0.87)	-0.42	-0.26	-0.16	(0.78)	0.47	-0.31
	SBMP	-0.43	-0.15	-0.28	(0.67)	-0.44	0.02	-0.46	(0.55)	1.06	-1.14
	(No.IPOs)	(82)				(52)					
Non-VC	KOSDAQ	-0.38	-0.42	0.04	(1.07)	-0.23	-0.36	0.13	(1.20)	-0.70	-0.59
	SIMF	-0.38	-0.15	-0.22	(0.74)	-0.23	-0.06	-0.17	(0.82)	-0.32	-1.25
	SBMP	-0.39	-0.04	-0.35	(0.64)	-0.20	0.10	-0.30	(0.73)	-0.37	-0.31
	(No.IPOs)	(55)				(107)					
		24 Month									
VC	KOSDAQ	-0.56	-0.68	0.12	(1.37)	-0.62	-0.67	0.06	(1.18)	0.35	-1.51
	SIMF	-0.56	-0.37	-0.19	(0.69)	-0.62	-0.16	-0.45	(0.46)	1.11	-0.76
	SBMP	-0.57	0.00	-0.57	(0.43)	-0.63	0.25	-0.87	(0.30)	1.40	-0.96
	(No.IPOs)	(36)				(27)					
Non-VC	KOSDAQ	-0.66	-0.69	0.03	(1.10)	-0.19	-0.64	0.46	(2.27)	-2.73***	-2.60***
	SIMF	-0.66	-0.31	-0.35	(0.49)	-0.19	-0.09	-0.10	(0.89)	-0.94	-1.34
	SBMP	-0.67	0.25	-0.92	(0.27)	-0.19	0.45	-0.64	(0.56)	-1.23	-0.64
	(No.IPOs)	(18)				(45)					

Source: Korean Information System, IPO prospectuses

Note: Asterisks denote significant levels at the level of 1% (***), 5% (**), and 10% (*)

Table 7.6(3) BHARs by VC-backing and non-VC-backing grouped by market capitalisation on KOSDAQ 1999–2001

		Small				Big				T-Statistics by t-test	Z-scores by Mann-Whitney Test
		Raw	Benchmark	Adjusted	(WR)	Raw	Benchmark	Adjusted	(WR)		
12 Month											
VC	KOSDAQ	-0.14	-0.52	**0.38**	(1.78)	-0.60	-0.50	**-0.10**	(0.81)	2.98***	-4.50***
	SIMF	-0.14	-0.14	**0.00**	(1.00)	-0.60	-0.40	**-0.20**	(0.66)	1.34	-1.18
	SBMP	-0.17	0.12	**-0.29**	(0.75)	-0.62	-0.23	**-0.39**	(0.50)	0.62	-1.14
	(No.IPOs)	(55)				(79)					
Non-VC	KOSDAQ	-0.14	-0.35	**0.21**	(1.33)	-0.50	-0.42	**-0.07**	(0.87)	2.39**	-2.81***
	SIMF	-0.14	0.03	**-0.16**	(0.84)	-0.50	-0.28	**-0.22**	(0.69)	0.34	-0.96
	SBMP	-0.12	0.21	**-0.33**	(0.73)	-0.50	-0.20	**-0.30**	(0.62)	-0.17	-1.30
	(No.IPOs)	(98)				(64)					
24 Month											
VC	KOSDAQ	-0.49	-0.68	**0.18**	(1.56)	-0.70	-0.68	**-0.03**	(0.92)	1.23	-1.42
	SIMF	-0.49	-0.28	**-0.22**	(0.70)	-0.70	-0.28	**-0.43**	(0.41)	0.89	-0.90
	SBMP	-0.51	0.30	**-0.81**	(0.38)	-0.70	-0.15	**-0.55**	(0.35)	-1.14	-2.31**
	(No.IPOs)	(36)				(27)					
Non-VC	KOSDAQ	-0.20	-0.66	**0.46**	(2.35)	-0.61	-0.65	**0.04**	(1.11)	2.76***	-3.37***
	SIMF	-0.20	-0.06	**-0.14**	(0.86)	-0.61	-0.36	**-0.25**	(0.61)	0.44	-1.21
	SBMP	-0.19	0.67	**-0.86**	(0.49)	-0.64	-0.22	**-0.43**	(0.46)	-1.97*	-1.54
	(No.IPOs)	(44)				(19)					

Source: Korean Information System, IPO prospectuses

Note: Asterisks denote significant levels at the level of 1% (***), 5% (**), and 10% (*)

Table 7.6(4) BHARs by VC-backing and non-VC-backing with industry on KOSDAQ 1999–2001

		High-tech				Non-high-tech				T-Statistics by t-test	Z-scores by Mann-Whitney Test
		Raw	Benchmark	Adjusted	(WR)	Raw	Benchmark	Adjusted	(WR)		
12 Month											
VC	KOSDAQ	-0.43	-0.51	0.08	(1.16)	-0.36	-0.51	0.15	(1.31)	-0.39	-0.81
	SIMF	-0.43	-0.30	-0.13	(0.82)	-0.36	-0.28	-0.09	(0.88)	-0.25	-0.02
	SBMP	-0.45	-0.10	-0.35	(0.61)	-0.38	-0.06	-0.32	(0.66)	-0.16	-0.02
	(No.IPOs)	(98)				(36)					
Non-VC	KOSDAQ	-0.36	-0.39	0.03	(1.05)	-0.21	-0.37	0.16	(1.25)	-1.03	-0.58
	SIMF	-0.36	-0.23	-0.12	(0.84)	-0.21	0.02	-0.24	(0.77)	0.65	-1.05
	SBMP	-0.36	-0.04	-0.32	(0.67)	-0.19	0.13	-0.32	(0.72)	-0.02	-1.05
	(No.IPOs)	(74)				(88)					
24 Month											
VC	KOSDAQ	-0.58	-0.68	0.10	(1.30)	-0.60	-0.68	0.08	(1.25)	0.09	-1.43
	SIMF	-0.58	-0.40	-0.18	(0.71)	-0.60	-0.01	-0.58	(0.41)	1.65	-1.06
	SBMP	-0.59	0.16	-0.75	(0.36)	-0.59	0.00	-0.59	(0.41)	-0.65	-1.06
	(No.IPOs)	(43)				(20)					
Non-VC	KOSDAQ	-0.50	-0.68	0.18	(1.54)	-0.21	-0.64	0.43	(2.21)	-1.71*	-1.68*
	SIMF	-0.50	-0.41	-0.10	(0.84)	-0.21	0.01	-0.22	(0.79)	0.48	-0.28
	SBMP	-0.51	0.10	-0.61	(0.45)	-0.22	0.57	-0.79	(0.50)	0.86	-1.69*
	(No.IPOs)	(24)				(39)					

Source: Korean Information System, IPO prospectuses

Note: Asterisks denote significant levels at the level of 1% (***), 5% (**), and 10% (*)

BHARs of non-VC-backed IPOs (0.46) are significantly higher than big firms BHARs (0.04) at 1 per cent level by t-test and Mann-Whitney test.

Even though the SBMP-adjusted BHARs show that big firms outperform small firms using twenty-four months returns, this seems to be caused by the considerable underperformance of the big firm benchmark returns rather than the performance of IPO firms, as was stated in sub-section 7.2.4. Since the big firm benchmark comprised big-sized firms, this indicates that benchmark firms also performed worse than small-sized firms by following the underperformance patterns of big IPO firms.

Table 7.6(4) compares the long-term performance of VC-backed IPOs and non-VC-backed IPOs by industry. For twelve-month returns, there is no significant difference between high-tech and non-high firms in both VC-backed and non-VC-backed IPOs. However, as was shown in sub-section 7.2.5, twenty-four months BHARs show that non-high-tech firms outperform high-tech firms significantly. The KOSDAQ-adjusted non-high-tech BHARs of non-VC-backed IPOs (0.43) are significantly higher than those of high-tech BHARs (0.18) at 10 per cent level by t-test and Mann-Whitney test. Even though SBMP-adjusted non-high-tech BHARs (−0.79) for non-VC-backed IPOs is significantly lower than high-tech BHARs (−0.61) at 10 per cent level by Mann-Whitney test, This is mainly caused by the considerable outperformance of benchmarks. The comparison of the twenty-four month returns between high-tech and non-high-tech firms seem to confirm the finding in Section 7.2.5 that high-tech firms in KOSDAQ experienced a fall of stock price in the long run.

7.4 Long-term performance by institutional difference of VC-backing

Table 7.7 compares the long-term performance according to the institutional difference of VC-backing: bank-affiliated-VC-backed IPOs, security-company-affiliated-VC-backed IPOs, other-institutions-affiliate-backed IPOs (excluding bank-affiliated and security company-affiliated) VC and non-VC-backed IPOs. This analysis aims to test the hypothesis H3b (the impact of bank-affiliated VCs on the long-term performance) and H4b (the impact of security company-affiliated VCs on the long-term performance). The comparison of the long-term performance is carried out for all IPOs, the IPOs brought to stock market in the hot-market period, and the IPOs brought to stock market in the cold-market period, respectively, by Kruskal-Wallis test, as was explained in Chapter 4.

For all IPOs, it is shown that bank-affiliated IPOs outperform other types of IPOs after twelve and twenty-four months. For twelve-month KOSDAQ-adjusted return, bank-affiliated BHAR is 0.36, followed by 0.10 of the non-VC-backed, 0.05 of other institution-affiliated and − 0.18 of security-affiliated. The significance appears between bank-affiliated and security company-affiliated at 5 per cent level, between other institution-affiliated and security company-affiliated at 5 per cent level and between non-VC-backed and security company-affiliated at 10 per cent level by Kruskal Wallis Test. SIMF-adjusted and SBMP-adjusted BHARs also show the same

Table 7.7 BHARs by institutional affiliation in VC-backing on KOSDAQ 1999–2001

	Mean	Median	Mean	Median	Mean	Median	Mean	Median	Significance of Mean Difference by Kruskal Wallis Test
	Bank–affiliated VC (a)		Security Company–affiliated VC (b)		Other Institution–affiliated VC (c)		Non–VC–backed (d)		
Panel A: Total									
12 Month									
KOSDAQ	0.36	–0.03	–0.18	–0.19	0.05	–0.07	0.10	–0.03	a>b at 5%
SIMF	0.06	–0.22	–0.14	–0.01	–0.17	–0.16	–0.19	–0.15	c>b at 5%
SBMP	–0.18	–0.34	–0.43	–0.40	–0.39	–0.41	–0.32	–0.35	d>b at 10%
(No.IPOs)	(29)		(13)		(92)		(162)		(KOSDAQ)
24 Month									
KOSDAQ	0.39	–0.03	–0.11	–0.18	0.03	–0.07	0.33	0.14	d>b at 5%
SIMF	0.21	–0.13	–0.55	–0.27	–0.43	–0.20	–0.17	–0.06	d>c at 1%
SBMP	–0.53	–0.64	–0.68	–0.51	–0.75	–0.64	–0.72	–0.51	(KOSDAQ)
(No.IPOs)	(13)		(5)		(45)		(63)		d>c at 10% (SIMF)
Panel A: Hot Market Issue									
12 Month									
KOSDAQ	0.75	–0.04	0.07	–0.04	0.11	–0.03	0.35	0.01	
SIMF	0.34	–0.22	–0.12	–0.01	–0.28	–0.20	–0.20	–0.07	
SBMP	–0.04	–0.67	–0.42	–0.23	–0.53	–0.45	–0.41	–0.42	
(No.IPOs)	(13)		(5)		(45)		(63)		
24 Month									
KOSDAQ	0.39	–0.03	–0.11	–0.18	0.03	–0.07	0.33	0.14	d>b at 5%
SIMF	0.21	–0.13	–0.55	–0.27	–0.43	–0.20	–0.17	–0.06	d>c at 1%
SBMP	–0.53	–0.64	–0.68	–0.51	–0.75	–0.64	–0.72	–0.51	(KOSDAQ)
(No.IPOs)	(13)		(5)		(45)		(63)		d>c at 10% (SIMF)
Panel A: Cold Market Issue									
12 Month									
KOSDAQ	0.05	–0.01	–0.33	–0.28	–0.01	–0.21	–0.06	–0.14	a>b at 5%
SIMF	–0.17	–0.20	–0.16	–0.04	–0.06	–0.07	–0.18	–0.20	d>b at 10%
SBMP	–0.29	–0.29	–0.43	–0.41	–0.25	–0.39	–0.26	–0.28	(KOSDAQ)
(No.IPOs)	(16)		(8)		(47)		(98)		

Source: Korean Information System, IPO prospectuses

Note: Asterisks denote significant levels at the level of 1% (***), 5% (**), and 10% (*)

patterns of long-term performance according to the institutional difference, but no significance appears by Kruskal Wallis Test among the four groups. The twenty-four month KOSDAQ-adjusted BHARs also show that bank-affiliated case (0.39) is higher than security company-adjusted (–0.11), other institution-affiliated (0.03) and non-VC-backed (0.33), but difference of the BHARs among the groups is significant only between non-VC-backed and security company-affiliated at 5 per cent level and between non-VC-backed and other institution-affiliated at 1 per cent level by Kruskal Wallis Test. SIMF-adjusted BHARs show that non-VC-backed IPOs outperform other institution-affiliated IPOs at 10 per cent level by the same test.

For the IPOs brought to the stock market in the hot-market period, bank-affiliated BHARs are higher than any other BHARs in all cases. However, the difference between bank-affiliated and the other BHARs is not significant by Kruskal Wallis test. Moreover, the security company-affiliated BHARs are generally lower than any other BHARs. The significant differences appear among twenty-four month returns.

The non-VC-backed IPOs are significantly higher than security company-affiliated at 5 per cent level and than other institution-affiliated at 1 per cent level when the BHARs are adjusted by KOSDAQ. The non-VC-backed IPOs also show the significantly higher BHARs than other institution-affiliated BHARs for SIMF-adjusted case at 10 per cent level.

In the cold-market IPOs, the differences of BHARs among the four groups are narrowed compared with the hot-market IPOs. However, the twelve-month KOSDAQ-adjusted bank-affiliated BHAR (0.05) is significantly higher than the other three KOSDAQ-adjusted BHARs. The bank-affiliated BHAR (0.05) is significantly higher than security company-affiliated (–0.33) at 5 per cent level, while the non-VC-backed (–0.06) BHAR outperform significantly the security company-affiliated (–0.33) at 10 per cent level.

The comparison of long-term performance among the four groups divided by the institutional difference of VC-backing supports H4b. The IPOs backed by security company-affiliated VC performs worse than other IPOs in the long run. This may be evidence that the potential conflict of interest that the security company-affiliated VC may cause between investor and issuing firms by bringing overvalued IPO firms to the stock market (Gompers and Lerner, 1999; Hamao, packer et al., 2000). It is not very clear that the informationally advantageous role of bank-affiliated VC is reflected in the long-term performance. Even though the bank-affiliated VC shows the highest long-term performances in almost all of the cases, it is significantly higher than only security company-affiliated VC in a couple of cases. Therefore, the hypothesis on the better long-term performance by bank-affiliated VC is partly supported in the univariate analysis.

7.5 Long-term performance in hot and cold markets by different types of IPOs

Table 7.8(1) compares the long-term performances of hot and cold markets across IPOs grouped by VC-backing. For twelve months returns, there are no significant difference between VC-backed IPOs and non-VC-backed IPOs.

Table 7.8(1) BHARs in hot and cold markets by VC-backing on KOSDAQ 1999–2001

		Mean	Median	Mean	Median	T-Statistics by t-test	Z-scores by Mann-Whitney Test
		VC-backed		Non-VC-backed			
12 Month							
HOT	KOSDAQ	0.24	−0.03	0.35	0.10	−0.54	−1.19
	SIMF	−0.14	−0.20	−0.20	−0.07	0.24	−1.64
	SBMP	−0.42	−0.45	−0.41	−0.45	−0.05	−0.31
	(No.IPOs)	(63)		(64)			
COLD	KOSDAQ	−0.03	−0.21	−0.06	−0.14	0.42	−0.23
	SIMF	−0.10	−0.07	−0.18	−0.20	0.77	−1.25
	SBMP	−0.28	−0.39	−0.26	−0.28	−0.30	−0.81
	(No.IPOs)	(71)		(98)			
24 Month							
HOT	KOSDAQ	0.09	−0.07	0.33	0.14	−2.15**	−3.45***
	SIMF	−0.31	−0.18	−0.17	−0.06	−0.81	−1.78*
	SBMP	−0.70	−0.64	−0.72	−0.51	0.16	−0.90
	(No.IPOs)	(63)		(63)			

Source: Korean Information System, IPO prospectuses

Note: Asterisks denote significant levels at the level of 1% (***), 5% (**), and 10% (*)

However, for twenty-four month BHARs, benchmark-adjusted abnormal returns of IPOs that were brought in the hot-market period show that non-VC-backed IPOs performed better than VC-backed IPOs. The KOSDAQ-adjusted BHAR of non-VC-backed IPOs is 0.33, significantly higher than 0.09 of VC-backed IPOs at 5 per cent level by t-test and 1 per cent level by Mann-Whitney test. The SIMF-adjusted BHAR of non-VC-backed IPOs (−0.17) also shows significantly higher returns than that of VC-backed IPOs (−0.31). The difference is significant at 10 per cent level by Mann-Whitney test.

As in sub-section 7.2.1, this result rejects the hypothesis H1b. The VC-backed IPOs do not result in the better firm performance in the long run. This may imply that venture capitalists do not play a role in adding value by retaining ownership and intervening in the management.

Otherwise this may indicate that the share price of IPOs backed by venture capitalists increased sharply at the initial stage of IPOs higher than non-VC-backed IPOs, thus leading the worse long-term BHAR which is calculated by the difference between the closing price that did not hit the maximum upper limit for the first time and the long-term share price.

Table 7.8(2) shows that old firms performed better than young firms that were brought to KOSDAQ in the same hot-market period. For the twelve-month BHARs in the hot-market period, the KOSDAQ-adjusted old firms BHAR is 0.34, which is significantly higher than 0.24 of young firms BHAR. The difference

Table 7.8(2) BHARs in hot and cold markets by age on KOSDAQ 1999–2001

		Mean	Median	Mean	Median	T-Statistics by t-test	Z-scores by Mann-Whitney Test
		Young		Old			
12 Month							
HOT	KOSDAQ	0.24	*–0.03*	0.34	*0.12*	–0.48	–1.80*
	SIMF	–0.19	*–0.20*	–0.15	*0.09*	–0.17	–1.67*
	SBMP	–0.37	*–0.36*	–0.45	*–0.50*	0.32	–0.90
	(No.IPOs)	(55)		(72)			
COLD	KOSDAQ	–0.06	*–0.21*	–0.04	*–0.13*	–0.20	–1.17
	SIMF	–0.11	*–0.15*	–0.18	*–0.14*	0.63	–0.08
	SBMP	–0.26	*–0.34*	–0.27	*–0.33*	0.13	–0.34
	(No.IPOs)	(82)		(87)			
24 Month							
HOT	KOSDAQ	0.09	*–0.06*	0.31	*0.12*	–1.91*	–3.39***
	SIMF	–0.25	*–0.16*	–0.23	*–0.10*	–0.08	–1.02
	SBMP	–0.69	*–0.63*	–0.73	*–0.57*	0.27	–0.05
	(No.IPOs)	(54)		(72)			

Source: Korean Information System, IPO prospectuses

Note: Asterisks denote significant levels at the level of 1% (***), 5% (**), and 10% (*)

is significant at 10 per cent level by Mann-Whitney test. This is also found in the SIMF-adjusted return. The SIMF-adjusted BHAR of old firms (–0.15) is higher than that of young firm (–0.19) significantly at 10 per cent level by Mann-Whitney test. For the twenty-four month BHARs, old firms also outperformed young firms that started trading in the same hot-market period. The KOSDAQ-adjusted old firms BHAR is 0.31, significantly higher than 0.09 of young firms at 10 per cent level by t-test and 1 per cent by Mann-Whitney test. However, I cannot find any significant difference between old firms and young firms in the cold market issue.

From this result, I can see that the outperformance of old firms over young firms that was found in sub-section 7.2.3 was mainly caused by the outperformance of old firms that got listed in the KOSDAQ in the hot-market period.

Table 7.8(3) also confirms the conflicting results of KOSDAQ-adjusted and SBMP-adjusted BHARs between small firms and big firms. While KOSDAQ-adjusted BHARs show the outperformance of small firms over big firms, SBMP-adjusted BHARs show vice-versa. For the twelve-month BHARs of the IPOs brought to KOSDAQ in the hot-market period, KOSDAQ-adjusted BHARs show that the abnormal return of small firms is 0.49, significantly higher than – 0.03 of big firms at 1 per cent level by t-test and Mann-Whitney test. Twenty-four month KOSDAQ-adjusted BHARs in the hot-market period also shows the significant outperformance of small firms (0.34) relative to big firms (0.00) at 1 per cent level by t-test and Mann-Whitney test.

Table 7.8(3) BHARs in hot and cold markets by market capitalisation on KOSDAQ 1999–2001

		Mean	Median	Mean	Median	T-Statistics by t-test	Z-scores by Mann-Whitney Test
		Small		**Big**			
12 Month							
HOT	KOSDAQ	0.49	*0.14*	−0.03	*−0.08*	2.62***	−4.66***
	SIMF	−0.12	*−0.10*	−0.25	*−0.18*	0.55	−1.59
	SBMP	−0.42	*−0.53*	−0.40	*−0.29*	−0.08	−2.57**
	(No.IPOs)	(80)		(47)			
COLD	KOSDAQ	0.03	*−0.05*	−0.11	*−0.19*	1.86*	−1.33
	SIMF	−0.08	*−0.14*	−0.19	*−0.15*	1.03	−0.74
	SBMP	−0.19	*−0.26*	−0.32	*−0.36*	1.75*	−1.00
	(No.IPOs)	(73)		(96)			
24 Month							
HOT	KOSDAQ	0.34	*0.10*	0.00	*−0.09*	2.92***	−3.81***
	SIMF	−0.17	*−0.18*	−0.35	*−0.10*	1.05	−0.65
	SBMP	−0.83	*−0.68*	−0.50	*−0.47*	−2.18**	−2.59***
	(No.IPOs)	(80)		(46)			

Source: Korean Information System, IPO prospectuses

Note: Asterisks denote significant levels at the level of 1% (***), 5% (**), and 10% (*)

However, this outperformance of small firms compared with big firms is reversed when the raw returns are adjusted by SBMP. The twelve-month small firms SBMP-adjusted BHAR is − 0.42, lower than − 0.40 of big firms significantly at 5 per cent level by Mann-Whitney test. The twenty-four month small firms SBMP-adjusted BHAR is also significantly lower for small firms (−0.83) than for big firms (−0.50).

As was stated in sub-section 7.2.4 and section7.3, it seems that this occurs because the benchmark portfolio matched with big IPO firms, being constituted by big firms too, underperform small-sized benchmark portfolios, rather than because the small firms did not show better long-term performance than the old firms.   A noteworthy point is that the outperformance of small firms relative to big firms were led by the IPO firms that were brought to KOSDAQ in the hot-market period. Although the twelve-month BHARs of IPOs in the cold-market issues show that small firms outperformed big firms significantly, the difference of returns between the two groups was narrowed.

Table 7.8(4) shows the outperformance of non-high-tech firms compared with high-tech firms as in the sub-section 7.2.5. The twenty-four month non-high-tech KOSDAQ-adjusted BHAR is 0.31, which is significantly higher than 0.13 of high-tech firms at 1 per cent level by Mann-Whitney test. An interesting point is that SIMF-adjusted BHAR of high-tech firms in the cold-market period out-performs those of non-high-tech firm significantly at 5 per cent level by Mann-Whitney test. Actually, this significance did not appear in sub-section 7.2.5 when

Table 7.8(4) BHARs in hot and cold markets by industry on KOSDAQ 1999–2001

		Mean	Median	Mean	Median	T-Statistics by t-test	Z-scores by Mann-Whitney Test
		High-tech		Non-high-tech			
	12 Month						
HOT	KOSDAQ	0.26	*0.02*	0.34	*0.04*	−0.40	−0.29
	SIMF	−0.16	*−0.17*	−0.17	*−0.05*	0.04	−1.30
	SBMP	−0.40	*−0.38*	−0.43	*−0.51*	0.11	−0.60
	(No.IPOs)	(67)		(60)			
COLD	KOSDAQ	−0.07	*−0.18*	−0.02	*−0.11*	−0.63	−0.61
	SIMF	−0.10	*−0.10*	−0.21	*−0.28*	1.02	−2.16**
	SBMP	−0.30	*−0.36*	−0.21	*−0.27*	−1.05	−0.37
	(No.IPOs)	(105)		(64)			
	24 Month						
HOT	KOSDAQ	0.13	*−0.05*	0.31	*0.13*	−1.65	−3.02***
	SIMF	−0.15	*−0.12*	−0.34	*−0.21*	1.16	−0.46
	SBMP	−0.70	*−0.57*	−0.73	*−0.65*	0.18	−0.34
	(No.IPOs)	(67)		(59)			

Source: Korean Information System, IPO prospectuses

Note: Asterisks denote significant levels at the level of 1% (***), 5% (**), and 10% (*)

the BHARs between high-tech and non-high-tech were compared throughout the whole sample period. This may imply that the high-tech firms brought to KOSDAQ in the cold-market period did not suffer from the loss of firm value as seriously as the high-tech firms in the hot market that experienced the serious downfall of share prices in line with bursting of dot.com bubble.

7.6 Long-term Performance between low and high underpricing groups by state of the market and VC-backing

Table 7.9 compares the long-term performance of low and high underpricing groups[12] across IPOs cross-classified by state of the market and VC-backing.

Panel A shows that, in both hot and cold markets, the IPOs that belonged to the low underpricing group recorded significantly higher long-term performance than those of high underpricing group. For twelve-month BHAR in the hot market, the KOSDAQ-adjusted BHAR of low underpricing group is 0.64, significantly higher than 0.13 of high underpricing group at 5 per cent level by t-test and 1 per cent level by Mann-Whitney test. The SIMF-adjusted BHAR of low underpricing group also shows significantly higher return (0.13) than high underpricing group (−0.31). This outperformance of low underpricing group also appears in the cold market. The twelve month KOSDAQ-adjusted BHAR of low underpricing group in the cold market (0.08) performs better than that of high underpricing group (−0.22) at 1 per cent level. The SIMF- and SBMP-adjusted

Table 7.9 BHARs between low and high underpricing groups by state of the market and VC-backing on KOSDAQ 1999–2001

		Mean	Median	Mean	Median	T-Statistics by t-test	Z-scores by Mann-Whitney Test
		Low Underpricing		High Underpricing			
Panel A: by State of the Market							
12 Month							
HOT	KOSDAQ	0.64	0.32	0.13	−0.05	2.48**	−5.53***
	SIMF	0.13	0.01	−0.31	−0.21	1.78*	−3.90***
	SBMP	−0.41	−0.60	−0.42	−0.37	0.06	−1.17
	(No.IPOs)	(41)		(86)			
COLD	KOSDAQ	0.08	−0.01	−0.22	−0.30	3.87***	−5.03***
	SIMF	−0.07	−0.10	−0.24	−0.21	1.63	−1.98**
	SBMP	−0.15	−0.23	−0.42	−0.50	3.58***	−5.05***
	(No.IPOs)	(97)		(72)			
	24 Month						
HOT	KOSDAQ	0.50	0.29	0.08	−0.07	3.60***	−6.06***
	SIMF	−0.01	−0.09	−0.35	−0.16	1.93*	−1.77*
	SBMP	−0.84	−0.73	−0.65	−0.56	−1.17	−1.03
	(No.IPOs)	(41)		(85)			
Panel B: by VC-backing							
12 Month							
VC-backed	KOSDAQ	0.18	0.09	0.05	−0.10	0.77	−2.54**
	SIMF	0.07	−0.04	−0.24	−0.22	1.99**	−3.51***
	SBMP	−0.24	−0.30	−0.41	−0.49	1.03	−3.48***
	(No.IPOs)	(52)		(82)			
Non-VC-backed	KOSDAQ	0.29	0.10	−0.11	−0.17	3.44***	−4.38***
	SIMF	−0.06	−0.06	−0.33	−0.20	1.55	−2.14**
	SBMP	−0.22	−0.26	−0.42	−0.40	1.53	−1.68*
	(No.IPOs)	(86)		(76)			
	24 Month						
VC-backed	KOSDAQ	0.25	0.19	0.05	−0.10	0.92	−3.48***
	SIMF	−0.07	−0.08	−0.36	−0.20	0.98	−1.82*
	SBMP	−0.60	−0.59	−0.72	−0.64	0.44	−0.70
	(No.IPOs)	(12)		(51)			
Non-VC-backed	KOSDAQ	0.60	0.41	0.11	−0.05	3.56***	−4.23***
	SIMF	0.02	−0.18	−0.33	−0.02	1.46	−0.76
	SBMP	−0.93	−0.74	−0.55	−0.42	−1.92*	−2.11**
	(No.IPOs)	(29)		(34)			

Source: Korean Information System, IPO prospectuses

Note: KOSDAQ IPO samples are grouped into Low Underpricing firms (when the underpricing is equal to or less than the median value, 1.05) and High Underpricing firms. This type of grouping applies to the remaining parts of the chapter. Asterisks denote significant levels at the level of 1% (***), 5% (**), and 10% (*)

BHAR in the cold market also shows the same significant outperformance of low underpricing group over high underpricing group. For twenty-four month BHAR, the better performance of low underpricing group is also observed. The KOSDAQ-adjusted BHAR is significantly higher for low underpricing group (0.50) than for low underpricing group (0.08) at 1 per cent level. The SIMF-adjusted BHAR shows the similar outperformance of low underpricing group (–0.01) over high underpricing group (–0.35).

This significant difference of long-term performance between low underpricing group and high underpricing group clearly shows the significantly negative relationship between underpricing and the long-term performance. As discussed in Chapter 3, global stock markets have reported that higher initial returns at the initial stage of IPO resulted in the poor long-term performance (Ritter, 1991; Loughran and Ritter, 1995). However, the poorer underperformance of high underpricing group of KOSDAQ IPO firms shows that it is more likely that the firms which experienced higher underpricing will suffer from the worse underperformance than those which went through lower underpricing. This phenomenon can be attributable to the hot issue market, but in the cold market, I also observe the same phenomenon. This may imply that, when the divergence of opinion that existed among investors disappears in the long run (Miller, 2000), the firms that had higher underpricing at the initial stage of IPOs are more likely to be subject to more acute deterioration of the stock prices in the long run.

This also may indicate that the IPO stocks whose value was overestimated at the initial stage of IPO by artificially created market demand turn out to show lower subsequent returns (Shiller, 1990).

Panel B compares the BHARs of low underpricing group and high underpricing group cross-classified by VC-backing. It appears that, in both VC-backed and non-VC-backed IPOs, low underpricing group shows higher return than high underpricing group. In the VC-backed group, the KOSDAQ-adjusted twelve-month BHAR is significantly higher for low underpricing group (0.18) than for high underpricing group (0.05). For the same period, the SIMF-adjusted BHARs show significant outperformance of low underpricing group (0.07) compared to high underpricing group (–0.24). The SBMP-adjusted BHARs of low underpricing group (–0.24) is significantly higher than that of high underpricing group (–0.41). Non-VC-backed IPOs twelve-month BHARs also show the significant outperformance of low underpricing group over high underpricing group for all three benchmarks. For twenty-four month returns, the outperformance of low underpricing group relative to high underpricing group is generally found. For VC-backed group, the KOSDAQ- and SIMF-adjusted BHARs are significantly higher for low underpricing group than high underpricing group. Non-VC-backed group shows conflicting results of long-term performance between low underpricing group and high underpricing group, depending on the benchmarks. While the KOSDAQ-adjusted BHAR shows the significant outperformance of low underpricing group over the high underpricing group, the SBMP-adjusted BHAR shows the significantly better performance of high underpricing group. Given the persistent pattern of outperformance of low underpricing group in Table 7.9, this exception is the result of the choice of benchmark.[13]

Table 7.10 compares the BHARs of low underpricing group and high under-pricing group cross-classified by the institutional affiliation with VC-backing. It appears that the outperformance of low underpricing group relative to high underpricing group is also observed in this analysis. For twelve-month return,

Table 7.10 BHARs between low and high underpricing groups by the institutional affiliation of VC-backing on KOSDAQ 1999–2001

		Mean	Median	Mean	Median	T-Statistics by t-test	Z-scores by Mann-Whitney Test
		Low Underpricing		High Underpricing			
	12 Month						
Bank-affiliated	KOSDAQ	0.27	*0.27*	0.41	*–0.08*	–0.21	–2.20**
	SIMF	0.13	*–0.05*	0.02	*–0.25*	0.18	–1.89*
	SBMP	–0.09	*–0.04*	–0.23	*–0.65*	0.19	–2.85***
	(No.IPOs)	(10)		(19)			
Security Company-	KOSDAQ	–0.14	*–0.23*	–0.21	*–0.15*	2.48**	–0.43
	SIMF	–0.12	*–0.04*	–0.16	*–0.01*	0.72	–0.14
	SBMP	–0.43	*–0.39*	–0.42	*–0.42*	–0.95	–0.29
	(No.IPOs)	(6)		(7)			
Other Institution-	KOSDAQ	0.20	*0.09*	–0.04	*–0.10*	2.31**	–2.14**
	SIMF	0.08	*–0.03*	–0.33	*–0.22*	3.54***	–2.93***
	SBMP	–0.24	*–0.33*	–0.48	*–0.47*	1.92*	–2.40**
	(No.IPOs)	(36)		(56)			
	24 Month						
Bank-affiliated	KOSDAQ	–	–	0.39	*–0.03*	–	–
	SIMF	–	–	0.21	*–0.13*	–	–
	SBMP	–	–	–0.53	*–0.64*	–	–
	(No.IPOs)	–	–	(13)		–	–
Security Company-	KOSDAQ	0.20	*0.20*	–0.19	*–0.20*	2.79*	–1.41
	SIMF	–1.43	*–1.43*	–0.32	*–0.14*	–0.84	–1.41
	SBMP	–1.48	*–1.48*	–0.48	*–0.46*	–0.74	–1.41
	(No.IPOs)	(1)		(4)			
Other Institution-	KOSDAQ	0.26	*0.17*	–0.05	*–0.10*	3.46***	–3.49***
	SIMF	0.05	*–0.07*	–0.59	*–0.30*	2.48**	–2.72***
	SBMP	–0.52	*–0.55*	–0.82	*–0.65*	1.43	–1.22
	(No.IPOs)	(11)		(34)			

Source: Korean Information System, IPO prospectuses

Note: Asterisks denote significant levels at the level of 1% (***), 5% (**), and 10% (*)

the SIMF-adjusted BHAR of bank-affiliated VC-backing is significantly higher for low underpricing group (0.13) than for high underpricing group (0.02) and the SBMP-adjusted BHAR of the same type of VC-backing shows a significantly higher performance for low underpricing group (–0.09) than for high underpricing group (–0.23).

However, the KOSDAQ-adjusted BHAR shows significantly higher performance of high underpricing group, which was caused by the underperformance of KOSDAQ benchmark matched with high underpricing group.[14]

The security company-affiliated KOSDAQ-adjusted BHAR shows a significantly higher performance of low underpricing group. The other institution-affiliated BHAR shows significantly higher performance of low underpricing group for all three benchmarks. For twenty-four month returns, the security company-affiliated KOSDAQ-adjusted BHAR and other institution-affiliated KOSDAQ- and SIMF-adjusted BHARs also show the significant outperformance of low underpricing group compared to high underpricing group.

7.7 Multivariate regression analysis of long-term performance[15]

So far I have considered univariate and bivariate analyses of long-term performance. In this section, I cover our multivariate analysis. I report the regression results of twenty-four month BHARs for IPOs that were listed in the hot-market period and of twelve-month BHARs for the IPOs that were listed in KOSDAQ in the cold-market period.[16] The IPO firms whose twenty-four month returns are available were listed in KOSDAQ in the hot-market period. Therefore, the regression analysis of twenty-four month BHARs for the hot-market IPOs is at the same time the regression analysis of all IPOs. Since our stock market data ends at March 2002, the long-term performance of the cold-market IPOs, which were listed after April 2000, was limited to the twelve-month BHARs. The regression tables of the twelve-month BHARs of the hot and cold combined and the hot-market IPOs alone were excluded in this sub-section, because the difference of coefficients turned out to be negligible in all three benchmark-adjusted BHARs regressions.[17]

The multivariate analysis addresses each of the groups of hypotheses I have set out. It follows the structure that was developed at the end of Chapter 4, which indicated the specification of regression models and the expected coefficients sign patterns. In each table in this section, I adopt the format set out in Chapter 4. Each table contains five regressions.

Model 1 tests for the impact of VC-backing (H1b) by including a dummy variable *VC* taking the value of 1 for VC-backed IPOs. *VC* is expected to show positive sign.

Model 2, in the first regime (which includes all sample firms), tests for the impact of VC-backing (H1b) by including *VC* and, in the second regime (which includes VC-backed firms only), tests for the impact of the reputation of VC-backing (H2b) by including dummy variables *VCk* and *VC3* which take the value of 1, when KTB and the big three venture capitalists respectively (KTB, KTI, and KDBC) back IPOs as lead venture capitalists, respectively. *VCk* and *VC3* are expected to show positive signs.

Models 3 and 4 test for the impact of institutional affiliation of VC (H3b and H4b) by including dummy variables *VCbank* and *VCsecu* which take the value of 1, when bank-affiliated VCs and security company-affiliated VCs back IPOs as lead venture capitalists, respectively. *VCbank* is expected to have positive coefficients and *VCsecu* to have negative coefficients.

Model 5 tests for the impact of reputation of underwriter and auditor (H5b and H6b) by including dummy variables *Und3* and *Aud3* which take the value of 1, when big three underwriters and big three auditors are involved with the IPO process and the auditing, respectively. *Und3* and *Aud3* are expected to show positive coefficients. Model 5 also tests for the impact of VC-backing (in the first regime) (H1b) and the reputation of VC-backing (in the second regime) (H2b).

Each of the five regressions is estimated with a constant term and nine variables controlling respectively for the effect of IPO company characteristics (age, market capitalisation, book-to-market ratio, the shareholdings of CEO and his related persons, and high-tech industry), stock market condition (number of IPOs, market index, and monthly change of market index) and underpricing.

7.7.1 *Regression analysis* of long-term performance for IPOs in the hot market

7.7.1.1 *Regression analysis of KOSDAQ-adjusted BHARs*

Table 7.11 shows the coefficients results of twenty-four month KOSDAQ-adjusted BHARs of IPO firms in the hot-market period. In Panel A, which provides estimates for all IPO firms, the age of IPO firms (*Lage*) has a positive relationship with twenty-four month KOSDAQ-adjusted BHARs at 5 per cent level in all model specifications of Panel A. Moreover, The market capitalisation (*LMC*), used as a proxy for firm size, shows negative relationship with KOSDAQ-adjusted BHARs at 1 per cent level in all models of Panel A. As was found in the univariate analysis, old firms and small firms outperformed young firms and big firms, respectively. These results are contrary to the findings in Hamao, Packer et al. (2000), who found the positive relationship of firm size with long-term performance and the negative relationship of age with long-term performance.

Gompers and Lerner (1999) also found that the size of the IPO firms is positively related to the long-term performances.[18] Moreover, it is found that underpricing (*UP*) has negative relationship with KOSDAQ-adjusted BHARs at 5 per cent or 10 per cent level in all model specifications of Panel A. This result is line with the finding suggested by Shiller (1990), who argued that the companies which experienced the higher initial returns should have the lower subsequent returns, because the higher initial returns do not reflect the true value of the firms, but were generated by the artificially created market demand. Our finding also supports hot-market theory. High initial returns can be a result of a temporary overvaluation by investors in the hot market. The poor long-term

Table 7.11 Cross-sectional regressions on twenty-four month KOSDAQ-adjusted BHARs in hot market

	Model 1		Model 2		Model 3		Model 4		Model 5	
Panel A: Regressions for All Sample Firms										
Intercept	2.53	(2.73)***	2.52	(2.74)***	2.24	(2.77)***	2.23	(2.77)***	2.69	(2.61)***
Lage	0.18	(2.26)**	0.18	(2.26)**	0.19	(2.39)**	0.19	(2.36)**	0.17	(2.04)**
LMC	-0.10	(-3.26)***	-0.10	(-3.29)***	-0.09	(-3.20)***	-0.09	(-3.17)***	-0.11	(-2.98)***
Bmr	-0.03	(-0.43)	-0.03	(-0.45)	-0.04	(-0.61)	-0.04	(-0.61)	-0.06	(-0.89)
SbCEO	-0.19	(-0.67)	-0.23	(-0.71)	-0.16	(-0.64)	-0.17	(-0.63)	-0.15	(-0.59)
UP	-0.04	(-2.07)**	-0.04	(-2.12)**	-0.04	(-1.95)*	-0.04	(-1.99)**	-0.03	(-2.14)**
High-tech	-0.07	(-0.77)	-0.08	(-0.78)	-0.04	(-1.26)	-0.04	(-1.21)	-0.08	(-0.82)
VC	-0.18	(-2.14)**	-0.19	(-2.25)**	-0.11		-0.10		-0.16	(-1.66)*
VCbank					0.15	(0.44)	0.15	(0.44)		
VCsecu					-0.33	(-4.11)***	-0.33	(-3.81)***		
VCetc					-0.23	(-2.45)**	-0.23	(-2.44)**		
Bank			0.00	(-0.02)			-0.05	(-0.20)		
Secu			-0.07	(-0.56)						
Und3									-0.04	(-0.36)
Aud3									0.17	(0.88)
AdjustedR	0.20		0.20		0.22		0.22		0.21	
Prob>F	0.00		0.00		0.00		0.00		0.00	
No.IPOs	126		126		126		126		126	

(Continued)

Table 7.11 (Continued)

	Model 1		Model 2		Model 3		Model 4		Model 5	
Panel B: Regressions for VC-backed Firms Only										
Intercept	1.26	(0.87)	1.25	(0.85)	0.33	(0.26)	0.30	(0.25)	1.55	(0.88)
Lage	-0.03	(-0.25)	-0.03	(-0.24)	-0.08	(-0.71)	-0.08	(-0.58)	-0.03	(-0.26)
LMC	-0.04	(-0.70)	-0.03	(-0.65)	0.00	(-0.06)	0.00	(-0.03)	-0.05	(-0.75)
Bmr	-0.16	(-0.21)	-0.15	(-0.20)	0.16	(0.30)	0.15	(0.27)	-0.32	(-0.36)
SbCEO	-0.11	(-0.26)	-0.14	(-0.25)	-0.21	(-0.46)	-0.23	(-0.41)	-0.03	(-0.08)
UP	-0.04	(-1.25)	-0.04	(-1.31)	-0.05	(-1.28)	-0.05	(-1.31)	-0.03	(-1.32)
High-tech	0.06	(0.42)	0.03	(0.21)	-0.05	(-0.59)	-0.05	(-0.58)	0.05	(0.35)
VCk	-0.21	(-1.09)								
VC3			-0.22	(-1.23)					-0.18	(-1.29)
VCbank					0.64	(1.55)	0.65	(1.43)		
VCetc					0.23	(2.07)**	0.24	(1.96)*		
Bank			0.03	(0.10)			-0.04	(-0.13)		
Secu			-0.07	(-0.64)						
Und3									-0.06	(-0.38)
Aud3									0.37	(0.87)
AdjustedR	0.07		0.08		0.11		0.11		0.12	
Prob>F	0.27		0.30		0.20		0.28		0.59	
No.IPOs	63		63		63		63		63	

Note: T-statistics in the parentheses are heteroskedasticity consistent. VCsecu in Panel B was dropped in the regressions. Asterisks beside t-statistics * , ** , *** denote significance at 10%, 5%, 1% level, respectively.

performance follows as a result of this overvaluation at the initial stage of IPOs (Aggarwal and Rivoli, 1990). In addition, Panel B, which yields the estimates for VC-backed firms only, does not show any significant coefficients for control variables.

I turn to the tests of our hypotheses and find that, in Panel A for the hot-market IPOs, Model 1 and Model 2 reject the effect for VC-backing for long-term performance. VC-backing was expected to have positive relationship with long-term performance (hypothesis H1b). On the contrary, VC-backing (*VC*) has significantly negative relationship with KOSDAQ-adjusted BHARs in Models 1 and 2. Model 2 also shows that the shareholdings of banks (*Bank)* and security companies (*Secu)* in addition to VC-backing have no effect on R-square and yield insignificant coefficients on those variables. This long-run underperformance of VC-backed IPOs relative to non-VC-backed IPOs in the hot market seems to show that the high underpricing effects of VC-backed IPOs in the hot market resulted in the poorer performance in the long-term. In model 3 which tests for the impact of different types of institutional affiliation of VC-backing, the result is in line with our hypothesis. In keeping with our univariate results I found a significantly minus coefficients for security company-affiliated VC (*VCsecu*) at 1 per cent level. This result is also found in Model 4. These significantly minus coefficients of security company-affiliated VC (*VCsecu*) support our hypothesis H4b (poor long-term performance by the backing of security company-affiliated VCs), although security company-affiliated VC showed the negative underpricing effects in the underpricing regression in the hot market. There is no evidence of better long-term performance by bank-affiliated VCs in Models 3 and 4, thus showing no support for the hypothesis H3b. Finally, Model 5, which tests for the impact of underwriter and auditor reputation, yields insignificant results. Panel B reveals that, for the VC-backed firms, there is no significant evidence of the impact of VC-backing, the reputation of VC-backing, the institutional affiliation of VC-backing and the reputation of underwriter and auditors, respectively.

The regression results show that there is little evidence supporting the H2b (the impact of the VC reputation on the long-term performance), H3B (the impact of bank-affiliated VC-backing) and the H5b and H6b (the impact of underwriter and auditor reputation on the long-term performance). However, I find the regression results in line with H4b (the impact of security company-affiliated VC-backing). Our results reject H1b (the impact of VC-backing). This underperformance of VC-backing IPOs is consistent with the finding in Kutsuna, Cowling et al. (2000)'s Japanese study.

7.7.1.2 *Regression analysis of SIMF-adjusted BHARs*

Table 7.12 exhibits the regression coefficients of twenty-four month SIMF-adjusted BHARs for all IPOs that were listed in KOSDAQ in the hot-market period.[19] For the impact of control variables,[20] it is shown the significant difference of firm age (*Lage*), which was shown in KOSDAQ-adjusted BHARs regressions, disappeared in SIMF-adjusted BHARs regressions. A notable

Table 7.12 Cross-sectional regressions on twenty-four month SIMF-adjusted BHARs in hot market

	Model 1		Model 2		Model 3		Model 4		Model 5	
Panel A: Regressions for All Sample Firms										
Intercept	1.07	(0.90)	0.98	(0.81)	1.06	(0.91)	1.00	(0.85)	1.11	(0.97)
Lage	0.02	(0.11)	0.01	(0.06)	0.04	(0.22)	0.03	(0.19)	0.00	(0.01)
Bmr	-0.09	(-0.90)	-0.09	(-0.87)	-0.11	(-1.05)	-0.11	(-1.03)	-0.17	(-1.50)
SbCEO	-0.63	(-1.33)	-0.50	(-0.95)	-0.59	(-1.29)	-0.54	(-1.13)	-0.53	(-1.16)
NumIPO	-0.01	(-1.34)	-0.01	(-1.36)	-0.01	(-1.20)	-0.01	(-1.27)	-0.01	(-1.23)
Kqindex	0.00	(-0.31)	0.00	(-0.31)	0.00	(-0.35)	0.00	(-0.32)	0.00	(-0.47)
Kqchange	-0.80	(-1.28)	-0.78	(-1.22)	-0.80	(-1.22)	-0.80	(-1.20)	-0.82	(-1.36)
UP	-0.04	(-1.46)	-0.05	(-1.55)	-0.05	(-1.56)	-0.05	(-1.58)	-0.04	(-1.26)
VC	-0.20	(-1.19)	-0.18	(-1.11)					-0.20	(-1.12)
VCbank					0.37	(1.09)	0.35	(1.02)		
VCsecu					-0.55	(-1.95)*	-0.54	(-1.87)*		
VCetc					-0.29	(-1.68)*	-0.29	(-1.66)*		
Bank			0.33	(1.35)			0.27	(0.96)		
Secu			0.10	(0.51)						
Und3									0.27	(1.77)*
Aud3									0.22	(1.12)
AdjustedR	0.09		0.10		0.13		0.14		0.11	
Prob>F	0.28		0.26		0.31		0.27		0.23	
No.IPOs	126		126		126		126		126	
Panel B: Regressions for VC-backed Firms Only										
Intercept	3.37	(1.71)*	3.21	(1.67)	4.12	(1.93)*	4.02	(1.84)*	3.87	(1.95)*
Lage	-0.09	(-0.29)	-0.13	(-0.40)	-0.10	(-0.33)	-0.15	(-0.48)	-0.20	(-0.69)
Bmr	-0.99	(-0.81)	-0.95	(-0.70)	-0.92	(-0.90)	-0.83	(-0.79)	-1.14	(-0.90)
SbCEO	-0.92	(-1.17)	-0.71	(-0.78)	-0.80	(-1.15)	-0.62	(-0.82)	-0.70	(-0.96)
NumIPO	-0.01	(-0.89)	-0.01	(-1.14)	0.00	(-0.42)	0.00	(-0.51)	0.00	(-0.24)
Kqindex	-0.01	(-1.44)	-0.01	(-1.42)	-0.01	(-1.58)	-0.01	(-1.51)	-0.01	(-1.77)*

Variable	(1)	(2)	(3)	(4)	(5)
Kqchange	−1.77 (−1.55)	−1.88 (−1.49)	−1.86 (−1.64)	−1.91 (−1.68)*	−2.04 (−1.70)*
UP	−0.04 (−1.06)	−0.04 (−1.17)	−0.04 (−1.11)	−0.05 (−1.16)	−0.03 (−0.83)
VCk	−0.17 (−0.67)				
VC3		−0.19 (−0.63)			−0.12 (−0.47)
VCsecu			−0.76 (−2.27)**	−0.71 (−2.02)**	
VCetc			−0.68 (−1.90)*	−0.66 (−1.74)*	
Bank		0.51 (1.81)*		0.43 (1.19)	
Secu		0.02 (0.10)			
Und3					0.28 (1.30)
Aud3					0.35 (1.25)
AdjustedR	0.23	0.25	0.31	0.33	0.27
Prob>F	0.42	0.30	0.30	0.22	0.46
No.IPOs	63	63	63	63	63

Note: T-statistics in the parentheses are heteroskedasicity consistent. VCbank in Panel B was dropped in the regressions. Asterisks beside t-statistics *, **, *** denote significance at 10%, 5%, 1% level, respectively.

result is that banking ownership (*Bank*) has a significantly positive relationship with SIMF-adjusted BHARs in a model of Panel B. This may be evidence that the banking institutions contributed to the value-adding of the IPO firms in which they hold shares, thus resulting in their better performance in the long run (Calomiris and Ramirez, 1996; Edwards and Fischer, 1994). However, unlike the regression of KOSDAQ-adjusted BHARs in which the control variables relating to stock market situation were excluded from the regression models, the regressions on the SIMF-adjusted BHARs included these variables and I find that the stock market situation is closely related to the long-term performance. It is also shown that monthly change of market index (*Kqchange*) has a negative relationship with SIMF-adjusted BHARs in two models of Panel B at 10 per cent level.

The market index (*Kqindex*) is also negatively related to SIMF-adjusted BHARs in a model of Panel B. This result clearly shows that the IPOs brought to KOSDAQ in the period when the stock market is hot experience the worse long-term performance in the long run (Ritter and Welch, 2002).

In Panel A, I find that Models 1 and 2 do not show any significant coefficients for VC-backing (*VC*), unlike the cases of regressions on KOSDAQ-adjusted BHARs. In Models 3 and 4, the coefficients of security-affiliated VC (*VCsecu*) display a significantly negative relationship with SIMF-adjusted BHARs at 10 per cent level. Although bank-affiliated VC-backing (*VCbank*) shows expected positive signs in the two models, they are insignificant. The other institution-affiliated VC-backing turned out to be negatively related to SIMF-adjusted BHARs at 10 per cent level. Model 5 shows that there is a significant reputational effect of underwriters for IPO firms. This is consistent with the finding in Carter, Dark et al., (1998) that the participation of reputable underwriters in the IPO process was associated with better long-term performance of IPO firms.

In Panel B, it is shown that the VC-backing (*VC*) and the reputation of VC-backing (*VCk, VC3*) do not have significant association with SIMF-adjusted BHARs in Models 1 and 2. However, in the regressions in Models 3 and 4 of Panel B, I find the security company-affiliated VC (*VCsecu*)'s significantly negative relationship with SIMF-adjusted BHARs. The coefficients of security company-affiliated VC are significant at 5 per cent level in Models 3 and 4. This negative relationship of security company-affiliated VC with long-term performance indicates that the IPO firms backed by venture capitalists having affiliation with security companies might cause conflict of interest between investors and issuing company by the security companies' intention to take advantage of investors by overvaluing the firms they back at the time of IPO. It is more likely that these IPO firms suffered from the poorer performance in the long run (Gompers and Lerner, 1999; Hamao, Packer et al., 2000).

The regressions on SIMF-adjusted BHARs in the hot market suggest that there is significant evidence in support of H4b (the impact of security company-affiliated VCs in the long-term performance) and H5b (the impact of underwriter reputation in the long-term performance).

7.7.1.3 Regression analysis of SBMP-adjusted BHARs

Table 7.13 shows the regression coefficients of SBMP-adjusted BHARs for all IPOs that were listed in KOSDAQ in the hot-market period. I find the lack of significant coefficients in the regression table as a whole, compared with those of KOSDAQ-adjusted and SIMF-adjusted BHARs.

As for the control variables,[21] while the significance of market index (*Kqindex*) is negligible and that of monthly change of market index (*Kqchange*) is not found in the SBMP-adjusted BHARs regressions unlike the SIMF-adjusted regressions, the other variable, such as the number of IPOs (*NumIPO*), used as a proxy of stock market situation, is found to have significantly negative relationship with SBMP-adjusted BHARs in almost of all models of Panel A and Panel B at 1 per cent, 5 per cent or 10 per cent level. This indicates that the IPOs, which were listed when the IPO market was witnessing the increasing number of IPOs, perform worse than others in the long run.

In the regressions, I find that the significant differences of the variables relating to the institutional affiliation of VC-backing are not shown in all model specifications, only except for the case of the reputation of auditor in Model 5 of Panel A. This finding may be evidence that the reputational auditor took a positive impact on the long-term performance of the IPO firms. The impact of VC-backing (*VC*) and the reputation of VC-backing (*VCk, VC3*) does not show any significant coefficients in the regressions. Although also insignificant, the signs of coefficients in Models 3 and 4 in Panel A and B still consistently show that the bank-affiliated VC (*VCbank*) have a positive relationship with long-term performance, while the security company-affiliated VC (*VCsecu*) has a negative relationship with long-term performance. Moreover, it is seen that the reputation of underwriter does not show significant coefficients in the regressions.

The regression results of SBMP-adjusted BHARs support the hypothesis H6b, but do not support H1b, H2b, H3b, H4b and H5b.

7.7.2 Regression analysis of long-term performance for IPOs in cold market

7.7.2.1 Regression analysis of KOSDAQ-adjusted BHARs

Table 7.14 shows the regression coefficients of twelve-month KOSDAQ-adjusted BHARs that were listed in KOSDAQ in the cold-market period.

For the control variables, market capitalisation (*LMC*) has a significantly negative relationship with KOSDAQ-adjusted BHARs in all models of Panels A and B at 1 per cent, 5 per cent or 10 per cent level. This finding is in line with the result in regressions of hot market issues. Book-to-market ratio (*Bmr*) is positively related to KOSDAQ-adjusted BHARs at 10 per cent level in Panel B. This implies that the IPOs, which experienced lower increase of share prices relative to book value of equity, outperformed in the long run. This is consistent with

Table 7.13 Cross-sectional regressions on twenty-four month SBMP-adjusted BHARs in hot market

	Model 1		Model 2		Model 3		Model 4		Model 5	
Panel A: Regressions for All Sample Firms										
Intercept	-1.80	(-1.45)	-1.87	(-1.46)	-1.81	(-1.43)	-1.84	(-1.43)	-2.03	(-1.71)*
Lage	0.02	(0.09)	0.01	(0.05)	0.02	(0.10)	0.01	(0.07)	-0.01	(-0.08)
ShCEO	-0.18	(-0.46)	-0.04	(-0.09)	-0.18	(-0.48)	-0.14	(-0.35)	-0.10	(-0.27)
High-Tech	0.01	(0.04)	0.01	(0.05)	0.00	(-0.03)	-0.01	(-0.10)	0.02	(0.11)
NumIPO	-0.01	(-3.63)***	-0.01	(-3.56)***	-0.01	(-3.50)***	-0.02	(-3.53)***	-0.01	(-3.69)***
Kqindex	0.01	(1.65)	0.01	(1.59)	0.01	(1.62)	0.01	(1.62)	0.01	(1.84)*
Kqchange	-0.24	(-0.44)	-0.22	(-0.39)	-0.22	(-0.36)	-0.22	(-0.36)	-0.03	(-0.06)
UP	0.00	(0.08)	0.00	(-0.06)	0.00	(-0.01)	0.00	(-0.08)	0.01	(0.29)
VC	0.00	(0.01)	0.02	(0.13)					0.06	(0.35)
VCbank					0.10	(0.24)	0.10	(0.22)		
VCsecu					-0.12	(-0.46)	-0.11	(-0.40)		
VCetc					-0.01	(-0.03)	0.00	(-0.02)		
Bank			0.17	(0.87)			0.18	(0.80)		
Secu			0.16	(1.03)						
Und3									-0.09	(-0.47)
Aud3									0.32	(1.67)*
AdjustedR	0.09		0.10		0.09		0.09		0.12	
Prob>F	0.03		0.03		0.08		0.08		0.03	
No.IPOs	126		126		126		126		126	
Panel B: Regressions for VC-backed Firms Only										
Intercept	-1.07	(-0.41)	-1.21	(-0.45)	-1.09	(-0.38)	-1.10	(-0.38)	-0.88	(-0.33)
Lage	-0.29	(-1.24)	-0.28	(-1.18)	-0.24	(-0.96)	-0.27	(-1.05)	-0.31	(-1.20)
ShCEO	-0.24	(-0.30)	-0.03	(-0.03)	-0.18	(-0.23)	-0.07	(-0.08)	-0.04	(-0.06)
High-Tech	-0.18	(-1.01)	-0.13	(-0.76)	-0.18	(-1.16)	-0.18	(-1.18)	-0.15	(-0.83)
NumIPO	-0.01	(-2.20)**	-0.01	(-2.16)**	-0.01	(-1.80)*	-0.01	(-1.82)*	-0.01	(-1.38)
Kqindex	0.01	(0.76)	0.01	(0.78)	0.01	(0.66)	0.01	(0.67)	0.01	(0.50)

	(1)	(2)	(3)	(4)	(5)
Kqchange	-1.27 (-1.47)	-1.25 (-1.33)	-1.29 (-1.26)	-1.36 (-1.33)	-1.01 (-1.14)
UP	0.00 (-0.06)	-0.01 (-0.39)	-0.01 (-0.26)	-0.01 (-0.35)	0.00 (0.00)
VCk	0.30 (1.59)				
VC3		0.09 (0.42)			0.19 (1.08)
VCbank			0.18 (0.41)	0.15 (0.33)	
VCetc			0.00 (-0.01)	-0.02 (-0.08)	
Bank		0.25 (0.95)		0.26 (0.81)	
Secu		0.11 (0.47)			
Und3					-0.18 (-0.60)
Aud3					0.53 (1.41)
AdjustedR	0.16	0.15	0.14	0.15	0.19
Prob>F	0.08	0.23	0.30	0.31	0.15
No.IPOs	63	63	63	63	63

Note: T-statistics in the parentheses are heteroskedasicity consistent. *VCsecu* in Panel B was dropped in the regressions. Asterisks beside t-statistics *, **, *** denote significance at 10%, 5%, 1% level, respectively.

Table 7.14 Cross-sectional regressions on twelve-month KOSDAQ index-adjusted BHARs in cold market

	Model 1	Model 2	Model 3	Model 4	Model 5
Panel A: Regressions for All Sample Firms					
Intercept	2.00 (2.45)**	2.40 (0.02)**	2.21 (0.03)**	2.23 (0.03)**	2.34 (0.02)**
Lage	-0.09 (-1.36)	-1.36 (0.18)	-1.42 (0.16)	-1.46 (0.15)	-1.42 (0.16)
LMC	-0.08 (-2.64)***	-2.56 (0.01)**	-2.36 (0.02)**	-2.38 (0.02)**	-2.47 (0.01)**
Bmr	0.25 (1.11)	1.10 (0.27)	1.20 (0.23)	1.20 (0.23)	1.20 (0.23)
SbCEO	0.16 (0.79)	0.72 (0.48)	0.68 (0.50)	0.71 (0.48)	0.98 (0.33)
UP	-0.10 (-3.01)***	-2.98 (0.00)***	-2.95 (0.00)***	-2.91 (0.00)***	-2.93 (0.00)***
High-tech	-0.08 (-1.02)	-0.92 (0.36)	-0.97 (0.34)	-0.97 (0.33)	-0.91 (0.36)
VC	0.13 (1.23)	1.08 (0.28)			1.16 (0.25)
VCbank			1.49 (0.14)	1.44 (0.15)	
VCsecu			-1.65 (0.10)	-1.62 (0.11)	
VCetc			1.30 (0.19)	1.23 (0.22)	
Bank		1.14 (0.26)		0.62 (0.54)	
Secu		-0.85 (0.39)			
Und3					0.56 (0.58)
Aud3					-0.37 (0.72)
AdjustedR	0.14	0.14	0.16	0.16	0.14
Prob>F	0.04	0.03	0.00	0.00	0.08
No.IPOs	169	169	169	169	169
Panel B: Regressions for VC-backed Firms Only					
Intercept	3.55 (2.13)**	3.75 (2.25)**	2.80 (1.53)	2.80 (1.52)	3.85 (2.21)**
Lage	-0.04 (-0.43)	-0.07 (-0.64)	-0.08 (-0.83)	-0.09 (-0.87)	-0.06 (-0.62)
LMC	-0.15 (-2.33)**	-0.16 (-2.45)**	-0.13 (-1.88)*	-0.13 (-1.87)*	-0.16 (-2.34)**
Bmr	1.08 (1.72)*	1.07 (1.71)*	1.14 (1.97)*	1.15 (1.98)*	1.02 (1.63)
SbCEO	0.42 (1.11)	0.44 (1.06)	0.34 (0.92)	0.37 (0.97)	0.43 (1.06)
UP	-0.16 (-2.79)***	-0.16 (-2.77)***	-0.16 (-2.63)**	-0.16 (-2.59)**	-0.16 (-2.84)***
High-tech	-0.11 (-0.93)	-0.09 (-0.72)	-0.08 (-0.71)	-0.08 (-0.68)	-0.09 (-0.74)

VCk	-0.11 (-1.01)	-0.01 (-0.08)			-0.01 (-0.12)
VC3					
VCbank			0.35 (1.96)*	0.34 (1.89)*	
VCetc			0.35 (2.14)**	0.34 (2.01)**	
Bank		0.13 (0.78)		0.05 (0.36)	
Secu		-0.08 (-0.50)			
Und3					0.03 (0.18)
Aud3					0.02 (0.12)
AdjustedR	0.45	0.45	0.48	0.48	0.44
Prob>F	0.00	0.00	0.00	0.00	0.00
No.IPOs	71	71	71	71	71

Note: T-statistics in the parentheses are heteroskedasicity consistent. *VCсец* in Panel B was dropped in the regressions. Asterisks beside t-statistics *, **, *** denote significance at 10%, 5%, 1% level, respectively.

the finding in Hamao, Packer et al., (2000) who found the same relationship of book-to-market ratio with the long-term performance. Underpricing (*UP*) is found to have a significantly negative relationship with KOSDAQ-adjusted BHARs at 1 per cent level in all model specifications of Panel A and B. As in the hot market, the firms with higher underpricing in the cold market led to the underperformance. It seems that this finding is consistent with the negative association of the worse performance with the higher underpricing which were found in Aggarwal and Rivoli (1990).

The regression result shows that the dummy variables relating to VC-backing (*VC*), the reputation of VC-backing (*VCk, VC3*), the security company-affiliated VC-backing (*VCsecu*) and the reputation of underwriter and auditor (*Und3, Aud3*) do not present any significant coefficients in all models of Panel A and Panel B. According, the results do not support hypotheses H1b (the impact of VC-backing on the long-term performance), H2b (the impact of the reputation of VC-backing on the long-term performance), H4b (the impact of security company-affiliated VC-backing) H5b (the impact of the reputation of underwriter on the long-term performance) and H6b (the impact of the reputation of auditor on the long-term performance).

On the contrary, it is apparent that bank-affiliated VC (*VCbank*) shows positive relationship with the KOSDAQ-adjusted BHARs in Model 3 and 4 of Panel B at 10 per cent level and that other institution-affiliated VC-backing (*VCetc*) is positively related to the KOSDAQ-adjusted BHARs at 5 per cent level in the same models. The coefficients of these two dummy variables are almost equal.

I note the significantly positive relationship of bank-affiliated VC in these results. This may be evidence that the bank-affiliated VC brings better-quality firms so as not to lose their reputation as a repeated financial player in the IPO market. Moreover, The IPOs backed by the bank-affiliated in KOSDAQ did not suffer from the potential conflict of interests between investors and issuing firms. This result is consistent with the lower underpricing by bank-affiliated VCs in the cold market, as was shown in the underpricing regressions in Table 6.8. This finding is consistent with our expectation that the information advantage provided by bank-affiliated VCs will contribute to the value-adding for the IPO firms (Aoki, 2000; Hellmann, Lindsey et al., 2003). While Hamao, Packet et al. (2000) did not find significant difference of bank-affiliated VCs on the long-term performances, I find that bank-affiliated VC's positive impact on the long-term performances is apparently present in KOSDAQ IPOs, especially in the cold market. The regression results support the H3b (the impact of bank-affiliated VCs on the long-term performance).

It seems that the regression results relating to the institutional affiliation of VC-backing in the cold-market IPOs are consistent those in the hot market. Although the security company-affiliated VC did not show significant underperformance in the cold market, unlike in the hot market, the signs of coefficients are consistently negative in both market period. Furthermore, although bank-affiliated VC-backing did not show significant relationship with KOSDAQ-adjusted BHARs in the hot-market IPOs, it shows significantly positive coefficients in the cold-market IPOs. In this case, the signs of coefficients are also consistently positive, regardless of whether the IPO firms were listed in the hot-market period or cold-market period. This indicates that short-term performance such as initial return is more sensitive to the stock market situation than long-term performance is. The long-term performance is concerned less with the stock market situation at the time of IPO than with the true value of the firms in the long run (Ritter, 1998).

7.7.2.2 Regression analysis of SIMF-adjusted BHARs

Table 7.15 shows the regression coefficients of SIMF-adjusted BHARs that were listed in the cold market.

For the control variables, the age of firm (*Lage*) turned out to be negatively related at 10 per cent level in Panel A. Considering the fact that the young and old firms SIMF-adjusted BHARs did not show any difference by hot- and cold-market issue in the univariate analysis of Section 7.5, this is likely to be caused by the interaction of the age of firm with other variables. The book-to-market ratio (*Bmr*) is positively related to SIMF-adjusted BHARs in all regressions of Panels A and B at 1 per cent or 5 per cent significance level. Unlike the regressions of the long-term performance in the hot-market IPOs, stock market situation (*NumIPO, Kqindex, Kqchange*) is not closely related to SIMF-adjusted BHARs. It is shown that the shareholdings of CEO and his related persons (*ShCEO*) are significantly related to SIMF-adjusted BHARs at 5 per cent or 10 per cent level in Panel B. Underpricing (*UP*) is found to have negative association with SIMF-adjusted BHARs at 10 per cent level in Panel A.

The coefficients estimates of regressions suggest that the VC-backing (*VC*), the reputation of VC-backing (*VCk, VC3*), the institutional difference of VC-backing (*VCbank, VCsecu*) and the underwriter reputation (*Und3*) do not show any significance, thus not supporting the hypothesis H1b, H2b, H3b, H4b, and H5b. The only coefficient that shows significance relating to the hypothesis is the reputation of auditor. In the Model 5 of Panel B, it is shown that the auditor reputation is negatively related to SIMF-adjusted BHARs at 10 per cent level. This rejects the H6b, but it is not very clear why this significantly negative relationship between auditor reputation and SIMF-adjusted BHARs appears in the regression, especially considering the fact that this in only one significant result that the auditor reputation appears as it is. In addition, other institution-affiliated VC-backing (*VCetc*) is found to have a significantly positive relationship with SIMF-adjusted BHARs at 10 per cent level in the Model 3 of Panel A.

7.7.2.3 Regression analysis of SBMP-adjusted BHARs

Table 7.16 shows the regression coefficients of SBMP-adjusted BHARs that were listed in KOSDAQ in the cold market.

The control variables relating to stock market situation (*NumIPO, Kqindex*) show significant coefficients, but the size of the coefficients is economically

Table 7.15 Cross-sectional regressions on twelve-month SIMF-adjusted BHARs in cold market

	Model 1		Model 2		Model 3		Model 4		Model 5	
Panel A: Regressions for All Sample Firms										
Intercept	-0.10	(-0.22)	-0.02	(-0.06)	-0.08	(-0.17)	-0.06	(-0.13)	-0.09	(-0.20)
Lage	-0.15	(-1.77)*	-0.15	(-1.66)*	-0.15	(-1.75)*	-0.16	(-1.79)*	-0.15	(-1.82)*
Bmr	0.52	(2.39)**	0.50	(2.26)**	0.52	(2.42)**	0.52	(2.37)**	0.53	(2.43)**
ShCEO	0.18	(0.83)	0.13	(0.57)	0.16	(0.73)	0.18	(0.81)	0.19	(0.90)
NumIPO	0.00	(0.22)	0.00	(0.18)	0.00	(0.18)	0.00	(0.19)	0.00	(0.26)
Kqindex	0.00	(0.20)	0.00	(0.20)	0.00	(0.23)	0.00	(0.17)	0.00	(0.19)
Kqchange	0.52	(1.11)	0.57	(1.18)	0.56	(1.18)	0.58	(1.21)	0.51	(1.08)
UP	-0.05	(-1.69)*	-0.06	(-1.74)*	-0.06	(-1.76)*	-0.06	(-1.68)*	-0.05	(-1.62)
VC	0.16	(1.49)	0.14	(1.28)					0.16	(1.44)
VCbank					0.09	(0.50)	0.09	(0.47)		
VCsecu					0.01	(0.09)	0.02	(0.12)		
VCetc					0.21	(1.73)*	0.20	(1.60)		
Bank			0.16	(1.27)			0.11	(0.91)		
Secu			-0.17	(-1.05)						
Und3									0.02	(0.15)
Aud3									-0.03	(-0.30)
AdjustedR	0.10		0.11		0.10		0.11		0.10	
Prob>F	0.01		0.01		0.02		0.03		0.01	
No.IPOs	169		169		169		169		169	
Panel B: Regressions for VC-backed Firms Only										
Intercept	-1.10	(-1.83)*	-1.09	(-1.79)*	-1.17	(-1.77)*	-1.17	(-1.75)*	-1.32	(-2.28)**
Lage	-0.07	(-0.71)	-0.13	(-1.04)	-0.08	(-0.83)	-0.09	(-0.88)	-0.13	(-1.26)
Bmr	1.59	(3.85)***	1.61	(4.01)***	1.58	(3.81)***	1.58	(3.80)***	1.63	(3.97)***
ShCEO	0.77	(1.96)*	0.84	(1.95)*	0.71	(1.76)*	0.75	(1.75)*	1.02	(2.30)**
NumIPO	0.01	(0.70)	0.01	(0.71)	0.01	(0.55)	0.01	(0.55)	0.01	(1.08)
Kqindex	0.00	(1.62)	0.00	(1.57)	0.00	(1.61)	0.00	(1.59)	0.00	(2.00)**

	(1)	(2)	(3)	(4)	(5)
Kqchange	0.47	0.36	0.56	0.56	0.31
UP	-0.06 (-1.04)	-0.06 (-0.97)	-0.07 (-1.03)	-0.07 (-1.01)	-0.05 (-0.87)
VCk	0.00 (-0.03)				
VC3		0.11 (0.75)			0.10 (0.72)
VCbank			0.11 (0.46)	0.10 (0.44)	
VCetc			0.17 (1.11)	0.17 (1.03)	
Bank		0.11 (0.60)		0.05 (0.29)	
Secu		0.04 (0.31)			
Und3					0.24 (1.27)
Aud3					-0.31 (-1.85)*
AdjustedR	0.34	0.35	0.35	0.35	0.40
Prob>F	0.01	0.02	0.01	0.02	0.01
No.IPOs	71	71	71	71	71

Note: T-statistics in the parentheses are heteroskedasicity consistent. VCsecu in Panel B was dropped in the regressions. Asterisks beside t-statistics *, **, *** denote significance at 10%, 5%, 1% level, respectively.

Table 7.16 Cross-sectional regressions on twelve-month SBMP-adjusted BHARs in cold market

	Model 1	Model 2	Model 3	Model 4	Model 5
Panel A: Regressions for All Sample Firms					
Intercept	0.05 (0.18)	0.07 (0.25)	0.07 (0.24)	0.07 (0.27)	0.00 (0.01)
Lage	-0.08 (-1.10)	-0.08 (-1.10)	-0.08 (-1.10)	-0.08 (-1.12)	-0.08 (-1.17)
ShCEO	0.14 (0.69)	0.13 (0.63)	0.12 (0.58)	0.13 (0.63)	0.17 (0.90)
High-Tech	-0.17 (-1.84)*	-0.17 (-1.79)*	-0.17 (-1.87)*	-0.17 (-1.88)*	-0.17 (-1.80)*
NumIPO	0.01 (2.07)**	0.01 (2.06)**	0.01 (2.04)**	0.01 (2.05)**	0.01 (2.02)**
Kqindex	0.00 (-1.72)*	0.00 (-1.75)*	0.00 (-1.71)*	0.00 (-1.76)*	0.00 (-1.68)*
Kqchange	0.44 (1.33)	0.46 (1.40)	0.48 (1.45)	0.50 (1.48)	0.44 (1.31)
UP	-0.05 (-1.48)	-0.05 (-1.44)	-0.05 (-1.47)	-0.05 (-1.42)	-0.04 (-1.38)
VC	0.05 (0.51)	0.04 (0.41)			0.05 (0.46)
VCbank			0.05 (0.49)	0.05 (0.47)	
VCsecu			-0.18 (-1.91)*	-0.17 (-1.90)*	
VCetc			0.09 (0.68)	0.08 (0.62)	
Bank		0.09 (0.90)		0.06 (0.56)	
Secu		-0.05 (-0.75)			
Und3					0.07 (0.60)
Aud3					0.00 (0.05)
AdjustedR	0.13	0.13	0.14	0.14	0.13
Prob>F	0.00	0.00	0.00	0.00	0.00
No.IPOs	169	169	169	169	169
Panel B: Regressions for VC-backed Firms Only					
Intercept	0.21 (0.36)	0.24 (0.38)	0.06 (0.10)	0.06 (0.11)	-0.09 (-0.14)
Lage	-0.05 (-0.46)	-0.04 (-0.33)	-0.07 (-0.63)	-0.08 (-0.61)	-0.07 (-0.59)
ShCEO	0.21 (0.37)	0.18 (0.27)	0.12 (0.22)	0.14 (0.23)	0.38 (0.67)
High-Tech	-0.35 (-1.44)	-0.33 (-1.33)	-0.34 (-1.38)	-0.34 (-1.36)	-0.31 (-1.27)
NumIPO	0.01 (1.17)	0.01 (0.98)	0.01 (1.02)	0.01 (1.03)	0.01 (1.22)
Kqindex	0.00 (-0.85)	0.00 (-0.86)	0.00 (-0.85)	0.00 (-0.87)	0.00 (-0.40)

	(1)	(2)	(3)	(4)	(5)
Kqchange	0.80 (1.45)	0.84 (1.50)	0.87 (1.32)	0.88 (1.38)	0.85 (1.41)
UP	-0.08 (-1.43)	-0.08 (-1.38)	-0.09 (-1.35)	-0.09 (-1.30)	-0.07 (-1.17)
VCk	-0.08 (-0.51)				
VC3		-0.03 (-0.26)			-0.01 (-0.08)
VCbank			0.23 (1.78)*	0.23 (1.70)*	
VCetc			0.29 (1.96)*	0.28 (1.72)*	
Bank		0.11 (0.59)		0.03 (0.16)	
Secu		-0.14 (-0.87)			
Und3					0.19 (0.95)
Aud3					0.03 (0.17)
AdjustedR	0.14	0.15	0.16	0.16	0.16
Prob>F	0.31	0.59	0.54	0.49	0.66
No.IPOs	71	71	71	71	71

Note: T-statistics in the parentheses are heteroskedasicity consistent. VC_{secu} in Panel B was dropped in the regressions. Asterisks beside t-statistics *, **, *** denote significance at 10%, 5%, 1% level, respectively.

insignificant. The dummy variable of high-tech shows negative coefficients at 10 per cent level. It may imply that the high-tech stocks were still suffering from the decline of share prices even in the cold-market period.

The findings in the regressions show that the institutional affiliation of VC-backing apparently has significant relationship with SBMP-adjusted BHARs. The bank-affiliated VC (*VCbank*) shows significantly positive association with SBMP-adjusted BHARs in Models 3 and 4 of Panel B at 10 per cent level, while the security company-affiliated VC (*VCsecu*) is negatively related in Models 3 and 4 of Panel A at 10 per cent level. These results also confirm the value-adding role of bank-affiliated VCs (Aoki, 2000) and the possible conflict of interests incurred by security company-affiliated VCs (Gompers and Lerner, 1999). It seems that, considering the fact other institution-affiliated VC (*VCetc*) also shows the significantly positive coefficients, the underperformance of security company-affiliated VC are clearly seen by the KOSDAQ IPO data.

While the regression analysis of SBMP-adjusted BHARs supports the hypothesis H3b and H4b, it does not suggest any significant association of VC-backing (*VC*), the reputation of VC (*VCk, VC3*) and the reputation of underwriter and auditor (*Und3, Aud3*), thus not supporting the H1b, H2b, H5b and H6b.

7.8 Summary of the chapter

This chapter presents the results of univariate and multivariate analysis of long-term performance (BHAR).

Section 7.2.1 compares the long-term performance by different types of IPOs. I find that the non-VC-backed IPOs outperformed that VC-backed IPOs in the long run. This result does not support the hypothesis H1a (the impact of VC-backing on the long-term performance) and is not consistent with the finding in Brav and Gompers (1997). However, this result is consistent with the finding in Kutsuna, Cowling et al. (2000), who found that Japanese VC-backed IPOs underperformed in the long run. It is clearly shown that KOSDAQ IPO firms show poor long-term performance in the similar way that was found in other studies (Ritter, 1991; Loughran and Ritter, 1995; Ritter and Welch, 2002). Section 7.2.2 compares the long-term performance between the IPOs brought to KOSDAQ in the hot market and those in the cold market, and finds that there are conflicting results of the comparison, depending on the selection of the benchmarks. The aggravating performance of hot-market IPOs from the twelve months to twenty-four months seems to be in line with the findings in Ibbotson, Sindelar et al. (1994) and Aggarwal and Rivoli (1990), who found that hot market issues experienced the worse long-term performances. Section 7.2.3 compares the long-term performance between young and old firms and show that young firms underperform old firms after twelve month and twenty-four month significantly for some benchmark-adjusted BHARs. Section 7.2.4 analyses the BHARs of small and big firms, and showed the outperformance of small firms over big firms. This result is contrary to the finding of Ritter (1991) and DeBondt and Thaler (1987), who documented that smaller offers had the worst long-term performances. Section 7.2.5 compares the BHARs of high-tech and non-high-tech firms and finds that high-tech firms underperformed significantly non-high-tech firms after twenty-four months. This difference of BHARs between high-tech and non-high-firms may be evidence that high-tech firms, including the information and communication technology firms, were overvalued at the time of IPO, and thus suffered from the decline of the firm performance in the long run (Hand, 2000).

The more detailed analysis of the long-term performance of VC-backing and non-VC-backed IPOs respectively in relation to the different types of IPOs in Section 7.3 generally confirms the results that were found in Section 7.2. There are conflicting results of differences between hot and cold market issues for VC-backed and non-VC-backed IPOs respectively. The old firms show significantly better performance than the young firms in the long run, whether they are VC-backed IPO or non-VC-backed IPOs, and the small firms significantly outperformed the big firms irrespective of VC-backing. The univariate analysis of the BHARs between high-tech and non-high-tech firms shows that non-high-tech firms showed significantly better performance in the long term than high-tech firms for the case of non-VC-backed IPOs after twenty-four month.

Section 7.4 compares the long-term performance according to the institutional difference of VC-backing. For all IPOs, it is shown that bank-affiliated VCs outperform other types of IPOs in all cases and that the security company-affiliated VCs generally underperform the other types of IPOs. The significant difference appears between bank-affiliated and security company-affiliated. For the IPOs brought in the hot-market period, bank-affiliated BHARs are higher than any other BHARs in all cases and the security company-affiliated BHARs are generally lower than any other BHARs. While the significant differences between bank-affiliated VCs and other types of VCs are not found, the security company-affiliated VC show significant underperformance over other types of IPOs. In the cold-market IPOs, the differences of BHARs are narrowed compared with the hot-market IPOs. It is shown that bank-affiliated VCs show better performance generally and that security company-affiliated VCs show worse performance generally. The significant difference appears between bank-affiliated and security company-affiliated, too. The results support the hypothesis H3b (the impact of bank-affiliated VC-backing on the long-term performance) and H4b (the impact of security company-affiliated VC-backing on the long-term performance).

Section 7.5 compares the long-term performance of hot and cold markets with the different types of IPOs. The results that were found in this section are consistent with the findings in the Sections 7.2 and 7.3.

Section 7.6 compares the long-term performance between low underpricing and high underpricing group cross-classified by state of the market and VC-backing. The results show that the IPOs which experienced lower underpricing led to outperformance compared to the IPOs which went through higher underpricing.

Section 7.6 reports the regression coefficients of long-term performance for IPOs in the hot market and the cold market. In the regressions on the twenty-four month hot-market IPOs, I find that VC-backing has significantly negative relationship with the long-term performance (KOSDAQ-adjusted BHARs), thus rejecting H1b. However, I find that that there is evidence that supports the H4b. The security company-affiliated VC shows significantly negative coefficients of the long-term performance (KOSDAQ-adjusted BHARs and SIMF-adjusted BHARs). The significantly positive relationship of the reputation of underwriter with the long-term performance (SIMF-adjusted BHARs) suggests that there is evidence in support of H5b. I also find significantly positive impact of the reputation of auditor on the long-term performance (SBMP-adjusted BHARs), which suggests evidence supporting H6b. The regressions on the twelve-month BHARs in the cold market also show evidence that support the hypotheses. It is apparently shown that the bank-affiliated VC has significantly positive relationship with the long-term performance (KOSDAQ-adjusted BHARs, SBMP-adjusted BHARs). On the contrary, the security company-affiliated VC shows significantly negative coefficients (SBMP-adjusted BHARs). These results in the cold market also support H3b and H4b. The positive impact of bank-affiliated VC on the long-term performance is consistent with our expectation that the information advantage provided by bank-affiliated VCs will make a difference in the quality of the IPO firms (Aoki, 2000; Hellmann, Lindsey et al., 2003). The negative impact of security company-affiliated VC on the long-term performance may be evidence of the conflict of interest that the security company-affiliated VC cause in the process of IPOs, thus with the IPO firm performance experiencing the decline in the long run (Gompers and Lerner, 1999). This negative impact of security company-affiliated VC is consistent with the finding in Hamao, Packer et al. (2000) who found that VC-backed IPOs in Japan showed worse performance when the lead venture capitalist was affiliated with a security company. Furthermore, it appears that control variables are less related to the long-term performances than to the underpricing. However, some variables such as market capitalisation and underpricing are found to have a significant negative relationship with the long-term performance in a good many model specifications.

Notes

1 At the time of this analysis, the IPO firms whose twenty-four month returns were available had been listed in KOSDAQ in the hot-market period. Therefore, the twenty-four month returns include only hot-market IPOs, while the twelve month returns include both hot and cold-market IPOs.

2 The benchmarks used in order to adjusted raw BHARs are KOSDAQ index (KOSDAQ), KSE index (KSE), size and industry matched firm (SIMF), size and book-to-market ratio matched firm (SBMF) and size and book-to-market ratio matched portfolio (SBMP). In Section 7.2, I report all five benchmarks-adjusted BHARs, but from Section 7.3, I highlight only three benchmarks (KOSDAQ, SIMF, SBMP) -adjusted BHARs, mainly due to the limitation of writing space for this book and the similarity in results I obtained when using the excluded benchmark results.

3 Parts of univariate analysis in this chapter were extended to another analysis in Ch.26 "The Impact of Venture Capital Participation and Its Affiliation with Financial Institutions on the Long-term Performance of IPO Firm: Evidence from

Korea in Hot and Cold Market Periods" by Jaeho Lee from *Oxford Handbook of Venture Capital*, edited by Cumming, Douglas (2012) with different results.

4 Note that KOSDAQ and KSE benchmark returns are buy-and-hold returns, not the calendar time returns although they decrease after twelve- and twenty-four months following the trend of KOSDAQ index.

5 In an unreported analysis, the twelve- and twenty-four month *raw returns* of non-VC-backed IPOs are significantly higher than those of VC-backed IPOs at 1 per cent level. (In the following tables, I report only the results of univariate tests for the difference of the *adjusted BHARs* by the different types of groups)

6 As was stated in Chapter 4, we report wealth relatives in the tables of univariate tests in this chapter for reference. Wealth relative is another version of adjusted BHAR, both of which have the same meaning. A wealth relative of greater than (less than) 1.0 is interpreted as positive (negative) adjusted BHAR.

7 The raw returns that are calculated to match with SBMP-adjusted control groups are slightly different from the other original raw returns. To match each IPO return to a corresponding portfolio, the *first month return* of IPO is generated by compounding from the first day that did not hit the upper limit for the first time up to the end of second month following each IPO. For example, if a firm did not hit the upper limit on 15 January, the first-month IPO return is calculated by compounding the daily return from the 15 January to the end of February. The twelve- and twenty-four month raw returns in the case of SBMP do not show any statistically significant difference from the original IPO raw return. Hereafter, we just present the original raw returns when we need to mention raw returns.

8 Barber and Lyon (1997) stated that *new listing bias*, which arises from the fact that firms which constitute the market index used as benchmark include new IPO firms, and thus market index benchmark leads to higher benchmark return. This potential bias did not appear in KOSDAQ market, because of the severe under-performance of KOSDAQ market as a whole after March 2000.

9 Due to the limited availability of the stock price data at the time of this analysis, the IPOs that got listed in the cold market (after April 2000) have no 24-month BHARs. However, as stated and implied in the Chapter 4, one-year (12-month) BHARs can be a good indicator of showing the long-term performance of IPO companies.

10 This underperformance of big benchmark firms relative to small benchmark firms shows that SBMF and SBMP returns are closely related to their matched raw returns and that, as was shown in the previous sections, the bigger size firms underperformed small size firms. Therefore, the outperformance of SBMF- and SBMP-adjusted BHARs seems to be not so much the result of the long-term performance difference as the result of the benchmark selection that followed the same pattern with raw returns.

11 From this table, we report only KOSDAQ-, SIMF-, and SBMP-adjusted BHARs to save the writing space of the chapter. KOSDAQ represents market index benchmark, SIMF matched-firm benchmark and SBMP matched-portfolio benchmark. Since KSE and SBMF show similar patterns of benchmark returns with KOSDAQ and SBMP, as shown in the previous tables, the dropping of these two benchmarks does not affect the whole landscape of the univariate analysis.

12 I group total IPO firms into two groups: Low Underpricing firms (when the underpricing is equal to or less than the median value of underpricing of total IPOs, 1.05) and High Underpricing firms.

13 The raw IPO return of low underpricing group in non-VC-backed IPOs is significantly higher than that of high underpricing group. However, the SBMP benchmark return of low underpricing group is higher enough to offset this difference than that of high underpricing group. The low underpricing group of

non-VC-backed IPOs is made up of smaller firms than the high underpricing group. As market capitalisation declines in the long run, both groups are matched with smaller size portfolio, but low underpricing group was matched with smaller size groups, which showed a higher benchmark return.

14 All the firms in low underpricing group of bank-affiliated VC-backed IPOs were listed in the cold-market period, while more than half of the firms in high under-pricing group of bank-affiliated VC-backed IPOs were listed in the hot-market period. Since the KOSDAQ returns matched with the raw IPO returns in the hot-market period experienced sharp deterioration in the long run, this led to the underperformance of KOSDAQ benchmark return of high underpricing group.

15 Parts of multivariate analysis in this chapter were extended to another analysis in Ch.26 "The Impact of Venture Capital Participation and Its Affiliation with Financial Institutions on the Long-term Performance of IPO Firm: Evidence from Korea in Hot and Cold Market Periods" by Jaeho Lee from *Oxford Handbook of Venture Capital*, edited by Cumming, Douglas (2012) with different results.

16 The adjusted R-square in these equations are relatively low, which is common in the literature explaining BHARs movements, because if the stock markets are relatively efficient I would not be able to explain a high per centage of the variation in the stock price movements.

17 Only the coefficients on bank-affiliated VC-backing (*VCbank*) were positively significant in the regression based on the twelve-month KOSDAQ-adjusted BHARs for all IPOs taken together.

18 As was explained in the methodology section of Chapter 4, the control variables regarding stock market situation such as number of IPOs (*NumIPO*), market capitalisation (*Kqindex*) and monthly change of market index (*Kqchange*) were not included in the regressions, because KOSDAQ-adjusted BHARs already reflect the change of stock market situation by being adjusted by KOSDAQ index.

19 The adjusted R-square of Panel A of Table 7–10 (SIMF-adjusted regressions) decreased relative to that of Panel A Table 7–9 (KOSDAQ-adjusted regressions), while the R-square increased in Panel B.

20 The market capitalisation (*LMC*) and the dummy variable representing high-tech industry (*High-Tech*) were not entered in the SIMF-adjusted BHARs regressions, because SIMF-adjusted BHARs were already adjusted by size and industry.

21 The market capitalisation (*LMC*) and the book-to-market ratio (*Bmr*) were excluded in the regression, because SBMP-adjusted returns were already adjusted by the market capitalisation and book-to-market ratio.

8   Conclusion

8.1 Summary of the book

In this book, venture capital companies are considered as institutions that allevi-ate the information asymmetry inherent between issuing firms and investors and which enhance the value of firms through their ownership and management, thus leading to less underpricing and better long-term performance. This book has analysed how venture capital companies affected the underpricing and long-run performance of Initial Public Offerings (IPOs) on the Korean KOSDAQ market, the secondary stock market for the IPOs of high-tech based innovative firms. In order to test our hypotheses, I used data on 372 firms brought to IPO during the period of 1999–2001 in KOSDAQ. KOSDAQ had grown dramatically since 1999 and about half of the firms listed in KOSDAQ during this period were VC-backed. This provides a good testing ground for an empirical investigation. I ana-lysed how VC-backing, the reputation of VC companies and the affiliation of the VC with financial institutions (banks and security companies) affect the pricing and performance effects of IPO firms. Additionally, I also analysed the impact of reputable underwriters and auditors on pricing and performance. Given the sample period 1999–2001, when the KOSDAQ experienced both hot- and cold-market periods, I analysed separately the whole sample period, the hot-market period, and the cold-market period.

In Chapter 2, I set out the institutional aspects of the venture capital industry and the IPO market. First, I described the definition of venture capital and its primary features. Second, I overviewed the recent trend of the Korean and other countries' venture capital industry. The analysis showed that the Korean venture capital industry had experienced dramatic growth since the late 1990s, which was prompted by the government policy designed to enhance the role of technology-oriented SMEs. Korea ranks third in terms of venture capital investment as a share of GDP among the leading OECD countries over the period 1998–2001. During this period, the number of venture capital companies more than doubled from 72 in 1998 to 145 in 2001 and that of limited partnership funds more than quadrupled from 93 in 1998 to 395 in 2001. However, as in the cases of other major countries, the Korean venture capital industry experienced a sharp decline during 2001. The Korean venture capital industry was shown to be concentrated in the expansion stage rather than seed or start-up stage, which is also similar to the cases of other countries. It was also shown that the Korean venture capital industry was concentrated in the high technology sector as in other countries. Our analysis showed that the leading investors in Korean limited partnership funds were corporations, followed by financial institutions including banks and private individuals. In other countries, while pension funds were the leading type of limited partnership funds, banks were generally the main sources of limited partnership in other European countries. Finally, I reviewed the recent trend of Korean and other countries' IPO markets and showed that KOSDAQ is one of the most successful second-tier stock market in the OECD countries. In terms of the listed companies of 2002 year-end, KOSDAQ (843 companies) is bigger than any other second-tier stock market, except for the NASDAQ and Canadian Venture Exchange.

In Chapter 3, I reviewed the literature regarding underpricing and the long-term performance of IPO firms and the certification and value-adding role of venture capitalists, and derived the hypotheses for the empirical analysis. Numerous studies have documented that underpricing in the short run and underperformance in the long run are observed in the pricing of IPOs. While most of the discussion has concentrated on the information asymmetry problem that comes up between issuer, underwriter, and investor, it has been shown that a reputable financial player acting as certifying uncertain IPO firms can significantly reduce the information gap, thus decreasing the degree of underpricing. Furthermore, it has been argued that the IPO firms supported by reputable financial players will be expected to show outperformance in the long term, because in order to maintain their reputational capital they will only bring better-quality IPO firms to the market. Overall, venture capital companies have been considered as institutions that can take this role through their internal mechanisms to minimise the information asymmetry and the external activities with other financial players. However, I also assumed that the qualities of venture capitalists were not identical and discussed what would distinguish the good-quality venture capitalists from bad-quality venture capitalists. I also discussed the impact of institutional affiliation of venture capital companies with financial institutions such as banks and security companies by introducing a universal banking perspective. It has been suggested that security company-affiliated VCs can incur conflict of interests between investors and themselves by the security company's motivation to overprice an IPO firm. Commercial bank-affiliated VCs may effectively certify an IPO firm by the information advantage they have acquired through the parenting bank's on-going lending relationship with a number of firms including the IPO firm. From the literature review, twelve hypotheses regarding the VC-backing, the reputation of venture capitalists, the institutional affiliation of venture capitalists and the reputation of underwriter and auditor were derived.

In Chapter 4, I described the data and dealt with the problem of measuring underpricing when there is daily price limit. I dealt with the problem of regulated maximum daily price limit on KOSDAQ by defining underpricing as the difference between the offer price and the closing price on the first day that IPO stock did not hit the daily upper limit. After reviewing long-run return measurement, I set out the case for adopting a multi-benchmark approach. This involves two market index benchmarks (KOSDAQ index and KSE index), two control firm benchmarks (size-and-industry-matched-firm, and size-and-book-to-market-ratio-matched-firm) and a portfolio benchmark (size-and-book-to-market ratio-matched-portfolio). I also set out the specification of the multivariate regression model carried out in Chapters 6 and 7.

In Chapter 5, I presented a description of the characteristics of our IPO sample firms. From the comparison of IPO characteristics between VC-backed firms and non-VC-backed firms, I found that VC-backed firms are significantly younger and smaller than non-VC-backed firms. It was also found that VC-backed firms have less shareholdings by CEO's family and corporate venturing institutions than non-VC-backed firms do. As for the sources of funds, although VC-backed firms did not receive as much funding from banks and other financial institutions, and did not issue as many bonds and shares in the capital markets, as non-VC-backed firms did, the differences were small when normalised by the size of the firms. I also presented the financial and operating performances of IPO firms, in which VC-backed firms were found to be smaller in total assets and turnover than non-VC-backed firms were. It was also found that VC-backed firms were in a better short-term financial position, and they invested a higher proportion of their assets in R&D activities. I did not find any significant differences in profitability ratios. Finally, I compared the characteristics of KOSDAQ IPO firms with that of other major countries' data. I showed that IPO characteristics (market capitalisation, age, high-tech industry ratio and VC ownership) of KOSDAQ IPO firms were generally similar to that of other major countries and that the results of KOSDAQ case could be compared with those from other countries.

Chapters 6 and 7 contain the results of testing each of the hypotheses. In Chapter 6, I tested six hypotheses of underpricing. I hypothesise: VC-backed IPOs will be less underpriced (H1a); IPOs backed by more reputable venture capitalists will show less underpricing (H2a); IPOs backed by banks-affiliated VCs will show less underpricing (H3a); IPOs backed by security companies-affiliated VCs will show higher underpricing (H4a); Underwriter reputation is associated with less underpricing (H5a); Auditor reputation is associated with less underpricing (H6a). In Chapter 7, I tested six hypotheses of long-term performance. It was hypothesised: VC-backed IPOs will show a better long-term performance (H1b); IPOs backed by more reputable venture capitalists will show a better long-term performance (H2b); IPOs backed by banks-affiliated VCs will show a better long-term performance (H3b); IPOs backed by security companies-affiliated VCs will show a worse long-term performance (H4b); Underwriter reputation is associated with a better long-term performance (H5b); Auditor reputation is associated with a better long-term performance (H6b).

In Chapter 6, I presented the results of univariate and multivariate analyses of underpricing. This generated a large number of results, which are summarised in Table 8.1 and 8.2. Table 8.1 summarises the results of the univariate analysis of underpricing. The table shows that the underpricing of VC-backed IPOs was

Table 8.1 Summary of the hypotheses acceptance for univariate tests of underpricing

	Hypothesis								
	H1a			H3a			H4a		
	(VC-backing effect)			(Bank-affiliated VC effect)			(Security company-affiliated VC effect)		
Expected Sign	–			–			+		
	Sign	Sig.	Result	Sign	Sig.	Result	Sign	Sig.	Result
Whole period	+	√	Reject	+	×	Reject	–	×	Reject
Hot market	+	√	Reject	+	√	Reject	–	√	Reject
Cold market	–	×	Reject	–	×	Reject	+	×	Reject

Notes: Sign indicates the sign of mean difference of underpricing between VC-backed IPOs and non-VC-backed IPOs for H1a and that between an institutional affiliation of VC-backing and others for H3a and H4a, respectively. When the mean difference of underpricing between bank-affiliated VC-backing and security company-affiliated VC-backing respectively and others was positive (negative) at least in two cases, their signs were given + (–). Sig. indicates the presence of significance of mean difference using t-test or Mann-Whitney test. √ indicates the presence of significance and × indicates no significance. Asterisks denote significance levels at the level 1% (***), 5% (**), and 10% (*) in the binomial probability tests.

significantly higher than that of non-VC-backed IPO throughout the whole sample period and the hot-market period. This difference rejects hypothesis H1a. Contrary to our expectation, venture capitalists increase the extent of underpricing.

However, the univariate analysis in the cold market shows that the underpricing of KOSDAQ VC-backed IPO was lower than that of non-VC-backed IPOs, although their difference was insignificant.

Furthermore, the univariate analysis of institutional affiliation of VC-backing shows that the initial return of the bank-affiliated VC was significantly higher than the other groups in the hot-market period, while the IPOs backed by security company-affiliated VC showed significantly lower underpricing in the same period. This result is contradictory to our hypotheses H3a and H4a, which predict that the bank-affiliated case will show less underpricing and the security company-affiliated will show higher underpricing. However, in the cold market, the bank-affiliated VC showed the lowest underpricing and the security company-affiliated VC showed the second highest underpricing, although the differences of initial returns among the groups are insignificant. This analysis shows that the underpricing rank shown by bank-affiliated VC and security company-affiliated VC was reversed in the hot and cold market.

Table 8.2 summarises the results of the multivariate analysis of underpricing. I did not find any significant relationship of the VC-backing with underpricing in the whole sample period, the hot market and the cold market. This rejects H1a.

The bank-affiliated VC-backing and the security company-affiliated VC-backing did not show any significant results in support of H3a and H4a in the whole sample period and the hot market. Rather, they showed significantly conflicting results in these two periods. However, in the cold market, there is evidence in

Table 8.2 Summary of the hypotheses acceptance for multivariate tests of underpricing

		H1a (VC-backing effect)			H2a (Reputation of VC-backing effect)			H3a (Bank-affiliated VC effect)			H4a (Security company-affiliated VC effect)			H5a (Underwriter reputation effect)			H6a (Auditor reputation effect)		
Expected Sign		−			−			−			+			−			−		
		Sign	Sig.	Result	Sign	Sig.	Result	Sign	Sig.	Result	Sign	Sig.	Result	Sign	Sig.	Result	Sign	Sig.	Result
Whole period	All	−−−	×	Reject	NA		Reject	−−	×	Reject	−−	√	Reject	−	×	Reject	−	×	Reject
	VC	NA			−+−	×	Reject	++	×	Reject	NA		Reject	+	×	Reject	−	×	Reject
Hot market	All	+++	×	Reject	NA		Reject	++	×	Reject	−−	√	Reject	−	×	Reject	−	×	Reject
	VC	NA			−−−	×	Reject	+	√	Reject	−	√	Reject	+	√	**Accept**	−	×	Reject
Cold market	All	−−−	×	Reject	NA		Reject	−−	√	Reject	++	×	**Accept**	−	√	**Accept**	−	×	Reject
	VC	NA			+−−	×	Reject	NA		Reject	++	√	**Accept**	−	×	Reject	−	×	Reject

Note: Sign indicates the sign of dummy variable coefficients in the regressions. Multiple + and − signs in the Sign columns indicate how many regression were run in order to test each hypothesis. Sig. indicates the presence of significance in the regressions. √ indicates the presence of significance and × indicates no significance. Asterisks denote significance levels at the level 1% (***), 5% (**), and 10% (*) in the binomial probability tests.

support of H3a and H4a. In addition, the reduction of underpricing by reputable underwriter in the cold-market period in the case of the multivariate regressions supports H5a.

In Chapter 7, I presented the results of univariate and multivariate analysis of long-term performance (BHAR). Table 8.3 shows a summary of the results of the univariate tests. It shows that the VC-backed IPOs significantly underperformed non-VC-backed IPOs after twenty-four months for KOSDAQ-, KSE- and SIMF-adjusted BHARs. These results reject H1b. The tables also show that bank-affiliated VCs significantly outperformed other types of IPOs after twelve month in terms of the KOSDAQ-adjusted BHARs in the whole period issues and the cold period issues. The security company-affiliated VCs significantly underperformed the other types of IPOs after twelve month using KOSDAQ-adjusted BHARs in the whole period issues and in cold market issues, and after twenty-four month using KOSDAQ-adjusted BHARs in the whole period issues. These results support H3b and H4b.

Table 8.4 shows a summary of the results of the multivariate tests. There is no significant evidence that VC-backed IPOs outperformed non-VC-backed IPOs, thus rejecting H1b. However, I found evidence in support of H3b and H4b. The bank-affiliated VC-backing showed significantly positive coefficients for KOS-DAQ- and SBMP-adjusted BHARs in the cold market issues. The security company-affiliated VC showed significantly negative coefficients for KOSDAQ- and SIMF-adjusted BHARs in the hot market issues and for SBMP-adjusted BHARs in the cold market issues. Furthermore, the underwriter reputation and auditor reputation were found to have a significantly positive relationship with the long-term performance in only one case of the regressions. These results support H5b and H6b.

So far I have analysed each result of each test as an independent result on its own. However, it is interesting to consider them collectively. One way of thinking about this in a case where I have many insignificant results is to ask what the chances are of getting results of a similar sign (even if they are not significant) if there was no relationship. I might expect that, if there was no relationship, the signs would be equally distributed between positive and negative. A binomial test[1] on the distribution of positive and negative coefficients allows us to check this.

The binomial test for the signs of the univariate tests (See Table 8.3) shows that the individual signs of bank-affiliated VC-backing collectively tended to be positive at 5 per cent level and that those of security company-affiliated VC-backing were negative at 1 per cent level. The binomial test for the signs of the multivariate tests (See Table 8.4) shows that the individual signs of VC-backing coefficients collectively tended to be positive at 10 per cent level. This test also shows that the individual signs of bank-affiliated VC-backing and security company-affiliated VC-backing were likely to produce collectively positive and negative ones at 1 per cent and 5 per cent level, respectively. These results seem to strengthen the support of our hypotheses collectively, even though not all the individual results were significant.

In Table 8.5, I compare the results of the underpricing and the long-term performance analysis in our research with those of other studies which were carried

Table 8.3 Summary of the hypotheses acceptance for univariate tests of long-term performance

		Hypothesis								
		H1b (VC-backing effect)			H3b (Bank-affiliated VC effect)			H4b (Security company-affiliated VC effect)		
Expected sign		+			+			−		
		Sign	Sig.	Result	Sign	Sig.	Result	Sign	Sig.	Result
12 months										
Whole period	KOSDAQ	−	×	Reject	+	√	Accept	−	√	Accept
	KSE	−	×	Reject	NA			NA		
	SIMF	+	×	Reject	+	×	Reject	−	×	Reject
	SBMF	−	×	Reject	NA			NA		
	SBMP	−	×	Reject	+	×	Reject	−	×	Reject
Hot market	KOSDAQ	−	×	Reject	+	×	Reject	−	×	Reject
	SIMF	+	×	Reject	+	×	Reject	−	×	Reject
	SBMP	−	×	Reject	+	×	Reject	−	×	Reject
Cold market	KOSDAQ	+	×	Reject	+	√	Accept	−	√	Accept
	SIMF	+	×	Reject	−	×	Reject	+	×	Reject
	SBMP	−	×	Reject	−	×	Reject	−	×	Reject
24 months										
Hot market (Whole period)	KOSDAQ	−	√	Reject	+	×	Reject	−	√	Accept
	KSE	−	√	Reject	NA			NA		
	SIMF	−	√	Reject	+	×	Reject	−	×	Reject
	SBMF	−	×	Reject	NA			NA		
	SBMP	+	×	Reject	+	×	Reject	−	×	Reject
# of total tests		16			12			12		
# of tests showing expected signs		5			10			11		
Significance of binomial probability test					**			***		

Note: Sign indicates the sign of mean difference of BHAR between VC-backed IPOs and non-VC-backed IPOs for H1a and that between an institutional affiliation of VC-backing and others for H3a and H4a, respectively. When the mean difference of BHAR between bank-affiliated VC-backing and security company-affiliated VC-backing respectively and others was positive (negative) at least in two cases, their signs were given + (−). Sig. indicates the presence of significance of mean difference using t-test or Mann-Whitney test. √ indicates the presence of significance and × indicates no significance. Asterisks denote significance levels at the level 1% (***), 5% (**), and 10% (*) in the binomial probability tests.

Table 8.4 Summary of the hypotheses acceptance for multivariate tests of long-term performance

			Hypothesis																		
			H1b (VC-backing effect)			H2b (Reputation of VC-backing effect)			H3b (Bank-affiliated VC effect)			H4b (Security company-affiliated VC effect)			H5b (Underwriter reputation effect)			H6b (Auditor reputation effect)		
Expected sign			+			+			+			–			+			+		
			Sign	Sig.	Result	Sign	Sig.	Result	Sign	Sig.	Result	Sign	Sig.	Result	Sign	Sig.	Result	Sign	Sig.	Result
Hot market	KOSDAQ	All	– – –	√	Reject	NA			++	×	Reject	– –	√	Accept	–	×	Reject	+	×	Reject
		VC	NA			– – –	×	Reject	++	×	Reject	NA			–	√	Reject	+	×	Reject
	SIMF	All	– – –	×	Reject	NA			++	×	Reject	– –	√	Accept	+	×	Accept	+	×	Reject
		VC	NA			– – –	×	Reject	NA			– –	√	Accept	+	×	Accept	+	×	Reject
	SBMP	All	++	×	Reject	NA			++	×	Reject	– –	×	Reject	–	×	Reject	+	√	Accept
		VC	NA			+++	×	Reject	++	×	Reject	NA			+	×	Reject	+	×	Reject
Cold market	KOSDAQ	All	+++	×	Reject	NA			++	×	Reject	– –	×	Reject	+	×	Reject	+	×	Reject
		VC	NA			– – –	×	Reject	++	√	Accept	NA			+	×	Reject	+	×	Reject
	SIMF	All	+++	×	Reject	NA			++	×	Reject	++	×	Reject	+	×	Reject	–	×	Reject
		VC	NA			– + +	×	Reject	++	×	Reject	NA			+	×	Reject	–	√	Reject
	SBMP	All	+++	×	Reject	NA			++	×	Reject	– –	√	Accept	+	×	Reject	+	×	Reject
		VC	NA			– – –	×	Reject	++	√	Accept	NA			+	×	Reject	+	×	Reject
# of total tests			18			18			22			14			12			12		
# of tests showing expected signs			12			5			22			12			8			9		
Significance of binomial probability test			*						***			**								

Note: Sign indicates the sign of dummy variable coefficients in the regressions. Multiple + and – signs in the Sign columns indicate how many regression were run in order to test each hypothesis. Sig. indicates the presence of significance in the regressions. √ indicates the presence of significance and × indicates no significance. Asterisks denote significance levels at the level 1% (***), 5% (**), and 10% (*) in the binomial probability tests.

Table 8.5 Comparison of KOSDAQ data with other major countries

	Underpricing			Long-term performance		
	VC-backing	*Bank-affiliated VC-backing*	*Security company-affiliated VC-backing*	*VC-backing*	*Bank-affiliated VC-backing*	*Security company-affiliated VC-backing*
USA	$-^{1)}$, $+^{2)}$, NR$^{3)}$	N/A	NR$^{4)}$	$+^{5)}$	N/A	NR$^{4)}$
UK	NR$^{6)}$	N/A	$+^{6)}$	NR$^{6)}$	N/A	$+^{6)}$
Germany	NR$^{7), 8)}$	N/A	$+^{8)}$	NR$^{8)}$	N/A	NR$^{8)}$
Japan	$+^{9)}$	NR$^{9)}$	$+^{9)}$	$-^{10)}$	NR$^{9)}$	$-^{9)}$
Korea	+	+ (hot market) – (cold market)	– (hot market) + (cold market)	–	+	–

Sources: 1) Megginson and Weiss (1991) (sample period: 1983–1987); 2) Francis and Hasan (2001) (sample period: 1990–1993) and Smart and Zutter (2000) (sample period: 1990–1998); 3) Barry, Muscarella et al. (1990) (sample period: 1978–1987); 4) Gompers and Lerner (1999) (sample period: 1972–1992); 5) Brav and Gompers (1997) (sample period: 1972–1992); 6) Espenlaub, Garrett et al. (1999) (sample period: 1992–1995); 7) Franzke (2003) (sample period: 1997–2002); 8) Bessler and Kurth (2003) (sample period: 1998–2001); 9) Hamao, Packer et al. (2000) (sample period: 1989–1995); 10) Kutsuna et al. (2002) (sample period: 1995–1996)

Note: – and + indicate the sign of the significant impact of VC-backing, bank-affiliated VC-backing and security company-affiliated VC-backing in the studies. NR indicates no significant relationships.

out in the US, UK, Germany, and Japan. I cannot find any consistent difference between the Korean case and the stock market based financial systems (USA and UK) or consistent similarities with bank-based financial systems (Germany and Japan). The results may differ depending on research methods and timing (which I have shown affects the Korean results), as well as the country itself. A study which controlled for each of these factors would be necessary to make a proper comparison.

A notable point is that, despite the problems of comparability, security company (or underwriter/investment bank)-affiliated VCs were related to a large underpricing in many cases of venture capital research (four cases of five countries including Korea). This may imply that the security company or underwriter's intention to sell overvalued IPO shares tends to cause conflict of interests in the stock markets. It is also interesting that while Japanese and Korean IPOs backed by security company-affiliated venture capitalists showed a significant under-performance, in the other countries, underwriter or investment bank-affiliated VC-backing showed an outperformance or no significant relationship. There are very few research results comparing the impact of commercial bank-affiliated VC. While the study in Japanese IPOs did not find any significant results in relation to this, I find that commercial bank-affiliated VC-backing in KOSDAQ is related to less underpricing in the cold market and a better long-term performance.

8.2 Implication of the research

The core hypotheses tested in this book were that VC-backing, the reputation of venture capitalists and the institutional affiliation of VC-backing could make a specific impact on the IPO pricing and long-term performances by providing the IPO firms with certifying and value-adding roles. Specifically, it was hypothesised that this would result in less underpricing and better long-term performances.

I found in fact that the venture capital participation did not lead to the expected results. VC-backing was found to incur higher underpricing and poorer long-term performance. This result tended to be reinforced by the tests for the sample of the hot market issues. However, the analyses in the cold market showed the expected results, even though the findings were insignificant statistically on an individual basis. The contradictory findings of VC-backing in the hot and cold market imply that the information asymmetry theories fit in the cold market, where the demand for IPO shares is relatively low. The issuing firms should therefore allow for some underpricing in order to attract investors by assuring a high initial return. In this situation, reputable financial players can reduce the degree of underpricing by certifying the IPO firms. Our results for the hot market are consistent with an overreaction of investors pulling up the prices of IPO stocks when the demand for shares exceeds the supply of shares. In these circumstances, the conventional information asymmetry theory did not work well.

I also found results contradicting our hypotheses about the impact of bank-affiliated VC-backing and security company-affiliated VC-backing on pricing and long-term performance in the hot market. However, while the bank-affiliated VC-backing and security company-affiliated VC-backing did not lead to the expected results for underpricing in the hot market, they showed the right signs for underpricing in the cold market and were also statistically significant. In the cold market, for long-term performance, bank-affiliated VCs showed a consistent positive performance, while security company-affiliated VCs showed a consistent negative performance. In addition to the implication for information asymmetry theories mentioned above, this finding may be evidence that the institutional affiliation of VC-backing is closely related to the quality of IPO firms backed by venture capitalists. This may be especially so in an emerging stock market such as KOSDAQ which experienced a dramatic growth in a short period. It can be argued that bank-affiliated venture capitalists can bring a certifying and value-adding effect through the "information advantage" acquired through the process of lending relationships, while the security company-affiliated venture capitalists incur a conflict of interests between issuers and investors because of their motivation to overprice an IPO. In a situation such as of KOSDAQ experiencing a period of a remarkable growth, the quality of venture capitalists seems to be assessed by reference to their ownership. It is not clear that this difference of pricing and performance between bank-affiliated VC-backing and security company-affiliated VC-backing is a particular phenomenon in an emerging stock market or can be generalised in other established stock markets. However, in the Korean cases, these results show that the certification and value-adding role of a reputable large institution such as bank can lead to a specific advantageous effect to the IPO firms and their shareholders. However, I also see that when the IPO market is carried away by the overreaction of the investors, this impact was not found.

Note

1 The binomial test procedure compares the observed frequencies of the two categories of a dichotomous variable to the frequencies expected under a binomial distribution with a specified probability parameter (Conover, 1980). I set the probability parameter for both + and – groups as 0.5.

Glossary

The definition of variables in multiple regressions

Variable	Definition
Lage	Natural log of age of an IPO firm: years from the establishment date to IPO date
LMC	Natural log of market capitalisation of an IPO firm at IPO time
Bmr	Book-to-market ratio of an IPO firm at IPO time
ShCEO	Shareholdings of CEO and their related persons of an IPO firm at IPO time
Hi-Tech	A dummy variable representing if an IPO firm belongs to high-tech industry
NumIPO	Number of all IPOs in KOSDAQ on the last month prior to an IPO
Kqindex	Average of daily KOSDAQ index on the last month prior to an IPO
Kqchange	Monthly proportionate change of the average of the daily KOSDAQ index between the second last month and the last month prior to an IPO
UP	Underpricing
VC	A dummy variable representing VC-backing
VCk	A dummy variable representing the backing of KTB (Korea Technology Bank)
VC3	A dummy variable representing the backing of Big 3 venture capitalists
VCbank	A dummy variable representing bank-affiliated VC-backing
VCsecu	A dummy variable representing security company-affiliated VC-backing
VCetc	A dummy variable representing other institution-affiliated VC-backing
Bank	A dummy variable representing the direct bank ownership into an IPO firm
Secu	A dummy variable representing the direct security company ownership into an IPO firm
Und3	A dummy variable representing the backing of Big 3 underwriters
Aud3	A dummy variable representing the backing of Big 3 auditors

Bibliography

Abbott, S., and M. Hay, 1995, *Investing for the Future* (FT-Pitman, London).

Admati, A. R., and P. Pfleiderer, 1994, Robust Financial Contracting and the Role of Venture Capitalists, *Journal of Finance* 49, 371–402.

Aggarwal, R., 2000, Stabilization Activities by Underwriters After Initial Public Offerings, *Journal of Finance* 55, 1075–1103.

Aggarwal, R., and P. Rivoli, 1990, Fads in the Initial Public Offering Market? *Financial Management* 19, 45–57.

Akerlof, G. A., 1970, The Market for "Lemons": Quality Uncertainty and the Market Mechanism, *Quarterly Journal of Economics* 84, 488–500.

Allen, F., and G. Faulhaber, 1989, Signalling by Underpricing in the IPO Market, *Journal of Financial Economics* 23, 303–323.

Amir, E., and B. Lev, 1996, Value-Relevance of Nonfinancial Information: The Wireless Communications Industry, *Journal of Accounting and Economics* 22, 1–30.

Amit, R., L. Glosten, and E. Muller, 1990, Entrepreneurial Ability, Venture Investments, and Risk Sharing, *Management Science* 36, 1232–1245.

Aoki, M., 1994, Monitoring Characteristics of the Main Bank System: An Analytical and Developmental View, in M. Aoki, and H. Patrick, eds.: *The Japanese Main Bank System: Its Relevance for Developing and Transforming Economies* (Oxford University Press, Oxford).

Aoki, M., 2000, *Information, Corporate Governance, and Institutional Diversity: Competitiveness in Japan, the USA, and the Transitional Economies* (Oxford University Press, Oxford).

Arosio, R., G. Giudici, and S. Paleari, 2000, Why Do (or Did?) Internet-Stock IPOs Leave So Much 'Money on the Table'? *Working paper*, Politecnico di Milano, University of Bergamo and Politecnico di Milano.

Barber, B., R. Lehavy, M. McNichols, and B. Trueman, 1998, Can Investors Profit From the Prophets? Consensus Analysts Recommendations and Stock Returns, *Working paper*, University of California Davis and University of Berkeley.

Barber, B. M., and J. D. Lyon, 1997, Detecting Long-Run Abnormal Stock Returns: The Empirical Power and Specification of Test Statistics, *Journal of Financial Economics* 43, 341–372.

Barnes, E., and Y. McCarthy, 2002, Grandstanding in the UK Venture Capital Industry, *Working paper*, National University of Ireland and Credit Suisse First Boston.

Baron, D. P., 1982, A Model of the Demand for Investment Banking Advising and Distribution Services for New Issues, *Journal of Finance* 37, 955–976.

Baron, D. P., and B. Holmstrom, 1980, The Investment Banking Contrast for New Issues Under Asymmetric Information: Delegation and the Incentive Problem, *Journal of Finance* 35, 1115–1138.

Barry, C., R. Gilson, and J. R. Ritter, 1998, Initial Public Offerings and Fraud on the Market, *Unpublished TCU, Stanford and University of Florida working paper*.

Barry, C. B., C. J. Muscarella, J. W. Peavy III, and M. R. Vetsuypens, 1990, The Role of Venture Capital in the Creation of Public Companies: Evidence From the Going Public Process, *Journal of Financial Economics* 27, 447–471.

Beatty, R., 1989, Auditor Reputation and the Pricing of IPOs, *Accounting Review* 64, 693–709.

Beatty, R. P., and J. R. Ritter, 1986, Investment Banking, Reputation, and the Underpricing of Initial Public Offerings, *Journal of Financial Economics* 15, 213–232.

Berger, A. N., and G. F. Udell, 1998, The Economics of Small Business Finance: The Roles of Private Equity and Debt Markets in the Financial Growth Cycle, *Journal of Banking & Finance* 22, 613–673.

Berkman, H., and J. B. T. Lee, 2002, The Effectiveness of Price Limits in an Emerging Market: Evidence From the Korean Stock Exchange, *Pacific-Basin Finance Journal* 10, 517–530.

Bessler, W., and A. Kurth, 2003, The Performance of Venture-Backed IPOs in Germany: Exit Strategies, Lock-up Periods, and Bank Ownership, *Working paper*, Justus-Liebig-University Giessen.

Black, B. S., and R. J. Gilson, 1998, Venture Capital and the Structure of Capital Markets: Bank Versus Stock Markets, *Journal of Financial Economics* 47, 243–277.

Black, B. S., and R. J. Gilson, 1999, Does Venture Capital Require an Active Stock Market? *Journal of Applied Corporate Finance* 11, 36–48.

Booth, J., and R. Smith, 1986, Capital Raising, Underwriting and the Certification Hypothesis, *Journal of Financial Economics* 15, 261–281.

Bradley, D. J., B. D. Jordan, I. C. Roten, and H. C. Yi, 2001, Venture Capital and IPO Lockup Expiration: An Empirical Analysis, *Journal of Financial Research* 24, 465–492.

Brau, J. C., R. A. Brown, and J. S. Osteryoung, 2004, Do Venture Capitalists Add Value to Small Manufacturing Firms? An Empirical Analysis of Venture and Nonventure Capital-Backed Initial Public Offerings, *Journal of Small Business Management* 42, 78–92.

Brav, A., 2000, Inference in Long-Horizon Event Studies: A Bayesian Approach With Application to Initial Public Offerings, *Journal of Finance* 55, 1979–2016.

Brav, A., C. C. Geczy, and P. A. Gompers, 2000, Is the Abnormal Return Following Equity Issuances Anomalous? *Journal of Financial Economics* 56, 209–249.

Brav, A., and P. A. Gompers, 1997, Myth or Reality? The Long-Run Underperformance of Initial Public Offerings: Evidence From Venture and Nonventure Capital-Backed Companies, *Journal of Finance* 52, 1791–1821.

Brav, A., and P. A. Gompers, 2000, Insider Trading Subsequent to Initial Public Offerings: Evidence from Expirations of Lock-Up Provisions, *Working paper*, Duke University and Harvard Business School.

Brealey, R., and S. Myers, 1999, *Principles of Corporate Finance* (McGraw-Hill, New York).

Brewer III, E., H. Genay, W. E. Jackson III, and P. R. Worthington, 1996, How Are Small Firms Financed? Evidence From Small Business Investment Companies, *Economic Perspective*, 20, 2–18, Federal Reserve Bank of Chicago.

British Venture Capital Association (BVCA), 1990, *Report on Investment Activity* (BVCA, London).

Bygrave, W. D., M. Hay, and J. B. Peeters, 1994, *Realising Investment Value* (Prentice Hall, London).

Bygrave, W. D., M. Hay, and J. B. Peeters, 1999, *The Venture Capital Handbook* (Prentice Hall, London).

Bygrave, W., N. Fast, R. Khoylian, L. Vincent, and W. Yue, 1989, Early Rates of Return of 131 Venture Capital Funds Started 1978–1984, *Journal of Business Venturing* 4, 93–105.

Cai, J., and K. C. J. Wei, 1997, The Investment and Operating Performance of Japanese Initial Public Offerings, *Pacific-Basin Financial Journal* 5, 389–417.

Calomiris, C. W., and C. D. Ramirez, 1996, Financing the American Corporation: The Changing Menu of Financial Relationships, *NBER Working papers H0079*, National Bureau of Economic Research.

Canals, J., 1997, *Universal Banking: International Comparisons and Theoretical Perspectives* (Clarendon Press, Oxford).

Carow, K. A., 1999, Underwriting Spreads and Reputational Capital: An Analysis of New Corporate Securities, *Journal of Financial Research* 22, 15–28.

Carter, R., F. Dark, and A. Singh, 1998, Underwriter Reputation, Initial Returns, and the Long-Run Performance of IPO Stocks, *Journal of Finance* 53, 285–311.

Carter, R., and S. Manaster, 1990, Initial Public Offerings and Underwriter Reputation, *Journal of Finance* 45, 1045–1068.

Chan, Y. S., D. Siegel, and A. Thakor, 1987, Learning, Corporate Control and Performance Requirements in Venture Capital Contracts, *International Economic Review* 31, 365–381.

Chemmanur, T., and P. Fulghieri, 1994, Investment Bank Reputation Information Production and Financial Intermediation, *Journal of Finance* 49, 57–79.

Chemmanur, T., and P. Fulghieri, 1998, A Theory of the Going-Public Decision, *Review of Financial Studies* 12, 249–279.

Chen, C. R., and N. J. Mohan, 2002, Underwriter Spread, Underwriter Reputation, and IPO Underpricing: A Simultaneous Equation Analysis, *Journal of Business Finance & Accounting* 29, 521–540.

Conn, R., A. Cosh, P. Guest, and A. Hughes, 2003, The Impact on U.K. Acquirers of Domestic, Cross-Border, Public and Private Acquisitions, *ESRC Centre for Business Research Working Paper No. 276*, University of Cambridge.

Conover, W. J., 1980, *Practical Nonparametric Statistics* (John Wiley & Sons, New York).

Cooper, M. J., O. Dimitrov, and P. R. Rau, 2000, A Rose.com by Any Other Name, *Journal of Finance* 56, 2371–2388.

Cumming, D., 2002, Contracts and Exits in Venture Capital Finance, *Working paper*, School of Business, University of Alberta.

Cumming, D., and J. G. MacIntosh, 2003, A Cross-Country Comparison of Full and Partial Venture Capital Exits, *Journal of Banking & Finance* 27, 511–548.

DeBondt, W. F. M., and R. Thaler, 1987, Further Evidence of Investor Overreaction and Stock Market Seasonality, *Journal of Finance* 42, 557–582.

Demers, E., and B. Lev, 2000, A Rude Awakening: Internet Value-Drivers in 2000, *Working paper*, University of Rochester and New York University.

Diamond, D., 1991, Monitoring and Reputation: The Choice Between Bank Loans and Directly Placed Debt, *Journal of Political Economy* 99, 689–721.

Doukas, J. A., and H. Gonenc, 2003, Long-Term Performance of New Equity Issuers, Venture Capital and Reputation of Investment Bankers, *Working paper*, New York University.

Edwards, J., and K. Fischer, 1994, *Banks, Finance and Investment in Germany* (Cambridge University Press, Cambridge).

Ellis, K., R. Michaely, and M. O'Hara, 2000, When the Underwriter Is the Market Maker: An Examination of Trading in the IPO Aftermarket, *Journal of Finance* 55, 1039–1074.

Espenlaub, S., I. Garrett, and P. M. Wei, 1999, Conflicts of Interest and the Performance of Venture-Capital-Backed IPOs: A Preliminary Look at the UK, *Venture Capital* 1, 325–349.

Espenlaub, S., M. Goergen, A. Khurshed, and L. Renneboog, 2003, Lock-in Agreements in Venture-Capital-Backed UK IPOs, *Finance Working Paper No. 26/2003*, European Corporate Governance Institute.

European Venture Capital Association (EVCA), 2001, *EVCA 2000 Yearbook: Annual Survey of Pan-European Private Equity and Venture Capital Activity 2000*.

Fama, E. F., 1970, Efficient Capital Markets: A Review of Theory and Empirical Work, *Journal of Finance* 25, 383–417.

Fama, E. F., 1998, Market Efficiency, Long-Term Returns, and Behavioural Finance, *Journal of Financial Economics* 49, 283–306.

Fama, E., and K. F. French, 1993, Common Risk Factors in the Returns of Stocks and Bonds, *Journal of Financial Economics* 33, 3–56.

Fama, E. F., and K. F. French, 1995, Size and Book-to-Market Factors in Earnings and Returns, *Journal of Finance* 50, 131–155.

Fenn, G. W., and N. Liang, 1995, The Economics of the Private Equity Market, *Staff Report*, Board of Governors of the Federal Reserve System.

Field, L., and G. Hanka, 2000, The Expiration of IPO Share Lockups, *Journal of Finance* 56, 471–501.

Francis, B. B., and I. Hasan, 2001, Underpricing of Venture and Non Venture Capital IPOs: An Empirical Investigation, *Working paper*, University of South Florida and New York University.

Franzke, S. A., 2003, Underpricing of Venture-Backed and Non Venture-Backed IPOs: Germany's Neuer Market, *Working paper No. 003, Risk Capital and the Financing of European Innovative Firms*, London School of Economics.

Fried, V. H., and R. D. Hisrich, 1994, Toward a Model of Venture Capital Investment Decision Making, *Financial Management* 23, 28–37.

Gande, A., M. Puri, A. Saunders, and I. Walter, 1997, Bank Underwriting of Debt Securities: Modern Evidences, *Review of Financial Studies* 10, 1175–1202.

Gannon, M., 1998, VC Returns Strong, But for How Long? *Venture Capital Journal* www.venturecapitaljournal.net.

Garmaise, M., 1997, Informed Investors and the Financing of Entrepreneurial Projects, *Working paper*, Stanford University.

Gilson, R., 1996, Corporate Governance and Economic Efficiency, *Washington University Law Quarterly* 74, 327–345.

Gladstone, D., 1989, *Venture Capital Investing* (Prentice Hall, Eaglewood Cliffs, NJ).

Gompers, P., 1995, Optimal Investment, Monitoring, and the Staging of Venture Capital, *Journal of Finance* 50, 1461–1489.

Gompers, P., 1996, Grandstanding in the Venture Capital Industry, *Journal of Financial Economics* 42, 133–156.

Gompers, P., 1999, Resource Allocation, Incentives, and Control: The Importance of Venture Capital in Financing Entrepreneurial Firms, in Z. J. Acs, B. Carlsson, and C. Karlsson, eds.: *Entrepreneurship, Small and Medium-Sized Enterprises, and the Macroeconomy* (Cambridge University Press, Cambridge).

Gompers, P., and J. Lerner, 1997, Venture Capital and the Creation of Public Companies: Do Venture Capitalists Really Bring More Than Money? *Journal of Private Equity* 1, 15–30.

Gompers, P., and J. Lerner, 1998, Venture Capital Distributions: Short-Run and Long-Run Reactions, *Journal of Finance* 53, 2161–2183.

Gompers, P., and J. Lerner, 1999, Conflict of Interest in the Issuance of Public Securities: Evidence From Venture Capital, *Journal of Law and Economics* 42, 1–28.

Gompers, P., and J. Lerner, 2001, *The Money of Invention: How Venture Capital Creates New Wealth* (Harvard Business School Press, Boston).

Grinblatt, M., and C. Hwang, 1989, Signalling and the Pricing of New Issues, *Journal of Finance* 44, 383–420.

Hamao, Y., F. Packer, and J. R. Ritter, 2000, Institutional Affiliation and the Role of Venture Capital: Evidence From Initial Public Offerings in Japan, *Pacific-Basin Financial Journal* 8, 529–558.

Hand, J. R. M., 2000, Profits, Losses and the Non-linear Pricing of Internet Stocks, *Working paper*, University of North Carolina, Chapel Hill.

Hellmann, T., L. Lindsey, and M. Puri, 2003, Building Relationships Early: Banks in Venture Capital, *Working paper*, Stanford University.

Hellmann, T., and M. Puri, 2000, The Interaction Between Product Market and Financing Strategy: The Role of Venture Capital, *Review of Financial Studies* 13, 959–984.

Hellmann, T., and M. Puri, 2002, Venture Capital and the Professionalization of Start-Up Firms: Empirical Evidence, *Journal of Finance* 57, 169–197.

Holland, K., and J. Horton, 1993, Initial Public Offerings on the Unlisted Securities Market: The Impact of Professional Advisers, *Accounting and Business Research* 24, 19–34.

Ibbotson, R. G., J. Sindelar, and J. R. Ritter, 1994, The Market's Problems With the Pricing of Initial Public Offerings, *Journal of Applied Corporate Finance* 7, 66–74.

Jain, B. A., and O. Kini, 1995, Venture Capitalist Participation and the Post-Issue Operating Performance of IPO Firms, *Managerial and Decision Economics* 16, 593–606.

Jain, B. A., and O. Kini, 1999, On Investment Banker Monitoring in the New Issues Market, *Journal of Banking and Finance* 23, 49–84.

Jain, B. A., and O. Kini, 2000, Does the Presence of Venture Capitalists Improve the Survival Profile of IPO Firms? *Journal of Business Finance and Accounting* 27, 1139–1183.

James, C., and P. Wier, 1990, Borrowing Relationships, Intermediation, and the Costs of Issuing Public Securities, *Journal of Financial Economics* 28, 149–171.

Jegadeesh, N., M. Weinstein, and I. Welch, 1993, An Empirical Investigation of IPO Returns and Subsequent Equity Offerings, *Journal of Financial Economics* 34, 153–175.

Jelic, R., B. Saadouni, and R. Briston, 2001, Performance of Malaysian IPOs: Underwriters Reputation and Management Earnings Forecasts, *Pacific-Basin Financial Journal* 9, 457–486.

Jensen, M. C., and W. H. Meckling, 1976, Theory of the Firm: Managerial Behaviour, Agency Costs and Ownership Structure, *Journal of Financial Economics* 3, 305–360.

Johnson, J., and R. Miller, 1988, Investment Banker Prestige and the Underpricing of Initial Public Offerings, *Financial Management* 17, 17–29.

Kim, J. B., I. Krinsky, and J. Lee, 1995, The Aftermarket Performance of Initial Public Offerings in Korea, *Pacific-Basin Financial Journal* 3, 429–448.

Kim, J. I., and I. U. Park, 2002, Stock Market Condition and Pricing of Initial Public Offerings: A Theory and Evidence From the KOSDAQ Stock Market, *Korean Economic Review* 18, 349–371.

Kinney, W. R. Jr., 1986, Audit Technology and Preferences for Auditing Standards, *Journal of Accounting and Economics* 8, 73–89.

Kirkulak, B., 2002, Bubble IPO Underpricing, Evidence from Japan, *Working paper*, Hokkaido University.

Klein, P. G., and K. Zoeller, 2003, Universal Banking and Conflicts of Interests: Evidence From German Initial Public Offerings, *Working Paper No. 2003–06*, Contracting and Organizations Research Institute, University of Missouri-Columbia.

Korea Securities Dealers Association (KSDA), 2001, *2000 Securities Market in Korea.*

Korea Securities Dealers Association (KSDA), 2002, *2001 Securities Market in Korea.*

Korea Securities Dealers Association (KSDA), 2003, *2002 Securities Market in Korea.*

Korean Venture Capital Association (KVCA), 2001, *2001 Korean Venture Capital Yearbook: An Analysis of Korean Venture Capital.*

Korean Venture Capital Association (KVCA), 2003, *A Report on the Venture Capital Companies and Limited Partnership Funds.*

Kortum, S., and J. Lerner, 1998, Does Venture Capital Spur Innovation? *NBER Working papers* 6846, National Bureau of Economic Research.

KOSDAQ, 2003, Comparison of Major Yearly Statistics between KOSDAQ and KSE, www.kosdaq.or.kr.

Kothari, S. P., and J. B. Warner, 1997, Measuring Long-horizon Security Performance, *Journal of Financial Economics* 43, 301–339.

Kraus, T., H. Burghof, 2003, Post-IPO Performance and the Exit of Venture Capitalists, *Working paper*, University of Munich.

Kroszner, R. S., and R. Rajan, 1994, Is the Glass Steagall Act Justified? A Study of the US Experience With Universal Banking Before 1933, *American Economic Review* 84, 810–832.

Kroszner, R. S., and R. Rajan, 1997, Organization Structure and Credibility: Evidence From Commercial Bank Securities Activities Before the Glass-Steagall Act, *Journal of Monetary Economics* 39, 475–516.

Kutsuna, K., M. Cowling, and P. Westhead, 2000, The Short-Run Performance of JASDAQ Companies and Venture Capital Involvement Before and After Flotation, *Venture Capital* 2, 1–25.

Kutsuna, K., H. Okamura, and M. Cowling, 2002, Ownership Structure Pre- and Post-IPOs and the Operating Performance of JASDAQ Companies, *Pacific-Basin Finance Journal* 10, 163–181.

Lee, P., S. Taylor, and T. Walter, 1996, Australian IPO Pricing in the Short and Long Run, *Journal of Banking & Finance* 20, 1189–1210.

Lee, P. M., and S. Wahal, 2002, Grandstanding, Certification and the Underpricing of Venture Backed IPOs, *Working paper*, Emory University – Goizueta Business School.

Lerner, J., 1994, Venture Capitalists and the Decision to Go Public, *Journal of Financial Economics* 35, 293–316.

Levis, M., 2001, The UK IPO Market 2000, *Working Paper*, City University.

Li, X., and R. W. Masulis, 2003, Venture Capital Investments by IPO Underwriters: Certification or Conflict of Interest? *Working paper*, University of Miami and Vanderbilt University.

Ljungqvist, A. P, 1999, IPO Underpricing, Wealth Losses and the Curious Role of Venture Capitalists in the Creation of Public Companies, *Working paper*, Oxford University.

Ljungqvist, A. P., V. Nanda, and R. Singh, 2001, Hot Markets, Investor Sentiment, and IPO Pricing, *Working paper*, New York University, University of Michigan and University of Minnesota.

Ljungqvist, A. P., and W. J. Wilhelm Jr., 2003, IPO Pricing in the Dot-Com Bubble, *Journal of Finance* 58, 723–752.

Logue, D., 1973, On the Pricing of Unseasoned Equity Issues: 1965–1969, *Journal of Financial and Quantitative Analysis* 8, 91–103.

Logue, D., R. J., Rogalski, J. K. Seward, and L. Foster-Johnson, 2002, What Is Special About the Roles of Underwriter Reputation and Market Activities in Initial Public Offerings? *Journal of Business* 75, 213–243.

London Stock Exchange (LSE), 2003, Market Statistics, www.londonstockexchange.com.

Loughran, T., and J. R. Ritter, 1995, The New Equity Puzzle, *Journal of Finance* 50, 23–51.

Loughran, T., and J. R. Ritter, 2000, Uniformly Least Powerful Tests of Market Efficiency, *Journal of Financial Economics* 55, 361–389.

Loughran, T., and J. R. Ritter, 2002, Why Has IPO Underpricing Increased Over Time? *Working paper*, University of Notre Dame and University of Florida.

Loughran, T., J. R. Ritter, and K. Rydqvist, 1994, Initial Public Offerings: International Insights, *Pacific-Basin Financial Journal* 2, 165–199.

Loughran, T., J. R. Ritter, and K. Rydqvist, 2003, Initial Public Offerings: International Insights, *Working paper*.

Lowry, M., 2003, Why Does IPO Volume Fluctuate So Much? *Journal of Financial Economics* 67, 3–40.

Lowry, M., and W. Schwert, 2002, IPO Market Cycles: Bubbles or Sequential Learning? *Journal of Finance* 57, 1171–1200.

Lyon, J. D., B. M. Barber, and C. L. Tsai, 1999, Improved Methods for Tests of Long-Run Abnormal Stock Returns, *Journal of Finance* 54, 165–201.

MacMillan, I. C., L. Zemann, and P. N. Subbanarasimha, 1987, Criteria Distinguishing Successful From Unsuccessful Ventures in the Venture Screening Process, *Journal of Business Venturing* 2, 123–137.

Mayer, C., 2002, Financing the New Economy: Financial Institutions and Corporate Governance, *Information Economics and Policy* 14, 311–326.

Megginson, W. L., and K. A. Weiss, 1991, Venture Capitalist Certification in Initial Public Offerings, *Journal of Finance* 46, 879–903.

Michaely, R., and W. Shaw, 1994, The Pricing of Initial Public Offerings: Tests of Adverse Selection and Signalling Theories, *Review of Financial Studies* 7, 279–319.

Milhaupt, C., 1997, The Market for Innovation in the United States and Japan: Venture Capital and the Comparative Corporate Governance Debate, *Northwestern University Law Review* 91, 865–898.

Miller, E. M., 1977, Risk, Uncertainty, and Divergence of Opinion, *Journal of Finance* 32, 1151–1168.

Miller, E. M., 2000, Equilibrium With Divergence of Opinion, *Review of Financial Economics* 9, 27–41.

Mitchell, M. L., and E. Stafford, 2000, Managerial Decisions and Long-Term Stock Price Performance, *Journal of Business* 73, 287–329.

Moriarty, G., 1999, Venture-Backed Exits Move Toward M&A', *Venture Capital Journal*, www.venturecapitaljournal.net.

Murray, G., 1995, The UK Venture Capital Industry, *Journal of Business Finance & Accounting* 22, 1077–1106.

Muzyka, D., S. Birley, and B. Leleux, 1995, Trade-Offs in the Investment Decisions of European Venture Capitalists, *Journal of Business Venturing* 11, 273–287.

Myers, S., and N. F. Majluf, 1984, Corporate Financing and Investment Decisions When Firms Have Information That Investors Do Not Have, *Journal of Financial Economics* 13, 187–221.

NASDAQ, 2003, Listing Requirements and Fees: The NASDAQ Stock Market, www.nasdaq.com.

NASDAQ Newsroom, 2003, Market Performance, www.nasdaqnews.com.

National venture Capital Association (NVCA), 2001, *2001 National Venture Capital Association Yearbook*.

National Venture Capital Association, 2002, *Analysis of Recent Years' IPOs*.

OECD, 2003, Venture Capital Policy Review: United States, *Science, Technology and Industry Working paper*.

Palmrose, Z., 1988, An Analysis of Auditor Litigation and Audit Service Quality, *The Accounting Review* 63, 55–73.

Paudyal, K., B. Saadouni, and R. J. Briston, 1998, Privatisation Initial Public Offerings in Malaysia: Initial Premium and Long-Term Performance, *Pacific-Basin Financial Journal* 6, 427–451.

Perotti, E., and S. Rossetto, 2000, The Pricing of Internet Stocks: Portals as Platforms of Entry Options, *Working paper*, University of Amsterdam.

Petty, J., W. Bygrave, and J. Shulman, 1994, Harvesting the Entrepreneurial Venture: A Time for Creating Value, *Journal of Applied Corporate Finance* 7, 48–58.

Piccino, P., and A. Kierski, 1999, Quotation as an Exit Mechanism, in W. D. Bygrave, M. Hay, and J. B. Peeters, eds.: *The Venture Capital Handbook* (Prentice Hall, London).

Plummer, J. L., 1987, *QED Report on Venture Capital Financial Analysis* (QED Research Inc., Palo Alto, CA).

Porter, M., 1992, Capital Disadvantage: America's Falling Investment System, *Harvard Business Review* 46, 65–72.

Prowse, S., 1990, Institutional Investment Patterns and Corporate Financial Behaviour in the United States and Japan, *Journal of Financial Economics* 27, 43–66.

Puri, M., 1994, The Long-Term Default Performance of Bank Underwritten Security Issues, *Journal of Banking & Finance* 18, 397–418.

Puri, M., 1996, Commercial Banks in Investment Banking: Conflict of Interest or Certification Role? *Journal of Financial Economics* 40, 373–401.

Rajan, R., 1992, Insiders and Outsiders: The Choice between Informed and Arm's Length Debt, *Journal of Finance* 47, 1367–1400.

Rajan, R., and H. Servaes, 1997, Analyst Following of Initial Public Offerings, *Journal of Finance* 52, 507–529.

Rajgopal, S., Suresh K., and M. Venkatachalam, 2000, The Relevance of Web Traffic for Internet Stock Prices, *Working paper*, University of Washington.

Relander, K. E., A. P. Syrjanen, and A. Miettinen, 1994, Analysis of the Trade Sale as a Venture Capital Exit Route, in W. Bygrave, M. Hay, and J. Peeters, eds.: *Realising Investment Value* (FT-Pitman, London).

Rindermann, G., 2003, Venture Capitalist Participation and the Performance of IPO Firms: Empirical Evidence from France, Germany and the UK, *Working paper*, University of Muenster.

Ritter, J. R., 1991, The Long-Run Performance of Initial Public Offerings, *Journal of Finance* 46, 3–27.

Ritter, J. R., 1998, Initial Public Offerings, *Contemporary Finance Digest* 2, 5–30.

Ritter, J. R., and I. Welch, 2002, A Review of IPO Activity, Pricing, and Allocations, *Journal of Finance* 57, 1795–1828.

Rock, A., 1987, Strategy Versus Tactics From a Venture Capitalist, *Harvard Business Review* 65, 63–67.

Rock, K., 1986, Why New Issues Are Underpriced, *Journal of Financial Economics* 15, 187–212.

Roe, M., 1994, *Strong Managers, Weak Owners: The Potential Roots of American Corporate Finance* (Princeton University Press, Princeton).

Roll, R., 1996, Investment Banking, in P. Newman, M. Milgate, and J. Eatwell, eds.: *The New Palgrave Dictionary of Money and Finance* (MacMillan Press, London).

Rosa, R. S., G. Velayuthen, and T. Walter, 2003, The Sharemarket Performance of Australian Venture Capital-Backed and Non-Venture Capital-Backed IPOs, *Pacific-Basin Financial Journal* 11, 197–218.

Rutschmann, E., 1999, Going Public – European Markets and NASDAQ, in W. D. Bygrave, M. Hay, and J. B. Peeters, eds.: *The Venture Capital Handbook* (Prentice Hall, London).

Sah, R. K., and J. E. Stiglitz, 1986, The Architecture of Economic Systems: Hierarchies and Polyarchies, *American Economic Review* 76, 716–727.

Sahlman, W. A., 1990, The Structure and Governance of Venture-Capital Organizations, *Journal of Financial Economics* 27, 473–521.

Saunders, A., and I. Walter, 1996, *Universal Banking: Financial System Design Reconsidered* (Irwin, Chicago, London).

Schill, M. J., and C. Zhou, 1999, Pricing an Emerging Industry: Evidence From Internet Subsidiary Carve-Outs, *Working paper*, University of California at Riverside.

Schultz, P., 2003, Pseudo Market Timing and the Long-Run Underperformance of IPOs, *Journal of Finance* 58, 483–518.

Schultz, P., and M. Zaman, 2001, Do the Individuals Closest to Internet Firms Believe They Are Overvalued? *Journal of Financial Economics* 59, 347–381.

Shiller, R. J., 1990, Speculative Prices and Popular Models, *Journal of Economic Perspectives* 90, 55–65.

Simunic, D. A., and M. Stein, 1987, *Product Differentiation in Auditing: Auditor Choice in the Market for Unseasoned New Issues* (Monograph Prepared for the Canadian Certified General Accountant Research Foundation).

Singh A., 2003, Corporate Governance, Corporate Finance and Stock Markets in Emerging Countries, *Journal of Corporate Law Studies* 3, 41–72.

Singh, A., A. Singh, and B. Weisse, 2000, Information Technology, Venture Capital and the Stock Market, *Department of Applied Economics Discussion Papers in Accounting and Finance No. AF47*, University of Cambridge.

Small and Medium Business Administration (SMBA), 2001, *A White Book on Venture* (written in Korean).

Smart, S. B., and C. J. Zutter, 2000, Control as a Motivation for Underpricing: A Comparison of Dual- and Single-Class IPOs, *Working paper*, Indiana University.

Smith, C. Jr., 1986, Investment Banking and the Capital Acquisition Process, *Journal of Financial Economics* 15, 3–29.

Smith, S. C., and H. Chun, 2003, New Issues in Emerging Markets: Determinants, Effects, and Social Market Performance of Initial Public Offerings in South Korea, *Journal of Emerging Market Finance* 2, 253–286.

Stuart, T. E., H. Hoang, and R. C. Hybels, 1999, Interorganizational Endorsements and the Performance of Entrepreneurial Ventures, *Administrative Science Quarterly* 44, 315–349.

Suzuki, K., 2003, Conflicts of Interest Between Venture Capital Firms and Debtholders: Evidence From Japan, *Working paper*, Hitotsubashi University.

Titman, S., and B. Trueman, 1986, Information Quality and the Valuation of New Issues, *Journal of Accounting and Economics* 8, 159–172.

Trueman, B., M. H. Wong, and X. J. Zhang, 2000, The Eyeballs Have It: Searching for the Value in Internet Stock, *Journal of Accounting Research* 38, 137–169.

Tyebjee, T. T., and A. V. Bruno, 1984, A model of Venture Capitalist Investment Activity, *Management Science* 30, 1051–1066.

Venture Economics, 1988, *Venture Capital Journal*, www.venturecapitaljournal.net.

Venture Economics, 2002, *Historical Trend Data of Venture Capital Investment*.

Walsh, A., 1990, *Statistics for the Social Sciences: With Computer Applications* (Harper & Row, New York).

Wang, K., C. K. Wang, and Q. Lu, 2002, Differences in Performance of Independent and Finance-Affiliated Venture Capital Firms, *Journal of Financial Research* 25, 59–80.

Welch, I., 1989, Seasoned Offerings, Imitation Costs, and the Underpricing of Initial Public Offerings", *Journal of Finance* 44, 421–449.

Westhead, P., and D. J. Storey, 1997, Financial Constraints on the Growth of High Technology Small Firms in the United Kingdom, *Applied Financial Economics* 7, 197–201.

Williamson, O. E., 1988, Corporate Finance and Corporate Governance, *Journal of Finance* 43, 567–591.

Wright, M., and K. Robbie, 1996, Venture Capitalists, Unquoted Equity Investment Appraisal and the Role of Accounting Information, *Accounting and Business Research* 26, 153–168.

Wright, M., and K. Robbie, 1998, Venture Capital and Private Equity: A Review and Synthesis, *Journal of Business Finance & Accounting* 25, 521–570.

Wright, M., K. Robbie, Y. Romanet, S. Thompson, and R. Joachimsson, 1993, Harvesting and the Longevity of Management Buy-Outs and Buy-Ins: A Four-Country Study, *Entrepreneurship: Theory and Practice* 18, 90–109.

Wright, M., S. Thompson, and K. Starkey, 1994, Longevity and the Life Cycle of MBOs, *Strategic Management Journal* 15, 215–227.

Wruck, K., 1989, Equity Ownership Concentration and Firm Value: Evidence From Private Equity Financings, *Journal of Financial Economics* 23, 3–28.

Index

For Product Safety Concerns and Information please contact our EU
representative GPSR@taylorandfrancis.com
Taylor & Francis Verlag GmbH, Kaufingerstraße 24, 80331 München, Germany